Survival in the Academy:
A Guide for Beginning Academics

SCA Applied Communication Publication Program

Gary L. Kreps, Editor
Northern Illinois University

The SCA Program in Applied Communication supports the Speech Communication Association mission of promoting the study, criticism, research, teaching, and application of artistic, humanistic, and scientific principles of communication. Specifically, the goal of this publication program is to develop an innovative, theoretically informed, and socially relevant body of scholarly works that examine a wide range of applied communication topics. Each publication clearly demonstrates the value of human communication in addressing serious social issues and challenges.

Survival in the Academy:
A Guide for Beginning Academics

Gerald M. Phillips
Dennis S. Gouran
Pennsylvania State University

Scott A. Kuehn
Clarion University of Pennsylvania

Julia T. Wood
University of North Carolina

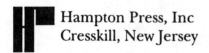

Hampton Press, Inc
Cresskill, New Jersey

Speech Communication Association
Annandale, Virginia

Printed in the United States of America

Library of Congress Cataloging-in-Publication Data

Survival in the academy : a guide for beginning academics / Gerald M.
    Phillips ... [et al.].
        p.   cm. – (SCA applied communication publication program)
    Includes bibliographical references (p.).
    ISBN 1-881303-69-1
    1. College teachers–United States. 2. First year teachers-
-United States. 3. College teaching–United States. I. Phillips,
Gerald M. II. Speech Communication Association. III. Series.
LB1778.2.S87   1994
378.1'2'0973–dc20   93-44472
                                                                          CIP

Hampton Press, Inc.
23 Broadway
Cresskill, NJ 07626

Contents

About the Authors

Dennis S. Gouran (Ph.D., University of Iowa) is Professor and Head in the Department of Speech Communication at The Pennsylvania State University. Professor Gouran teaches in the areas of communication theory and group communication. He is former President of both the Central State Communication Association and the Speech Communication Association. He is also past Editor of *Communication Studies* (formerly *Central States Speech Journal*).

He is the author of numerous books and articles focusing primarily on decision-making processes in groups. Professor Gouran has been recipient of the Speech Communication Distinguished Scholar Award, The Pennsylvania State University Faculty Scholar Medal in the Behavioral and Social Sciences, The Pennsylvania State University Howard B. Palmer Faculty Mentoring Award, the Speech Communication Association Robert J. Kibler Award for Professional Excellence, and the Speech Communication Association Distinguished Service Award.

Scott Kuehn (Ph.D., Pennsylvania State University) is Assistant Professor in the Department of Communication at Clarion University of Pennsylvania as well as Director of the Center for the Study of Computer Communication. He teaches communication research and theory and courses on the influences of new technologies in communication. His research interests are in adaptation in communication behavior resulting from computer-mediated settings.

Gerald M. Phillips (Ph.D., Western Reserve University) is Professor Emeritus of Speech Communication at Pennsylvania State University. He is author of 44 books and more than 200 articles. He is currently working as a freelance medical writer and editor and his most recent books in this area are *Living With Heart Disease* (with Robert Werman, MD) and *Communicating With Your Doctor, 2/e* (with J. Alfred Jones and Gary L. Kreps). He is also editor of *IPCT-J: An Electronic Journal for the Twenty-First Century*.

Julia T. Wood (Ph.D., Pennsylvania State University) is Nelson Hairston Professor of Communication Studies at the University of North Carolina,

Chapel Hill. Specializing in interpersonal relationships, communication, gender and culture, and feminist theory. She has published seven books, edited three others, and written over 100 articles and papers. She co-founded the National Conference on Gender and Communication Research and has won four Teacher Awards.

1

THE NATURE OF THE UNIVERSITY

Gerald M. Phillips

YOUR CAREER

Academic professionals just starting out may face a rocky future, or they may be part of the greatest educational boom in history. Writing a book like this demands the ability to predict the future, which, of course, is impossible. We compensate for this in this book by combining the forces of four authors who represent four different stages in the continuum. In chronological order, one is now retired emeritus after 42 years of professional service in academe. One is at the peak of his career; a past president of the national professional organization and chair of a major Ph.D.-granting department at a large university. The third is a newly minted Ph.D. on his first job. Our fourth author is a rising star, one of the most productive women in the discipline. Together, they represent points of view that provide different perspectives on the same world. Sometimes they are in conflict, sometimes not. What they agree on is that higher education will change dramatically in the next decade. The work rules under which we practice our profession will be drastically modified, the make-up of our student body will change, and even our mission will be modified to confront the new problems of the 21st century. But there will be constants also—the idea that our job is to discover and disseminate wisdom.

Now, how about you? The 1990s do not appear to be the best time begin a career. The future does not look especially optimistic at the moment. To enumerate:

There are money problems! Tax revenues are dwindling. Institutions funded with public money are cutting back, downsizing, and deselecting. At the beginning of 1992, many states announced budget cuts for higher education. Two major private universities, Yale and Stanford, came under heavy financial pressure. Smaller schools are struggling to stay afloat. Tuition is soaring; grants are dwindling. There is heavy competition for endowments. Some schools are exerting great pressure on alumni to help with expansion. Some are merely trying to stay alive. One of the most important indicators is questions about faculty pension funds. Many state-funded institutions are cutting their contributions, borrowing from the funds, and, in general, jeopardizing the secure future that is one of the main inducements for seeking a career as a professional academic.

In any case, it is clear that for most academics, the salad years may well be over. Some disciplines remain affluent because they are essential to industry. Most disciplines, however, must struggle to hold their own, for in a declining economy, higher education is one of the first enterprises to feel the pinch. It is smart to keep your eye on the media and consider carefully the consequences various news events might have on higher education. For example, if a politician advocates increased aid to public schools, will the funding come from the higher education budget? If the government reduces tax exemptions for charitable donations, what effect will changes in tax laws have on endowments for private universities? On the other hand, you must also consider demographics. The heavy influx of faculties from the 1960s/1970s is going to be the retirees of the early 21st century. There are prospects of an unprecedented boom in higher education. And, more and more older students are returning to institutions of higher education for retraining.

We do not know precisely what will happen, but we can see the directions the changes will take. We have already seen major alterations in hiring patterns. There has been a reduction of tenured faculty at some institutions. Colleges are hiring more and more adjunct and part-time faculty members, especially large institutions in major metropolitan areas. Many institutions are encouraging enrollment by foreign students. Both state and federal governments are modifying the way student loans and scholarships are granted and administered. There is ferment about the curriculum; no longer is there agreement on a common canon of instruction. We have also begun to see changes in enrollment patterns that show some institutions flourishing and others on the verge of bankruptcy. Changes in population patterns mean changes in geographic centers of instruction. The wise young academic professional will read the news carefully for precursors of change and will be prepared to adapt. This chapter is mainly about the alternatives and possibilities. It is not designed to predict the future, but to inform you about various possible futures.

There are political battles being fought. The newspapers regularly carry stories about the effect of defaults on student loans on future budgets for higher education. There are disputes about the regulations imposed by various accrediting agencies. These kinds of stories seem trivial to outsiders, but they can have serious ramifications for your career. For example, some accrediting agencies are beginning to demand compliance with regulations about what ought to be included in curricula to make instruction politically correct. This is but one aspect of a battle raging on many campuses about the extent to which "other voices," that is, minority groups and women, ought to be "heard" in the required curriculum. Should the works of black writers and women be taught alongside the traditional curriculum of Shakespeare and Melville?

Another argument concerns the extent to which instruction ought to focus on vocational preparation as opposed to the general humanistic curriculum characteristic of traditional higher education. There are also conflicts about freedom of expression and the rights of groups not only to be heard but also to be free of harassment. In the spring of 1992, for example, on the campus of a large state university, a black student published a column in the school newspaper calling for arming the black population and killing the white oppressors. This publication set off national reverberations. The issue was the right of individuals representing extreme points of view to be heard. These issues affect campus life in many important ways, and few faculty members can avoid becoming involved.

Institutions are diversifying. No longer can we stereotype the ivy-covered buildings on tree-shaded campuses offering up tired and traditional topics. Financial contingencies and local needs require schools to specialize and diversify. It is no longer sufficient for an aspiring professional to declare him- or herself to be "just interested in becoming a professor." The type of school that employs them will shape their lives, and they will be required to adapt to local constraints even while satisfying the intellectual demands of their discipline.

For example, the community college system was once a feeder system for 4-year schools. Their students were either locals who could not afford to go away to school or those who wanted special vocational training. Community colleges are now complex institutions, providing a variety of programs to all age groups and catering to specialized interests. On the other end of the spectrum, major institutions are cutting programs that are no longer viable, for example, dentistry and library science. New specialties like informatics are springing up, and there is competition both for students and financial resources.

College no longer has the perceived value it once had. Increasingly, graduates are disillusioned about what they gained from their college education. For one thing, college graduates find that it is not so easy to get employment. A cynical view is that many students go to college in order to qualify for employment. In a period of declining employment, many students feel that they have been cheated. Furthermore, as students become more crass about their education, they have fewer memorable instructional moments. In many cases, what they remember most frequently is something dramatic, or social occasions rather than academic experiences. The opportunities for employment for college graduates have been materially reduced by the recession and by general neglect of practical instruction. Employers are doing more on-the-job training because colleges are not keeping pace with advances in technology. Furthermore, in a period of cutbacks and unemployment, jobs are simply harder to find.

Even though some specialists seem to be able to secure positions and especially talented students are admitted to graduate and professional schools, for an increasing number of students, the college degree is viewed as the proverbial "hunting license." Furthermore, the traditional 4-year college education has become prolonged for many students who find it necessary to take time off periodically to work and possibly to "find" themselves.

The students are not what they used to be. College was once a privilege for the elite as opposed to a licensing organization. There are probably as many serious students as there were 50 years ago, but they are widely distributed. An apocryphal story has a college president responding to the question, "How many students do you have here?" with the answer, "About ten percent."

Recent studies claim students read less, although it is not clear what they are reading less of. One study indicated that only about 25% of college students actually used the library, compared to 70% 20 years ago. According to a news story in the *Chronicle of Higher Education* (November 20, 1991), students often complain about how much they are asked to read; many think of their education as a way to improve their employment prospects rather than a way of getting a "handle" on life. Teachers have expressed serious concern about the number of students who require remedial training if they are to have any hope of doing college-level work. To complicate the matter even more, special programs, once directed at those students who were not competent at reading and writing, are now specifically directed at blacks, Hispanics, women, and other groups once excluded from the mainstream of the college population.

This adds up to claims such as those aired by the major news services on February 6, 1992, about the deficiencies of American students on standardized exams compared to students in other countries. Presumably, this deficiency was caused by the American educational system. But the situation is not that clear. Large numbers of students are becoming technically proficient. When Gutenberg invented movable type, attention was taken away from the formal lecture and the sermon, and literacy became vital. Today's visual and computer technologies demand a new kind of literacy, and it seems fairly clear that American students are far ahead of their foreign counterparts in those areas. We are clearly in a period of change, in which the main media of instruction—lectures and books—are giving way to new methods based on video and the computer. What the ramifications of these changes will be for an instructor at the turn of the century cannot be predicted. What we can predict, however, is that prudence requires the professors of the future to be proficient in technologies of instruction that go beyond orality and literacy.

If students are in a "sorry state," and it is not clear that they are, their state is a logical culmination of events that have modified the teaching profession over the last 50 years. Higher education in America is no longer confined to elite institutions open only to the rich and cultured. Higher education is available to all, and its face has changed forever. These changes (and those we have been unable to predict) will mean a great deal to you as a beginning academic. You will have to become a seer and predict what will be required of you midway through your future. The professor who retired in the last five years has gone through two or three major changes during his or her career. Furthermore, economic recession and public criticism has removed higher education from its once favored position of being beyond reproach. Higher education has become the property, even the right, of the people, thus more and more, it has become responsive to their needs and wants. The vista is no longer that of a sinecure for professors who belong to a privileged class and are employed by institutions existing apart from society. The demands of vocational specialization and economic peril have resulted in diversification, which means that professionals who might be suited to one kind of institution would be superfluous or useless at another.

What this means is that you must be very aware of conditions at institutions that might hire you. If you have a choice at all, it is best to think in terms of the kind of job for which you are realistically best suited, in addition to your personal preferences as to geographical location and research interests. The work of the junior college faculty member is as different from that of the professor in the Ivy League as the work of an accountant is from a laboratory technician. A brief examination of the history of higher education in America will illustrate this point.

CONTEMPORARY TRENDS

Our current university structure has been shaped by a number of historical trends. Our academic traditions differ from those of the dignified dons of Oxford or the duelists at Heidelberg. Nothing academic in the

United States has been around all that long. Even august institutions such as Harvard have changed drastically from the way they were even as recently as the 1930s. Experimentation in higher education has been a way of life in America.

In less than 50 years, a college education has changed from being the privilege of an economic aristocracy to the right of the average citizen. The first colleges were founded in the United States to train ministers (and educate "Indians"). Some schools emulated the British model; others took the German universities as examples, but over the years the American higher education system has taken on its own flavor, one that is characterized by wide diversity and specialization. Although vestiges of the British and German traditions remain in some places, for the most part American colleges and universities have developed to meet the demands imposed on them by social trends and economic considerations. This has been especially important in the development of patterns of research that include everything from practical agriculture to theoretical physics.

The "rah-rah" films of the 1930s and 1940s are totally alien to today's students. Although the fraternity and sorority system remains and there are still pep rallies, college life is quite different from what it was 25 years ago. How many of you, for example, remember "house mothers" living in the women's dorms or deans of women?

Many students live in off-campus housing or commute. Many cohabit. Party time no longer means formal dating and community singing at the frat house, although a good deal of alcohol is consumed on most campuses. Few campuses are safe havens, even those tightly connected to religious institutions. Drugs are more common than we would like to believe, and one of the major issues facing college administrators is whether they should make crime statistics public. In the 1950s, debate raged about whether sex out of wedlock invalidated college students for further study. Today, the issue is not whether students should engage in sexual acts but how. The issue of AIDS and other sexually transmitted diseases makes socialization an epidemiological issue.

Furthermore, getting to college takes real effort for most students. Even with Pell Grants and student loans, there are relatively few students who can avoid working part time or who do not have student aid of some sort, and there are special efforts made to attract the kinds of students who were once summarily rejected. In fact, there are institutions such as Empire State College in New York that cater specifically to the needs of older students by providing education tailored to their individual specifications. Too often, the effort students must make to meet the financial requirements distracts them from serious intellectual effort. Older professors comment on how their syllabuses have become less and less demanding in recent years as they adapt to the constraints of time and interest that characterize today's students.

Before World War II, a college education was restricted to those who could afford it and a few gifted students from the lower socioeconomic classes. A middle-class family made considerable sacrifices to send a member to college. Often an older sibling worked in order to send a gifted younger brother or sister (but most likely a brother) off to college. Occasionally an unusually bright student from the lower socioeconomic classes slipped through on scholarship, but this was clearly an exception. Major Ivy League institutions were for males only. There were special colleges for women, and most southern states maintained exclusively black schools under the doctrine of "separate but equal."

Religion was also a major influence in higher education. Most Ivy League institutions were originally connected with Protestant churches. From the turn of the century up to World War II, their student bodies were made up of mainly white, Protestant, males from high income families. There were a great many small Catholic institutions staffed primarily by members of religious orders and run under strict discipline as virtual extensions of the parochial school system. Jews either "passed" or struggled with a rigid quota system. In fact, in the 1930s, Harvard instituted a policy of extending geographical quotas because there were fewer Jews in western states. The use of the quota system to exclude Jews is quite the opposite of the quota systems used today to provide opportunities for minority group members.

Academics are located in fields (a tribute to an agrarian tradition) or disciplines (the German model). The liberal arts and sciences are regarded as the "core," as part of a canon (in British fashion). But we have developed our own specialties, largely in response to vocational needs. Instead of developing a system of post-high school vocational training, as in Europe, we combined education for economic viability with education for cultural literacy. The goal that educators hoped for was well-read artisans and pragmatic intellectuals. In fact, however, schools took on their own character. Some became mainly vocational, and some remained quite effete. There are still a few schools that maintain a purely academic curriculum in the fashion of the original Ivy League, but most have instituted professional or vocational curricula as exemplified by colleges of business, engineering, or communications. Even the Ivy League is not "ivy" any more. Yale has its school of forestry; Harvard its colleges of business and education. Within large universities there are colonies of subject matter specialists and technological experts. Even the nature of the administrators varies; some emphasize educational programs, others specialize in fund raising. What is generally true is that even the smallest institutions have the administrative flavor of a corporate enterprise. They dispense a product (education) to consumers (students) for a price. They compete for students as well as football players. Schools that do not meet enrollment quotas can go bankrupt, just like a business that fails. At this writing, for example, the University of Bridgeport is quietly being disassembled and its parts parceled out to other colleges in the area. The University of Bridgeport could not meet its financial obligations. In 1991, the Japanese bought a bankrupt college in West Virginia to use for training businessmen on how to conduct business in America.

We might add that academic disciplines have the same economic constraints as their institutions. They must appeal to students, place their students in jobs, and maintain a viable research program in order to justify their existence within the university. Only a very few traditional subjects are regarded as absolutely essential in all universities. All have English and history departments, but speech communication and home economics are more often optional.

Furthermore, there are substantial differences in the way colleges and universities are organized. The older and more traditional schools maintain a semblance of the British model in which the academics remain in charge of subject matter and instruction. Those founded more recently on the land grant model or with public funding tend to follow the industrial model; some refer to their faculties as "the academic workforce." In any case, institutions of higher education are administered mostly by specialists. In many ways, the administration and the faculty are separate. Some professors feel that becoming a department head or dean is a step up. It may be a step up on the pay scale, but it is another career. The few institutions that have democratic administration on the department level surrender that democracy at the higher levels of control. The institution must be run by the administration. Beginning academic professionals are well advised to learn the governance pattern of the institution that employs them and adapt to it. Although employment can be a good deal more secure in academia than in the industrial world, there is still a chain of command, and those who do not attend to it carefully often run afoul of it.

Furthermore, the product of those institutions is in constant flux. Disciplines change their configuration, and courses change their content. Although the "core" disciplines of history, literature, and science (among others) have remained constant to their traditions, new courses have sprung up (computer science), and old disciplines have died out (philology). Sometimes this occurs because new knowledge replaces old. Sometimes, as in a large state institution, courses are sacrificed because of economic need. One major institution discarded its departments of linguistics and classics and distributed the tenured faculty to other departments in the university. They were fortunate. In some cases, tenured faculty have been dismissed when their departments were phased out. In today's world, budget considerations often guide academic decisions. In addition, the demands of industry for trained personnel combined with the urgent need of students to obtain employment as soon as they graduate have stimulated the growth of practical disciplines such as engineering and business administration.

Those who have had long careers in the academy refurbish themselves intellectually more than once. They must stay abreast not only of new knowledge, but of the administrative and political changes that are constantly taking place around them. Failure to acknowledge trends and changes and adapt to them can ruin one's career. Nowhere is this more true than in the communication (sometimes referred to with the barbarism "communications") disciplines including speech, speech communication, rhetoric, rhetorical theory, communication theory, interpersonal communication, and related areas.

These disciplines have gone through especially rapid changes in recent years. It is hard to predict the changes that are yet to come, but we will attempt to do so in the final chapter of this book. Suffice to say, currently in the dialectic between performance and theory, the latter is ascendant. The tilt toward the social sciences has become a definite leaning, and the performance end of rhetoric has been preempted by English departments in their writing courses. Twenty years ago, most of the professionals in rhetoric came from a performance background, but this discipline is now increasingly made up of people either with backgrounds in theoretical and experimental specialties loosely associated with the term social science, or those related to philosophy and literary criticism. They are tenuously connected through a shared literature and concern about the interpretation and understanding of motivation and meaning.

A Brief History

The history of higher education in America is almost like the biological principle that ontogeny recapitulates phylogeny. The changes that have come about in higher education provide a useful guide to help you understand your possible career choices. The following brief history is offered merely to illustrate some of the main differences among institutions. The missions of contemporary institutions vary. Some remain true to their original mission, whereas others have changed to meet current societal needs. Institutions of higher education are not static; 20 years after the fact most of us would hardly recognize the institutions from which we graduated.

The bottom line is that the early universities—Harvard, William and Mary, and Yale—educated ministers. This obligation is now met by schools devoted exclusively to that purpose. Although many major private universities still maintain seminaries, they no longer concentrate on graduating pulpit ministers. They focus their study on complicated theological issues. Dartmouth, originally founded to educate Native Americans, has become a school devoted to the liberal arts. American universities, during the first half of the 19th century, were bastions of elitism, reserved for the sons (mostly) and a few daughters of the first families. From these institutions came the doctors, lawyers, clergymen, and cultural elite that governed the nation and oversaw to its economic and diplomatic affairs.

Concurrently, normal schools were founded to meet the demand for public school teachers. As tax-supported elementary and secondary schools became the norm, it was necessary to find teachers to staff them. To service the public elementary and secondary schools, 2-year institutions were funded by the states to train and certify teachers. Today, 2-year schools devote a great deal of attention to vocational education. They fill the gap created when the normal schools became state colleges. The proprietary trade school system covered secretarial and mechanical training. The parochial school system ran in parallel, relying on members of religious orders to staff its institutions, but providing higher education facilities somewhat more versatile in orientation.

The Morrill Land Grant Act of 1862 represented the start of the great state universities. Some states, Virginia, for example, already provided public facilities that imitated the major liberal arts institutions, but the Morrill Act provided this capability to all of the states. Under its provisions, the federal government gave grants of land to the states to fund universities to train the "sons and daughters of the working class in agriculture and the mechanic arts." The schools founded under this act initially concentrated on their mission, but eventually grew into major state universities (Michigan State and Purdue, for example). Their existence made it realistic for ordinary students from the middle class to demand higher education, a demand that led many states to create elaborate publicly funded systems combining liberal arts and vocational traditions. Thus, the state of Michigan has Michigan State, a land grant institution, and the University of Michigan, a major university that is also funded by the state. In addition, it has several smaller comprehensive universities, most of which originated as normal schools. Pennsylvania has combined its land grant school and state university, and New York associated its land grant institution with Cornell, a private Ivy League school. Some states, like California, distributed the land grant money across a complex system of universities, colleges, and community colleges which, at least at its inception, guaranteed some form of higher education at low cost to all high school graduates. Large urban areas, like New York City, attempted to do the same with a system of city colleges which provided education without charge to resident high school graduates. However, current financial contingencies have required tuition fees, and there is currently no free higher education available anywhere in the country. Now, all students are expected to pay a share of the cost of their education. Moreover, the situation is complicated by a system of grants-in-aid and loans provided or guaranteed by legislatures and Congress itself. Thus, the public provides funding for private payment to public institutions of higher education. Those who receive public money are usually obligated to pay it back. A major administrative effort must be sustained by the Federal Government to ensure repayment of student loans.

The original thrust of the Land Grant Act has changed considerably over the years and has produced a bewilderingly complex system of institutions combining a variety of functions. Whatever the combination, however, each state has its multiversity, an all-purpose institution, which usually exists alongside private colleges and universities of various sorts together with an assortment of specialized state-funded institutions. The normal schools grew into 4-year quasi-liberal arts colleges and then into smaller multipurpose universities (mostly with limited graduate programs). The fiction is that large universities emphasize research, whereas smaller ones make teaching paramount. The situation is much more complicated than that. Virtually all schools at least give lip service to their teaching mission, and most 4-year schools pressure their faculties to do some research and to publish. The emphasis may differ from place to place, but most institutions evaluate their faculty members on their performance in some combination of the following four categories: teaching, research, professional activity, and service. The precise, albeit idiosyncratic, definitions of these terms in each institution are guides to acceptable performance to those who are employed by them.

Many churches also funded their own institutions dedicated to continuing their traditions of belief and observance. These coexisted with privately endowed liberal arts colleges, although many new combinations are now appearing. Colleges that traditionally limited their enrollment to women are now admitting men, and military-type colleges, responding to legal pressure, are now admitting women. A few schools in southern states cling to a tradition of predominantly black enrollment. Some African Americans have resisted attempts to homogenize these institutions. Most sizable cities have generated some form of community college system, which combines the efforts of public and private institutions. In many cases, the state has taken over these urban schools (for example, Ohio's establishment of Cleveland State by taking over Fenn, which was a YMCA-sponsored business college, or Michigan's making Wayne University into Wayne State University in Detroit). Institutions tend to take on the coloration of their region and specialize to meet the needs of the population they serve. In addition to all this, there are complex networks of 2-year branches of major universities granting associate degrees, community colleges, and proprietary schools providing general and vocational instruction. Adding to the complexity, most large universities maintain extensive continuing education programs and extension services. Each genre of institution offers its own particular type of opportunity to aspiring academic professionals.

The real growth in opportunity for employment in higher education came with the GI Bill, which democratized higher education by making it available to virtually everyone so that a college degree has now replaced the high school diploma as a basic requirement for many types of employment. The impetus to diversification by institutions was assured by the disbursement of funds to individuals to spend as they chose. Available funds meant a larger pool of students, and institutions adapted accordingly to obtain their share of the federal dollars. The GI Bill was not as altruistic an enterprise as it seemed. Its real purpose, in large part, was to prevent returning veterans from glutting the job market. Its effect was to expand higher education beyond anyone's wildest dreams.

The Requirements of Employment

The preceding capsule history of higher education in America makes one very important point: There is no way to educate a person, generally, for a career in higher education. Aspiring academics must identify the type of institution they seek as an employer and prepare for it, lest they be disadvantaged in the hiring process. More importantly, they need to be honest with themselves in assessing their abilities, qualifications, and motivations. It does one little good to aspire to the type of position for which one either has little prospect of success or the inclination to meet its expectations. Institutions will seek the kinds of people that meet their needs, specialized as they may be. Institutions are as widely varied as any other corporate enterprise. Adaptability is the critical element in success. There is, however, one anchor: the association with a discipline.

In addition to affiliating with an institution, academics must relate to their discipline. They have local allegiance to the place where they are trained and eventually employed. They have global allegiance to the subject matter and techniques of their specialty. Thus, the sine qua non of all academics is a subject matter specialty certified by an advanced degree. This requirement gives unity to an otherwise thoroughly confusing vista of potential employers.

Beginning academics may not be aware of how wide a range of choices they have regarding types of institutions. Whatever their preferences, however, they must adapt to the stated mission and operating practices of their eventual employer. This is not as easy as it sounds.

THE SINE QUA NON OF EMPLOYMENT

There are no real "job descriptions" for academics. In this book, we refer redundantly to "research, teaching, scholarship, and service" as the requirements for professional behavior and as the bases for evaluation.

The meaning of these four terms varies dramatically from place to place. Policy manuals are normally not explicit about what an institution demands in each category; criteria for success are often unclear, both to those who establish them and for those who have to live by them. It sometimes seems they are purposely phrased ambiguously. Survival often depends on your ability to read the requirements by observing the successful performance of others. Some aspiring academics may politicize their quest for success and attempt to gain tenure by currying favor with authorities or substituting success in one category for failure in another. Genuinely successful aspirants, however, carefully identify what is expected and concentrate on delivering it. If they do not approve of the requirements, they move on to another institution with whose expectations they are more harmonious.

The competition for positions at major universities can be intense, and once you are offered a position at a major institution, it can be very difficult to keep. On the other hand, good opportunities lie in strange places. Beginning academics must learn what is required of them both by the various institutions at which they might be employed, as well as by their discipline. In their search for positions, they must examine the confusing and often conflicting objectives of multiversities and comprehensive institutions, liberal arts colleges, vocationally specialized schools, and those serving specific communities and special-needs students. They must also understand the synthesis of public and private financing that characterizes higher education in America. They will serve many masters: trustees, alumni, administrators, colleagues, the voting public, students, and sometimes even the students' parents.

Major universities make many demands on their faculties, but they also provide for a wide variety of specializations. Full-time researchers work side by side with teachers. It is possible to devote yourself to minute details and esoterica in your subject matter area along with opportunities to teach complex, highly detailed, and arcane subject matter. There are hundreds of majors in dozens of disciplines; some devoted to preserving the wisdom of the past, others dedicated to training specialists and professionals.

There are "stars" and people who are "just passing through." Academics at major universities often refer to the "revolving door policy," in which young professionals are brought in, work a short term, and then are denied tenure and sent on their way (almost like being sent back to the minors). Major institutions also rely heavily on the work of graduate assistants and adjunct faculty (part-time workers not on regular appointment). It is difficult to obtain employment in a tenure-track position at such institutions. The competition is fierce, and a great deal is expected of those who are chosen. Before competing for a position at such a university, it is useful to consider how you would respond to their expectations if you got the job. Very often, young academics struggle for employment at a major institution only to find that they do not like the priorities and cannot take the pressure of meeting the high expectations their colleagues and administrators have for them.

Multiversities, such as Harvard or Stanford, or the elite of the "Big Ten" schools such as Michigan or Northwestern, represent the top of the academic heap. These institutions provide undergraduate (liberal arts, sciences, preprofessional), graduate (Ph.D.), professional (medicine, law), and vocational education (engineering, broadcasting, education). They also maintain a major research establishment (and often a major sports enterprise, as well). They have large endowments, and almost all have public funding in the form of grants and legislative appropriations. People who work for them exemplify the kind of pressure typical of such institutions. But the ability to withstand the pressure earns privileges and perks. Once tenured at them, an academic can be relatively secure in reputation and in the ability to follow his or her own intellectual muse. A regular appointment at such schools confers prestige; furthermore, they typically pay higher than average salaries, although, surprisingly, not nearly as high as prospective faculty members often think. In fact, some institutions located in desirable living areas place limits on salaries on the grounds that the ambiance of the area is, itself, sufficient to attract competent prospects.

The comprehensive universities (Southern Illinois, California State System) also provide a wide variety of options. Their research enterprise is not as extensive as in the multiversity, nor do they have the variety of graduate and professional programs, but they offer many services, have a large number of specialties, and cater to those students whose needs are often ignored by the multiversities. They are, for example, not as selective in their admission policy. In the multiversities, instructors presume the students will be more talented than those in smaller institutions. The comprehensive universities usually have diverse populations with a smaller proportion of gifted students. Faculty members often use comprehensive universities as springboards to "better" institutions. On the other hand, the academic who seeks to use them in this fashion must become a Stakhanovite and risk violating the work norms of those who make permanent careers there. Very often, they place a much heavier emphasis on teaching than the multiversities and tend to be a bit more relaxed about research and publications.

In smaller public colleges and universities it is possible to work out a very satisfactory "large fish in a small pond" kind of life. These colleges (Amherst, Vassar) focus on teaching the liberal arts canon to selected populations of highly qualified (and usually affluent) undergraduates. Some maintain small graduate enterprises, but most use their highly talented faculties to provide quality teaching to the "best" undergraduates. They are virtually all private (many are still church-related). They tend to be run as private clubs with "traditions" and networks of alumni providing support. The responsibilities of faculty members transcend mere academics. There is an implied duty to the culture of the school. Some of the private liberal arts colleges even require their faculty to participate in fund raising and recruitment of students as part of their job description.

Institutions with an emphasis on graduate studies (Rockefeller, Johns Hopkins, various medical and law schools, theological seminaries) have a variety of specializations. The research enterprise is often central, although professional training receives major emphasis as well. The pressures are very great here, both for conducting research and obtaining funding. These kinds of institutions cater to "stars" who are expected to produce "studies" and bring in money. The recent case of David Baltimore, President of Rockefeller University, who surrendered his position over an alleged case of scientific fraud indicates the kind of pressure one finds at a major research institution. Although somewhat smaller in scale, these same pressures can be encountered at major universities whether they have predominantly public or private funding.

Urban-centered universities (CUNY, Wayne State) attempt to maintain the services of comprehensive universities but are carefully tailored to meet the needs of the local communities they serve. They frequently provide special programs for minority and economically deprived students, and they tend to give more emphasis to vocational curricula than one would expect to find at most comprehensive institutions. It is almost as if the liberal arts and sciences are adjunct to the vocational and remedial aspects of the schools. The point is that it is important to be committed to the locale and its people in order to be satisfied working there.

Junior colleges and university branches in local communities specialize in the dissemination of lower level undergraduate education and associate degrees. They serve as feeders to larger and more specialized institutions and also provide for the vocational needs of local communities. Often there appears to be little difference between these schools and high school. Most of the students commute, and there is little campus life. However, most of them do not provide the protection of tenure to their faculties, nor do they usually demand that their faculties do much, if any, serious research and publication. Many are unionized. One of the newer features of life at institutions of this sort is the use of part-time and adjunct faculty, many of whom teach at two or more institutions and none of whom have a role in institutional governance. These teachers have few of the traditional protections and benefits enjoyed by those at major public and private institutions.

Aspiring academics must choose among available options within this wide variety of institutions; each of which offers a different kind of career path and opportunities for advancement. The ultimate frustration is finding yourself in an institution whose requirements you cannot or prefer not to meet. The problem when you begin your career is that often you do not have much choice. You apply for jobs for which you think you are qualified. You are interviewed only by institutions who agree with your assessment. There is no guarantee whatsoever that you will be offered a position at an institution with whose philosophy you agree. More often, it is necessary to make considerable accommodations on the first job. It becomes your burden to ascertain what your employer expects of you and to provide it. Your vita (and your future) is at stake. If you intend to use your first job as a stepping stone, it is important to meet expectations at that institution to keep your references in order.

SOME IMPORTANT ISSUES
AND QUESTIONS TO FACE

If you read professional publications regularly, you cannot help but be confused by the conflicting predictions about the future of "the academy." We raise some important issues here, without questioning their sources. All of them have been asserted by experts. The fact that there is so much conflict in the academy now should alert you to the importance of staying abreast of current events and piloting carefully through the provocative issues you will face.

The Future of Speech Communication

In the past four decades, the field of communication has changed considerably. Forty-five years ago, a typical "Speech" department included public speaking, speech correction, and theater. The latter two specialties have now become disciplines in their own right. In addition, specialties in broadcasting and film, now known collectively as "media," have passed through speech departments and have become independent departments, even separate schools and colleges. They have become the proverbial "tails that wag the dog." They attract the attention of the public and funding as well.

The wide variety of names for the field indicates that there is little consistency. There are departments of communication, communications, speech communication, communication studies, telecommunication, mass communication, and many more. There are very few departments of speech left.

It is possible to acquire a fairly accurate idea of the emphasis of particular schools and departments by examining their current catalogue. But you must read the course descriptions carefully. What is called "organizational communication" in one school may bear little resemblance to what is taught under the same name at another, and both may differ from the same course taught in the business college.

Whether the various disciplines will ever standardize is a moot question. At least for the foreseeable future, this patchwork of specialties and arrangements will continue. The communication professional will have to be sufficiently well informed in order to adapt to local conditions. We discuss this in detail in subsequent chapters.

The Question of Tenure

We deal with tenure in detail in a later chapter. Sufficient for now is the assertion that it is the most valuable prize academe has to offer. It goes without saying that there are satisfactions that come from the job. But tenure is the payoff for a job well done, at least in its ideal state. No other occupation provides a virtual guarantee of permanent employment (except perhaps for partners in a law firm). Earning tenure frees the academic professionally and permits him or her the luxury of thinking independently.

Tenure is not easily earned, especially at research-oriented universities. Each institution sets its own criteria, and often they are not terribly explicit. As we have noted, they generally refer to teaching, research, professional activity, and service. The balance among the four categories is shaped by the mission of the institution.

There are some institutions currently displaying doubt about the tenure process. Some say it protects incompetence. Others argue that it traps universities into retaining highly paid but nonproductive professionals. There have been suggestions in some legislatures that tenure be abolished. Whatever the doubts and reservations, however, tenure appears to be a secure institution for the foreseeable future, although it is entirely possible that the requirements one must meet to achieve it will become more rigorous. It is also possible that more institutions will do what a few do now, that is, restrict the proportion of the faculty that can be tenured at any one time. It is caveat emptor for you. It is imperative that you understand the rules for achieving tenure at your institution, for they will shape your professional future.

One of the greatest threats to tenure currently is the budget-cutting practice of hiring adjunct instructors on a temporary basis. This, coupled with the extensive use of graduate assistants as instructors (mostly in basic courses), keeps the number of tenured faculty under control. On the other hand, this practice interferes with the careers of the people employed in those temporary positions.

Tenure carries with it the added benefit of academic freedom. Tenure protects the professor's right to think freely, to speak out on public issues, and to take intellectual risks in his or her own field. This combination of privileges confers considerable responsibility. The tenured professor must be intellectually alive throughout his or her career.

There are professional organizations dedicated to the preservation of academic freedom and tenure. Even they seem to be bewildered at times about the future of the practice. Tenure and academic freedom have been considered in the courts, but despite the decisions, their privileges and responsibilities are matters of argument. It becomes part of your burden to be aware of local policies and practices and to be sure that you know your rights and what you have to do to earn them and retain them.

Where Do You Want to Work?

This can become a real issue. It is rare that academics find work in their hometown. Academic life, in fact, is notable for its lack of extended family. The beginning academic goes to the job; it almost never comes to the academic. Although there are numerous cases of professionals eventually returning to the school from which they graduated, most academics begin a new life far from home and must learn the norms of a new community in addition to accommodating to the professional requirements of their positions.

The employing institution has the advantage of being able to write its own job description and set criteria for the kind of person it would like to hire. As a candidate you must show how you fit the requirements, and often you must do this without really knowing what the institution is after. Most beginning professionals can tell stories about how many applications they sent out and how few positive responses they received. The suspense can build and become almost intolerable. Eventually, your job search will become an exercise in audience analysis. It would help, for example, to seek advice from people who work there already, and it helps if your vita contains items that meet the institution's criteria.

An old speech scholar, the late Wendell Johnson, used to talk of "IFD Disease." IFD stood for Idealization - Frustration - Demoralization. Although the authors of this book do not want to go on record as being opposed to dreaming, their advice is to stay open during the early days and ask the ultimately sensible question, "What kind of position am I prepared to handle?" Once you can answer this question, it is possible to scan the job announcements carefully and select those for which you have some reasonable hope of success. It is certainly not sensible to confine your expectations to one or two institutions, or even to a type of institution. Staying flexible and open will be decidedly to your advantage during the job search. It is important not to fall in love with an image. Images seldom live up to what we construct.

In the olden days, there was a caricature of professors as fumbling, impractical, absent-minded, almost comical. They used big words, and they worked in idyllic settings populated by cheerleaders, slow-witted football players, and some eager young men and women (of the type often portrayed by Mickey Rooney and Judy Garland). It never was like that any more than today's prep school resembles the one in *The Dead Poet's Society*. Most colleges are filled with middle-class students aspiring to move up economically, minorities struggling for identity and economic viability, and deadly serious young technologists struggling for qualifications and credentials to get them into graduate school. It is not always a lot of fun for students, and it is often financially draining for their families. Most students are not on the cheerleading squad, and professors are not especially comical. They are young professionals, most of them paying their own way with part-time work and loans. They are dedicated to something; some to money, some to fame, and some to solving the major problems of the world. Some are only concerned with surviving the college experience, receiving a degree, and getting to work. In most places, they spend surprisingly little time in contact with faculty.

Professors have their own agendas. They are required to meet the job requirements imposed on them by their employers. Many have their own dedication to research and publication; they consult, seek grants, give speeches, and labor in the community. In most cases, teaching is only part of their job description, and the time available for individual attention to students is very limited.

In 1958, so the story goes (and if it is not true, it ought to be), a member of the North Dakota legislature asked the president of North Dakota State how many hours the typical professor taught. "Twelve," replied the president. "Makes for a long day," was the apocryphal reply. Professors often teach 12 hours a week in branch campuses and small state colleges. In major institutions, they typically teach from one to four courses a year and are expected to do research and publish the results. They spend long hours in preparation for their teaching and equally long hours in their laboratories, or in the library, or in front of their word processors.

Attention to the realities of professional life is important to survival in the academy. Things are changing and no one can predict what the picture of higher education will look like 10 years from now.

Forecasting the Future

Things can change, but as the saying goes, the more they change, the more they stay the same. Some institutions will go under, new ones will spring up, but most institutions will continue under the same name and the same management. Their pattern of enrollment may change, however, and so may the requirements they impose on their faculties. Funding will make some changes mandatory. As this book is being written, public education is being challenged by budget cuts and competition from other interests for the tax dollar. Endowments are falling in many private institutions. As states experience fiscal difficulties, for example, some programs will have to be cut and patterns of employment may change. Tuition may rise, and this may affect the pattern of enrollment. Institutions that once had the luxury of allowing their faculties to specialize in research may have to assign them to increased teaching loads. Universities and colleges will be compelled to compete for funds compounded by demands for health care, unemployment compensation, and other forms of welfare. The infrastructures of society will also affect funding. There are bridges and roads to repair, slums to clear, the wilderness to protect. Education is but one of many demands on the public and eleemosynary dollars.

The types of courses offered are, even now, beginning to change. Current debates about political correctness, the termination of some programs because of diminished public demand or lack of funds, and the intellectual changes that require disciplines to evolve will all have an effect on your career. Cognitive science may displace philosophy; linguistics may give way to English as a Second Language. Although parts of academic institutions seem to remain inviolate, for the most part they change to reflect changes in the society they serve. If present trends continue, you can expect to see several major changes during your career, and you will have to adapt to them.

It will be your responsibility to stay alert to changes and accommodate them. Your career in an academic institution is, for the reasons presented above, as fragile as it would be in industry. In the chapters to follow, we discuss the issues that you will confront as you seek a job and then during your first years of teaching. We will be speaking in four voices: one explaining how to work within the system, one explaining how to work the system, one—a chronicle of the system itself—a personal narrative of professional quest, and one speaking of diversity and change in the academy.

◆ RESPONSE TO CHAPTER ONE

DENNIS S. GOURAN

Of the many points Professor Phillips makes in his discussion of the nature of institutions of higher education, there are only two matters about which I wish to offer further comment. In the first instance, I seek merely to underscore my colleague's observations about the importance of considering positions for which one's credentials and interests are best suited. In the second, I hope to bring a different perspective to the matter of tenure, which some of Professor Phillips's comments might otherwise lead one to believe is the *raison d'etre* of college and university life. I have more to say about this subject in my response to Professor Kuehn's chapter on tenure.

Most colleges and universities now consider the Ph.D. degree (or equivalent) as a precondition for employment in a tenure-track position. The reasons for this insistency are not altogether clear. What is clear, however, is that many administrators believe that a high proportion of doctoral-degree holders assures a higher quality faculty and, hence, level of instruction. The validity of this assumption may be debatable, but on its face, it appears to be reasonable. Whether the assumption is valid or not, however, it is increasingly difficult to secure employment in institutions of higher education without a doctoral degree and, preferably, the Doctor of Philosophy.

The Ph.D. is a research degree, and the vast majority of institutions do not offer it. Because most require it for employment, however, degree recipients tend to think of employment in terms of the types of institutions in which they pursued doctoral study, even if they are not especially interested in doing research. For those who are primarily interested in teaching and who have limited desire to establish ongoing programs of research and publication, seeking employment in the types of institutions from which they received their degrees can be a serious mistake. Nothing can be more frustrating and unfulfilling than carrying the burden of doing research when one is either not well-equipped for it or feels that he or she has to rather than wants to.

Although the Ph.D. degree is a research degree, its value is not restricted to one's preparation to do research. The knowledge to which doctoral candidates are exposed, if used properly, can have considerable value in teaching and in a professor's continuing education. Most institutions, moreover, no matter how vocationally oriented, pay attention to the need for the general education of their students. Doctoral training can equip faculty to deliver a meaningful program of general education. Hence, one's degree is not wasted if he or she fails to secure employment in a research university.

The point I am emphasizing is that many individuals would profit from seeking employment commensurate with both their interests and talents. Lacking in the inclination, desire, or ability to become research scholars, many individuals new to the profession who are successful in securing positions requiring research become easily demoralized. They devote a considerable amount of time to making allegations about the unfairness of the institutions and exaggerating their performance in other aspects of their jobs. Most people in the profession can do what they want to do. The problem with many individuals is their failure to appreciate that they have less freedom when it comes to choosing where to do it. They appear to feel that any institution has the responsibility to accommodate itself to their particular professional desires. Why be miserable when there are personally rewarding jobs available in which one can thrive, experience a sense of accomplishment, and have excellent prospects for advancement?

The second matter I wish to address has to do with the achievement of tenure as the fundamental motive for professional activity. Unfortunately, far too many individuals in higher education see tenure as a goal rather than as a consequence of their performance. (Indeed, some even view it as an entitlement.) Even more unfortunately, institutional norms frequently tend to promote this view. There is certainly nothing wrong with wanting to achieve tenure. The problem arises when it becomes the driving force behind practically all that a person does professionally. Nonpossession of tenure creates among some aspirants an obsessive concern with its achievement and leads to choices based almost exclusively on assessments of how certain activities will "count" toward it. As with other forms of social behavior, the vicarious reinforcing properties of tenure often become the end toward which activity is directed. (Who among us has not encountered the student who "needs an A?") The confusion of the symbol with what it symbolizes in this case, and the attendant motivation it induces, can make one's professional existence a chore rather than a pleasure and even have damaging effects on one's relationships with others.

Let me state emphatically that achieving tenure should not be the only, or even a major, reason for taking a position in higher education. Tenure is rather a benefit accruing from performance that an institution considers sufficiently promising to warrant continued employment beyond a probationary period, typically six years. I know of no other profession that has this benefit or the approximately 18 months one is permitted to secure other employment upon denial of tenure. Again, my observations are not intended to suggest that tenure is a trivial matter, but merely to put the awarding of it into a reasonable perspective. When tenure becomes a preoccupation ("the goal" in my colleague's words), the effects on an individual's performance are more likely to be injurious than helpful. Students, colleagues, programs, and the untenured faculty member him- or herself are apt to be victims of the obsession.

I should add two other observations here. First, relatively few college and university professors—whether tenured or not—remain in one position for an entire career. Despite financial difficulties, being a college or university professor remains one of the most mobile of all professions. Second, in over 25 years in higher education, I have encountered no one who, upon being denied tenure, has failed to secure another position at least as good as the one he or she vacated. More often than one might suspect, the consequence of a tenure denial is finding an even better position elsewhere.

◆ RESPONSE TO CHAPTER ONE
JULIA T. WOOD

Professor Phillips has offered an insightful, albeit rather negative, perspective on the nature of contemporary universities. I agree with most of his observations, although I believe there are also some very positive trends in academe to which he gave less than adequate attention. In invigorating and expanding academic life, emergent trends make this era one with great promise for the academy and those who participate in it.

In my response, I wish to do three things. First, I echo Professor Gouran's comments on the nature of tenure at academic institutions. I find his views of the meaning and process of tenure much more compatible with my own than are those of Professor Phillips. More often than not tenure, as Professor Gouran points out, follows from steady, good work over a period of years. It is also more a means than an end in itself, as it creates conditions that enable faculty to continue to do their work unencumbered by political and economic constraints. Thus, more than being a goal in itself, tenure is recognition of an individual's achievements and potential, and it is insurance against infringement on academic freedom as one continues to teach and conduct research.

Let me now address two other matters in greater detail. First, I wish to add to Professor Phillips's views of the contemporary academic scene by noting a positive emergent tendency. Second, I call attention to some issues that are uniquely important to women and minority faculty's decisions of where to locate, but which were not salient in Professor Phillips's experience and, thus, were muted in the perspective he offered.

Perhaps, as Professor Phillips claims, the "salad days" are over for universities. Then again, perhaps not. It is true that budgets are being cut and, with them, programs and services that have long been counted on by faculty, students, and staff. At the same time, new programs, services, and priorities are emerging, and these promise to reconfigure academe in exciting ways.

Perhaps the most remarked on ascendant priority in academic life is the move toward "multiculturalism," which is recontouring academic institutions in many ways. Contrary to some critics' caricatures, multiculturalism is not an effort to "wrest power from the dominant white male majority" and to sacrifice intellectual depth for politically correct subject matter. It is neither a rejection of traditional goals of education, nor an unqualified dismissal of long-revered traditions in our culture.

Most supporters of multicultural education believe it will add in vital ways to the intellectual integrity and social value of the academic enterprise. What is advocated is not throwing out "the great works" or "the canons." Instead, the goal is to augment existing curricula by including traditions, materials, and viewpoints long repressed in Western society. Knowledge of human nature and its communicative expression are impoverished when they exclude, for example, African-American history, women's developmental patterns, interaction in gay and lesbian relationships, and communicative rituals of Third World women. All of these— and other—areas of study have been neglected in higher education, whereas the thought, values, and experience of one privileged group has been equated with all knowledge, morality, and perspective. Whether one sees multicultural education as promising or portentous may depend more on individuals' standpoints than on any intrinsic merit of the issues: Those who have long enjoyed the privilege of having their lives, values, and experiences regarded, studied, and taught as universals of cultural life may be less than enthusiastic about giving up this territory. On the other hand, those whose lives, values, and experiences have been disregarded resoundingly by partial representations of "common culture" are likely to welcome a more comprehensive, more collaborative vision of what knowledge is and of ways to create and share it.

As Professor Phillips points out, there is controversy about multiculturalism, and faculty are often deeply divided in their attitudes. Thus, this is political ground. No faculty—old or new—can avoid being affected, involved, and taking stands. You either do or do not include women's leadership styles in a group communication course; you either do or do not discuss African-American family structure in your class on interaction in families. You either do or do not try to educate yourself about the lives, experiences, and resulting kinds of thinking that are part of people different than you. Either way, you take a political stand.

Multiculturalism is invigorating many academic fields and faculty. Women and minority faculty are discovering their perspectives, ideas and concerns are given some hearing, and, increasingly, faculty are experiencing levels of credibility and respect not previously conferred on them. Many universities have departments or programs in Women's Studies and African-American Studies. More and more faculty are experimenting with ways to make their teaching and research more reflective of multiple viewpoints and life positions. Although some efforts are yet mechanical and inadequate, they are starts, and this matters. These developments reflect acknowledgment—sometimes grudging, sometimes eager—that there are other voices and other perspectives than those which have for so long held sway, and that "our common heritage" entails a much broader set of people and practices than traditionally has been appreciated.

For women and minority faculty, the trend toward multiculturalism promises to make academic institutions more hospitable, more receptive, and more supportive of their professional concerns and personal requirements. Thus, this major development is viewed differently, depending on how it affects faculty: Those who traditionally have enjoyed a privileged position at the center of academic (and cultural) life understandably may feel displaced and defensive, whereas those who conventionally have found doors and ears closed to them sense a new openness and, with that, possibilities for positive intellectual and cultural innovation. Of course, there are exceptions to these tendencies. Some members of historically marginalized groups seek assimilation into "mainstream" culture and, thus, do not wish to call attention to how they differ from it. Similarly, some members of the historically dominant group welcome and want to participate in enlarged understandings of culture and communication.

A second matter upon which I wish to comment is issues obscured in Professor Phillips's discussion of conditions at institutions new Ph.D.s might consider for employment. Although I have no criticism of what he does cover, I do want to fill in gaps in his commentary. In addition to matters he highlighted that all beginning academics should consider, there are issues uniquely germane to women and minority candidates. Particularly important in considering institutions for employment is assessing the climate toward minorities and women. This is not something that has to be evaluated by individuals whose identity and value enjoy presumptive and longstanding legitimacy. Unfortunately, it remains something that women and minority individuals must take into account in their decision making.

There are some obvious clues to notice: Are there other women and minorities on the faculty that is interviewing you? Do the catalogs describing graduate and undergraduate curricula include many (or any) courses that address minority and women's traditions and concerns? Do you see many women and minority students on the campus? I say more about ways to check out campus climate in my response to Chapter 3. For now, my point is simply that it is prudent for nontraditional academics to consider issues that need not be part of traditional academics' concerns.

◆ RESPONSE TO CHAPTER ONE
SCOTT A. KUEHN

I believe Professor Phillips makes a number of important observations in this chapter. I wish to concur with him on the importance of remaining adaptable, with my comments focused on the perspective from a small public university.

My three colleagues have commented on finding the right type of job and working toward tenure, so I am responding on the tenure issue here (I present more in Chapter Four). I think my colleagues' warnings about the difficulty of achieving tenure at multiversities and comprehensive universities are valid, but not the whole picture. Tenure is becoming more difficult to achieve everywhere, not just at the big name universities. Professor Phillips points out that budgets are not secure for most universities. Part-time and adjunct faculty are gaining in number. Small universities tend to suffer the same economic realities, even with their smaller budgets. Limits on the number of tenured faculty can be placed by the smallest as well as the largest of universities.

Tenure is no longer a "shoo-in" (if it ever was) at smaller, teaching-oriented colleges and universities. Small universities put a major emphasis on teaching quality in tenure requirements. Although different institutions use different measures of teaching quality, the implications should be clear—one should not seek to follow the tenure track at a small university if he or she is not prepared to perform proficiently in the classroom. I recently observed a case at my small university in which a good researcher was almost denied tenure for being ineffective in the classroom. I believe that toughening of tenure standards means that ineffective teachers who are also unsuccessful researchers/writers will find only adjunct positions viable. The future holds the promise that no longer will the "minor leagues" (small universities) be an automatic ticket for those denied tenure at the major research universities, unless they are effective teachers.

Why do many faculty consider getting tenure a major career goal? Perhaps because a major appeal of tenure is academic freedom. Again, working from a point made by Professor Phillips, adjunct and part-time faculty without tenure are not as secure as their tenured colleagues. Tenure was created to protect academic freedom. Those without tenure are denied this protection. This have/have not situation may, in the future, create a class system of those who can teach freely and those who teach freely at the discretion of their employers. Part-time and adjunct faculty who have no chance at tenure have none of the guarantees of academic freedom that tenure brings. This is evident in a number of court decisions on academic freedom such as the Roth (*Board of Regents* v. *Roth*, 92 S.Ct. 2701 1972) and Sindermann (*Perry* v. *Sindermann*, 92 S.Ct. 2717 1972) cases. In these instances the courts failed to uphold academic freedom privileges that were not specified by contract (as in tenure). Although it does not happen often, both Roth and Sindermann were fired for speaking out on issues that displeased their administrations (Hemmer, 1986). They would have had protection had they been tenured.

Given this climate, I have little wonder at the fact that many see tenure as a goal, although I agree with Professor Gouran that it should not be the primary motive for one's entry into academe. Providing proof that one is a fine teacher/scholar or researcher/scholar would be terribly difficult if a person does not enjoy what he or she is doing. Besides, tenure does not provide total job security. Tenured faculty can still be fired, retrenched, or laid off. But, with fewer tenure track positions available relative to the growing number of temporary and adjunct positions, many view the academic freedom provided by tenure as a worthwhile achievement. Professor Gouran notes that some even see tenure as an entitlement. I believe we will find fewer representations of this view as the relative number of non-tenure-track positions increases in the future. Just as major research universities seek to tenure the best qualified researchers/scholars, so will the teaching institutions seek to tenure the best teachers/scholars.

Beyond the tenure issue, I would like to add to Professor Phillips's description of smaller public colleges and universities. Many smaller universities cater to the needs of a fairly diverse group of students. Usually, however, these students have lower academic skills than those accepted at the multiversities and comprehensive universities. In some states, these small universities are overcrowded and face tight budgets (Mercer, 1992, p. 1). In other states, there is intense competition for decreasing numbers of post-baby boom students. Thus, most states see the need for managed growth of their public 4-year campuses. We are going to witness more specialization in some state regency systems, in which each campus will be given authorization to grow in some disciplines and to phase out areas on some campuses. Tight budgets also mean higher tuition. Students will likely become more consumer conscious as they encounter growing costs. To teach at smaller universities one must be prepared to address consumerism by providing professional skills to disadvantaged students and by stimulating critical thinking and motivation in the classroom.

2

ISSUES FACING ALL
BEGINNING ACADEMICS

Gerald M. Phillips

As Aristotle pointed out, "man (sic) is a political animal." Academics often refer to the "real world" as though academic life was some sort of fantasy. Aristotle is right, and the academics who differentiate between the academy and the real world are wrong. Professing is a real occupation, and it takes place in a real setting, a setting which is usually highly political; the battles that are fought can be fierce, and the stakes are as much "for keeps" as in any other occupation. The personal issue all academics must face is the dialectical tug between our professional conscience and the exigencies of survival at our employing institutions. It is hard to distinguish personal integrity from institutional loyalty as bases of our professional decisions.

On the simplest level, one must survive economically. That means the job must be done competently or better according to the rules of your employer. But economic survival is not quite enough. There is also self-survival, the feeling that you are a whole human, a true professional, a person unfettered by compromises made in the interest of institutional regulations. This is not to imply that all institutions force professionals to make personal compromises. On the contrary, most institutions are thoughtful and careful about what they require, and not all professionals behave professionally when they do their job. The point is, there is often apparent conflict, and in order to survive with a clear head, it is important that such conflicts be resolved in a satisfactory manner.

The author of this chapter takes a very cynical view of most campus political issues. He has been a perennial outsider, a protester, and was twice denied tenure. At the rural college that first employed him, the reason was not clear. It may have been for having catsup on his shirt and unshined shoes. It may have been for speaking out against what he regarded as fraud in one of the colleges. At the second institution, a state university, he was denied tenure on the sole authority of his department head because he was heavily involved in ACLU activity. It is important to note here, however, that his publication record generated support from the graduate dean, and instead of being dismissed, his case was deferred. He waited until his political and legal protests won the day, and he was granted tenure before he quit and moved on. So, this chapter must be understood in that light. It is cynical and assumes the worst. It is sometimes sarcastic, and often facetious. But it offers one point of view as a basis for your consideration of the issues. And, it must be noted, the author did indeed achieve tenure and promotion to the highest rank at a quality university. This was in recognition of his research and publications (not to speak of a few grants) and in spite of his attempt to organize a faculty labor union and his continued activity with the ACLU. There will be an answer to this chapter; perhaps a counterpart, not a rebuttal.

Campus Politics

It is difficult for those new to academics to understand campus politics. Few academic issues are clear (and, as C. P. Snow noted, few are genuinely important). Most internal disputes in any organization are about issues that appear meaningless to outsiders. When academics argue about how to divide up the paper clips, they are as silly as employees in industry arguing about the same thing. But, academics rarely argue about such matters. They have to deal with the division of valuable resources such as time allotments, assignment of courses, the composition of a major, secretarial help, the promotion and tenure of their colleagues, and various awards and prizes. For example, the courses we are assigned to teach may shape our career, and thus certainly control the way we spend our valuable work time. The outcome of these arguments may be critical to the individuals involved. Their professional lives may hang in the balance. Outsiders simply do not understand the stakes.

There are many academic professionals who are immune to politics. They mind their own business and take what comes. There are others who engage in campus politics because they believe it is their duty or who feel that they can do something that matters. It is a personal choice. The true question on any campus is, "Who has the power, really?" In most cases, professors have little real power, but they can argue intensely about foolishness and feel relevant even though little or nothing they say has an effect on major decisions. When faculty members are truly threatened, when their tenure is challenged or their salaries are in jeopardy, they can sometimes make an impact, although it is immensely difficult to unite them. In any case, however you regard campus politics, they will affect you, and you will be constrained by them. You will be unable to avoid taking a stand on some issues. In many cases, silence is a commitment.

Academic life is not a sinecure. Academics, or at least those worth their salt, work long hours, and their work is often physically hard and emotionally taxing. Advancement is difficult, and the material rewards are rarely proportional. There are, however, some important issues at stake. For example, academics can, if they work at it, achieve job security that surpasses anything currently found in industry. Here it is, tenure again.

To digress for a moment about the long hours demanded of academics. There are really few mandatory hours. Perhaps an academic has a 4-course load. That is actually 12 hours in the classroom. There are some academics who coast. All of us have stories about academics with yellow notes that are never revised, who do not modify their lectures, and whose tests remain the same over the years.

Once you get that golden plum of tenure, there is a temptation to sit back and relax. If you can curb your ambition, you can then hold out with nominal raises, no advancement, and little work. This is an option chosen by more people than we care to think about, but certainly nowhere near the majority. Most academics work very hard. Even to achieve tenure requires sufficient commitment to satisfy the requirements your employer establishes to qualify for tenure. Tenure confers the benefits of self-employment with few of the responsibilities. Normally, when you have it, seniority permits you to teach the courses you enjoy and do the research that interests you. From that perspective, it is a sinecure. There are few positions (except perhaps the civil service) more secure than that of tenured college professor.

The preceding paragraph does not, by any means, characterize the whole professorate. Most members of college faculties continue to work hard at both their teaching and research after they have earned tenure. There are some who fail to achieve tenure for no fault of their own. Some are caught in economic vicissitudes; others come to the wrong place at the wrong time. The most demanding lessons to be learned by a newcomer are how to retain intellectual integrity, comply with the requirements of the "system," and produce work of genuine value. Even while trying to earn tenure at Institution A, you need to be working on your vita in the event that you need to seek a position at Institution B. Tenure is becoming harder and harder to acquire, and its future is in doubt, at least at some institutions.

One of the reasons tenure is so hard to achieve is that not only employers but colleagues are involved in the decision-making process. The tenure system is supposed to reward merit by providing professionals who qualify with protection so they can think and act as their intellect and conscience direct them. Still, there is an aspect reminiscent to pledging an old-time college fraternity. You must please the powers that be, who then vote. You can be blackballed on any level. Your colleagues or your department head can vote against you. The college committee can reject you, or the union might find reasons to block you. Finally, the upper echelons of administration have their say. This means you not only have to do your job well (by objective standards), but you have to convince the influential people who hold your fate in their hands that you have done so. All the people who have input can control the outcome. The same holds true for other crucial decisions in the university.

"Input" is a buzz word in university politics meaning the ability to block action. Everyone wants it, especially regarding issues that affect them. In most cases, however, it is irrelevant. There are a great many institutional decisions that are autocratically made, in which the faculty has only an advisory voice. There are autocrats everywhere, and the political climates of colleges vary widely. It would be facile to warn you, as you begin your job search, to try to gain an insight into that climate. Moreover, the people you meet will be as varied as the climates. Some will act like veritable members of the Chamber of Commerce, and others will regale you with their troubles. You cannot get a sense of place until you have been around for a while.

This uncertainty, of course, seems to make "kissing up" a requirement for beginning professors. This is an abrasive notion to confront, but it is an important lesson. Some people in authority are susceptible to flattery. One alternative for a new academic appointee is to play the political game well under the caveat that it is very hard to see one's individual merit so early in one's career. Scholars progress slowly over many years to earn their reputations through diligent teaching, taxing research, and consistent publishing. These qualities may not become apparent during the brief probationary time before the tenure decision is made. On the other hand, many of those that cannot earn tenure campaign for it. Said one cynic, the second most important thing in the academy is "competence. " The most important is making people believe you are competent.

POLITICS IS POWER

There are different kinds of power up for grabs in the university. One is the power to control your own destiny. The other is the more traditional power embodied in controlling events, making decisions that affect others, and in general, being a "big shot. " Both take considerable time and effort to accomplish. The first comes as a result of outstanding performance at teaching, research, and so on. The second comes as a result of skilled politics, including service on committees and performance of subordinate administrative tasks. Occasionally, an academic excels in both areas, but it is rare.

There are also perks at stake. Very few are granted to beginning professors, but once you attain a certain position in the university, you gain a modicum of budget control. You get a better office, secretarial service and research assistance, travel expenses to conventions, and, perhaps, a title. Although the fate of nations does not hang on any decision made within the university, in the final analysis, an academic institution can be very influential in the community at large, and those who are important in it can be important in the world. Certainly the scientists, physicians, and law professors in the university carry their status into the world. It is important to remember that academic institutions are not remote islands of introspection, but live communities, active with ideas that penetrate the world around them.

It is hard for beginners to understand that academic politics, university Senates, the committee system, and even collective bargaining are often little more than displays. The same is true in the world at large. Industrial organizations do not give very much power to the lower echelons. Even administrators with high status have little control over major policies. Most academic institutions employ some sort of industrial model, and although they appear to encourage participation, they often pay little attention to it once they get it. The important thing is not to waste your time in your early years. When you get your first position, there will be blandishments to serve on this committee or supervise that program. Some of you will not be able to avoid this. But every political task takes time from teaching and research. Your dilemma will be to adjudicate among the demands of the four criteria for advancement and decide where to invest your time. Especially in the political arena, beginners must learn to distinguish between the appearances of politics and what is really important. In the long run, the big budget items are decided by trustees. Few faculty members have the political clout to participate, and the high rollers rarely consider the faculty in their final decisions.

Faculty members get to play with pennies; the trustees make sure there is enough loose change rolling around so that faculty members can be kept occupied fighting about it. The trustees will spend millions on a new sports complex, whereas within the department, the faculty fights over who gets a new PC or a choice parking space. These are perks worth fighting for. But oddly enough, the upper echelons also tend to leave the academic program alone. The professor, in a sense, is in complete charge in his or her classroom and within the perimeters of what is allowable under the rubric of academic freedom, he or she is free to think, to be innovative, and to study.

But the novice knows very little of this at the outset. Most novices are naive, idealistic, and ready to give their all for alma mater and the bright-eyed students who sit before them. They are tempted by the political plums, and there is no denying that a few of them will make successful careers based in campus politics. But it takes a while for them to discover that to the "higher ups," they are marks on an organization chart, manipulable and expendable. These days, many high-powered schools are literally revolving doors for beginners; they are in and out in about seven years. Once their salary goes up and they do not bring in grant money, they are turned out and replaced by lower salaried beginners. When a major university spots a star elsewhere, they often pay the price to get him or her.

So, there is a paradox. Tenure is the goal—but many do not achieve it at their first-choice school. Some who achieve it go slack and reduce their efforts. And, standing apart from the herd, there are the stars, consistent performers for whom political issues are irrelevant. They are immersed in their work, committed to their profession, and high achievers. They are the models who set the standards by which newcomers are judged.

Actually, the picture is not quite so bad as it looks. If you make a good career choice and get a job for which your talents match expectations, you can look forward to a rewarding career. Earning tenure gives you both intellectual freedom and the power to make decisions about your professional life. It is worth working for and once it is earned, it is worth justifying by quality teaching and productive research. This is where the academy is very different from industry. Your university is not likely to go bankrupt or be sold out from under you. Once you have earned your patent of security, you may use it as a protecting shield from distractions from your main job of teaching and research. Your own noblesse oblige will guide your political activities.

THE NATURE OF THE POLITICAL GAME

Whether we like it or not, even the most effete institutions must be governed, and most operate on an industrial model. There is a lot of money coming in and out and a great many ongoing operations that have nothing to do with instruction and research. Buildings and grounds must be maintained, the legislature must be lobbied, and funds must be secured. The lawn must be mowed and the snow removed. Consequently, there must be an organization. The professors are not going to do the routine work.

There is a board of trustees that operates much like a corporate group. They control the money, and, although they do not initiate the important decisions, they have veto power. Many trustees are appointed by state governors; in private institutions, trustees are often elected. Some private institutions, especially those that are church-related, often have their parent body appoint the trustees. Trustees are often political people with agendas. They delegate the administrative details, but they set the policy that guarantees the institution meets the mission imposed on it by its constituency. The role of the trustees is primarily economic; their mission is to provide the "grease" to keep the wheels spinning. That means that individual and human interests are often subordinated to what appear to be cold economic realities. Their job is to keep the institution going. No one works for an organization that is out of business; thus, their work is vital and their power is substantial.

Doing the day-to-day work of administration is a cadre of officials: presidents, vice presidents, chancellors, provosts, and deans. Whatever their titles, they are arrayed by rank and specialty. There are those responsible for budgets, others for academic programs, and still others for alumni relations. Some even look after the welfare of students. They are ostensibly responsible to the trustees, but the president (or the head person) is the interface between the administration and the trustees. These people decide on how money is to be spent, including faculty salaries. This gives them considerable influence over the behavior of the faculty.

In a sense, those in the upper echelons of administration do not really care about what the faculty does. If the courses do not sound too crazy and do not get bad publicity in the press, the faculty is pretty much free to pursue its own muse. Faculty (as a body) can design a curriculum, specify requirements, and as individuals, follow their own line of research. The administration often rubber stamps the faculty's decisions exactly as the trustees rubber stamp administrative decisions. Still, it does not pay to forget the line of authority. If you attract the attention of the upper brass early in your career, it is prudent that it be for something distinguished such as getting a development grant for your research.

One of the most critical issues is deciding on your own political aspirations. It is possible to exist in an academic institution without being political, but it is often not much of an existence. If you do not look out for yourself, no one else will. Many new academics look about for a "mentor" to advise and protect them. This may be an illusion. Mentors rarely act for altruistic reasons. We discuss mentors in detail shortly.

Even at the beginning level, there is a lot you can gain by being sensitive to the distribution of power and by understanding who makes decisions about what. We are not advocating that you butter up the big shots (although this is easy to do and not particularly demeaning), but we do caution you to be careful about whom you challenge about what issues. There is a great deal of academic business over which those new to the institution have little influence, and it is senseless to jeopardize your political position by engaging in fights that, at best, can only bring pyrrhic victories. You may believe that Prof. Oldteimer's course is out of date and should be replaced as a requirement, and you may even scare up enough votes to accomplish it, but you cannot be sure the replacement will be any better, and you may have earned Oldteimer's opposition when the promotion and tenure committee meets. The political issues you will face are sometimes that clear-cut and simple, and they can be resolved only by weighing your own ethical code against the possibility of victory and the shape of your future.

One of the most important elements in attaining political power is finding knowledgeable advisors and protectors. The name "mentor" is often used to describe this role, but the metaphor is inappropriate. Mentor was the loyal selfless servant of Odysseus whose job it was to train Telemachus, son of Odysseus, in the art of war. In the academy, mentoring does not come cheap. There may be some altruists who take a "youngling" under their wings, but for the most part there is a price to be paid for mentoring. For all the idealism associated with the word, mentoring is a political process by which older members of the faculty gain the support of younger members in exchange for advice and sometimes influence. Beginning faculty members are often too optimistic about it; they do not really want advice at all, they want protection and patronage. They want powerful older members of the faculty to intercede for them and push the buttons that bring important things their way.

Very often, the weakest person in the organization is the first person to greet the newcomer. The person who need allies most makes a concerted effort to get them by offering blandishments to the beginners. There are perils associated with accepting these offers. For one thing, you might find yourself in a weak political party. For another, the person who offers friendship may have little else to offer, and in fact may be weaker than you are. Much of the political jockeying in the academic organization appears to be socializing. This is far from the case. What appears to be random socialization normally does not occur out of affinity or even curiosity, but out of the perceived demands of the political structure.

But this brings up the issue of collegiality. You have to get along with your colleagues. We could take the position that "some people got it and some don't," but that would be the easy way out. We do caution, however, that people in the academy are not different from people with whom you might work anywhere. They have their own motives and goals. You may be a potential friend to them, but at the minimum, you are a co-worker and you must be accounted for. To a large extent, political power in an academic department depends on the alignment of allegiances and factions that grow up around issues as they arise. Those who want to expand the course offerings (to include their pet courses) may have to group together and support each other. Those who feel their entrenched courses are imperiled by new courses may form another faction. The department then experiences conflict.

Many communication professionals, presumably, specialize in group problem solving, but often they remain sufficiently theoretical that they do not address the issues that affect their own lives. You do not get much mileage out of reminding them of this. The people who point a cautionary finger usually find themselves consigned, like Jeremiah, to be buried to the neck in mud. Most departments attempt to obviate problems arising from absolutely essential disagreements by setting up some sort of formal decision-making system. In some cases, the department head is supreme and rules on all issues.

Other departments may function through an apparently democratic committee system in which people with common interests are formed into decision-making groups. Some go as far as to turn all controversial issues into agendas for departmental meetings. This kind of decision making works well as long as it can be confined to the department. If intradepartmental disagreements become public currency, the whole administrative system can collapse. Thus, it is sometimes politic to lose graciously rather than challenge a mature decision-making system. On the other hand, in matters of greater moral consequence, each individual can appeal to the next administrative level and hope for the best. There is, however, no formal appellate jurisdiction. An academic community is self-contained, but although it contains an obvious executive body and sometimes a legislature, a judiciary is notoriously lacking.

Genuine democratic decision making is rarely found, however, because any pretense at equality and equity is lost in the hierarchical system that prevails within the faculty. Professor, associate professor, tenured assistant professor, untenured assistant professor on tenure track, fixed-term instructor—it is almost like the military. There are commissioned officers, non-coms, and the troops. The junior (nontenured) members of the department are dependent on the goodwill of the senior members for their award of tenure, and consequently are not often characterized by their courage in standing up to the power structure. In fact, in a quest for patronage, younger members of the department often ally themselves with seniors they perceive as powerful and able to protect them from unfortunate decisions to be made later on.

In short, what we are trying to tell you is that life in the academy, like life in the real world, is far from abstractly theoretical, and it is sometimes brutal. You are responsible for the consequences of the decisions you make and the people with whom you choose to ally yourself. We might also offer the caution that there is very little to be gained from coming into a new department and advising about how things were done at your old school. No one is interested, and such talk may mark you as a hopeless moralist or doctrinaire or be used as grounds to subject you to various indignities (or at least, suspicion). This paranoid view of departmental politics runs counter to the image of the ideal university, but it represents what goes on at some, perhaps most, institutions. Faculty may learn to solve their problems with grace and dignity, but they often "duke it out" as if engaged in a street corner brawl.

The counterpart of this is that there is a great deal to be gained from collegiality. The goodwill of senior colleagues can be helpful when tenure decisions are made. More importantly, senior members can help you understand your new profession and the complex workings of your institution, and they can be helpful in consoling you in times of professional disappointment. Your own peers in age and rank can become lifelong friends and collaborators.

One axiom well worth following is that power derives from performance. At some institutions, one way to acquire power is to gain distinction in the profession at large. By publishing in quality journals and appearing on programs at important meetings, you acquire standing in your department. At others, you may be judged by your contribution to the educational program. Professional productivity, no matter how the institution defines it, is the currency of power. The same holds true for teaching. Even though you may not get too much credit for being a "great" teacher (there are really very few "great" teachers), a major gaffe in the classroom can hurt you seriously. In a later chapter, we talk about some of the requirements maintaining quality teaching performance. For now, the Hippocratic injunction—"above all, do no harm"—applies. Take care with teaching, and make it up to date, well planned, considerate of student needs, and loose enough to allow reasonable appeals and criticisms.

Another important issue is for you to discover what is of value to your institution. Then you must decide whether you can and will provide it. If you can, your future is hopeful. If you cannot or choose not to, it may be wise to seek another position. Where research and publication are paramount, being awarded grants is a way to power. Where teaching is the major criterion, winning the approval of your students is your ticket. Senior members of the faculty can guide you in understanding what your choices are, but you are the only one who can make them. You have choices in the goals you set, and it does not hurt to try to make your personal goals compatible with those of your employer.

One last word on politics. There are both internal and external politics. Some years ago, the terms "cosmopolitans" and "locals" were used to refer to different types of employees. A cosmopolitan paid attention to the profession, whereas a local was concerned about the institution. More recently, in an article in a popular paper, an employee of a small state university complained that his colleagues were annoyed with him because he was publishing too much and was too active in professional associations, whereas the major players in the professional associations paid no attention to him because he was employed by a small university. His plight illustrates what happens when a person who is cosmopolitan in outlook is employed in an institution that rewards locals. Conversely, in major research universities, locals do the grunt labor, but cosmopolitans win the major rewards.

The issue of basic allegiance is one you must resolve for yourself. Do academics owe primary loyalty to their academic discipline or to their institution? You may elect to be the big fish by becoming important nationally, through major research contributions or as an officer of important organizations. On the other hand, you may wish a smaller pond and seek importance on your own campus via service through committee membership and other contributions to the local mission. There is no uniformly "better" choice; it is a matter of personal commitment, but it is important that the commitment be made and understood by the beginning academic.

Whatever your choice, you cannot escape your institution's mission. Some institutions are clearly bound by externally imposed obligations. Public institutions are sensitive in their goal setting to the legislative commitments of the body that funds them. Church-related schools are often obligated to the ethical commitments of the church that supports them. Schools locked into communities, such as urban community colleges, have a burden to meet the local needs for employment and services. The instructor who is out of step with such commitments may find him- or herself "in the soup," not only with the authorities, but with colleagues as well. The academic we referred to above, who sought distinction in the national arena despite his employment by a local college, is an example of how conflict in commitment can pose problems—sometimes serious ones—in a career.

By the same token, you cannot ignore your obligation to your own self-interest. Despite the ostensibly eleemosynary nature of the college teaching profession, it is necessary for the academic to meet living expenses and maintain a properly ambient lifestyle. That means that you must pay some attention to your income and expenses. The question of how you can rise economically in the institution becomes very important. Augmenting your income through consulting or other outside employment is also an issue. For example, many large institutions maintain extensive continuing education programs, and faculty members are paid extra money for teaching courses in them. This is one way to increase your income, but it could materially interfere with the amount of time you have available for your students or to apply to your research. Similarly, consulting is usually gratifying. Being paid in exchange for something you know is both flattering and provides a warm feeling in the wallet. On the other hand, the use of institutional facilities to support private consulting is risky, not to mention illegal in many places. Consulting can also distract you from your main obligation. One may put a little money in the bank through continuing education and consulting, but an academic will rarely be promoted because of it. Senior professors, near the end of their career and not involved in any major new research, can more easily afford to be major players in the consulting game and often are.

A distinguished professor once advised the younger faculty that a good article published in a major journal during the first year or two of employment could be worth $250,000 in a lifetime. The article enhances your value and raises your pay, which, in turn, raises your retirement annuity. To continue this pattern of publication means further increasing your value on the market, which will either get you a better job or motivate your home institution to raise your pay, at least at institutions not having fixed salary schedules. In short, economic prudence demands maximum performance on the job. The extras which look so tempting can prove to be distractions.

However, the importance of income cannot be denied. You need enough money on which to live. Without adequate income, it is not possible to think and perform as effectively as your institution would expect. Some younger faculty members, in the rush to raise a family, buy a house, or pay off undergraduate and graduate debts, occasionally get themselves trapped in the money chase; they lose sight of their professional obligations and spend the bulk of their time hunting "bucks." In one such case, a smart young academic, five years into his profession and a husband and father, on the verge of tenure, found himself with a lucrative but time-consuming consulting contract. He did well at the consulting, but when it came time for his evaluation for tenure, his teaching ratings were low, and he had nothing in print. He is once again job hunting. His chances of another academic job at a comparable institution are very slim, but there is some chance that his consulting client may hire him full time. When this happens, the question of whether or not you are ready for a career change becomes very important.

PERSONAL GRATIFICATION AND SERVICE

The preceding story brings us to the central moral issue of an academic's professional career: the obligations of professionalism. A career in the academy is not for everyone. There is a mission to be fulfilled; only those who are gratified personally by fulfilling that mission ought to undertake it.

We said earlier that there are some (actually very few) academics who are well-to-do as a result of their scholarly work. Most of the well-to-do academics I have met, however, have inherited a good stock portfolio. Few get rich in the academy. If you have the right employer, you have security, decent benefits, and a regular job that you cannot easily lose, but you will not become wealthy. In fact, one does not seriously consider an academic career for the money. There are exceptions in the case of scientists who make prodigious discoveries and share in the patents, but these instances are rare and mostly serendipitous.

Most young academics choose their career because they are captivated with the lifestyle. Some have been influenced by their own professors and want to follow in their path. They may make the choice without having the vaguest notion of what this professor does when he or she is not in his classroom. Often, those who choose the career based on hero worship do not understand the research and publication obligation, nor do they realize how difficult it is to teach well. What seems to be the leisurely pace of academic life is what captivates them.

The academic life is considerably more demanding than most people expect. One prolific researcher even declared, "It is an unhealthy life. You sit a lot." Academics spend a lot of time alone, the profession is sedentary (unless you are a coach), it is highly competitive, and it calls for a constant state of mental alertness and attention to world events. An academic is expected to be well informed, especially in his or her specialty.

The bottom line for those who choose an institution that demands research productivity is that one's dissertation is repeated several times in the course of a career. Life is a process of designing studies, gathering data, writing up results, and in many cases, procuring the funding as well. Writing is a slow and painful process for most. Articles and books are not accepted at first writing, the process of editing and revising is time-consuming, and the suspense of waiting to find out whether a piece is accepted can be unbearable. There must be a genuine love of the process to make it palatable.

In Chapter 1 we talked about the North Dakota legislator who referred to 12 hours of teaching as a "long day." The typical college teacher is responsible for the equivalent of 12 hours of instruction a week. In some cases, this is divided between teaching and research. Let us consider what is involved in 12 hours of teaching. Twelve hours a week normally translates into 36 hours or more, given that it takes roughly 2 hours to prepare for 1 hour in the classroom. And, that is a bare minimum. Faculty members are expected to be up to date in their discipline, to maintain active contact with colleagues elsewhere, and to constantly be alert to new ways to prepare and distribute information to students, many (if not most) of whom may not be terribly interested in what is going on. They must also keep office hours to see the students who are interested or who have complaints. They are also expected to do their share of committee duty and to make themselves generally useful in the college community.

College teachers rarely face classes full of bright-eyed, eager youngsters, hungry for knowledge. Those who teach required courses know the sullen expressions and bored yawns all too well. Overcoming resistance to the instruction process is not an easy task. It calls for a good physical constitution and mental agility on the level of a stand-up comic.

The issue of fraternization and relationships with students has also become a serious public issue. Questions of sexual harassment and evangelism by professors are both troublesome. The new academic must decide what posture to take on these and similar issues such as those regarding discrimination because of race, gender, religion, and sexual orientation. They must also take a position on freedom of speech, political correctness, and affirmative action. Add to all this the obligation as a beginning academic to serve on committees and tend to the daily business of the university, and it makes for a long week of long days. College faculty members rarely work a 40-hour week. All that time off that looks so alluring at the outset is usually spent being buried in the library, pouring over notes, gathering data, or writing. What time there is left is usually devoted to evaluating students' work. What this adds up to is the demand for serious dedication to the process.

One senior professor, about to retire, commented about life during the prime of his career. He was an officer of a national professional organization which required his attendance at a dozen national and regional meetings. He served on the committee to review sabbatical applications. This committee, he estimated, took about 10 hours a week for a period of 3 months. He was in the midst of gathering data for a major book and responsible for administering and teaching a section in the college honors program. He also taught a demanding seminar required of many graduate students. Each semester he had to fill out a card estimating the hours he had worked. This would eventually be submitted to the legislature. He discovered that he was working in the neighborhood of 80 hours per week. He had no time for a movie, to play catch with his sons, to take his wife to dinner. He simply had to endure the pressure and hope that during the summer term it would let up.

Although most academics will not achieve this level of stress, they will all come close. They will all have national commitments and local obligations. They will be torn between their commitments to teaching and research and their private life. It is as taxing as being an executive of a corporation, but nowhere near as lucrative.

Put this into a context in which you are constantly confronted with difficult ethical issues to resolve, and you will have some understanding of what it is really like to be a faculty member. To put it bluntly, we must now declare C. P. Snow wrong. The decision about whether to pass a borderline Ph.D. candidate is not trivial, nor is figuring out what to do with a prominent athlete about to flunk your course. The young adults you serve bring you their problems and expect you to help, and you may feel like a coward if you back off. Any decision you make about perks, or course assignments, or rewards of any kind mean denial of those privileges to others. There is no escape from pressure.

It is small wonder that so many aspirants drop out while still in graduate school and why there is attrition of those who do not achieve tenure or who are drawn away by the financial blandishments of private industry. Let us consider in detail some of the serious issues you have to confront in your academic life.

THE CONTROVERSIAL ISSUES OF THE ACADEMY

There is a question of whether the college classroom is a "bully pulpit." There are unlimited opportunities for college faculties to influence the impressionable. In fact, the opportunity to be "in control" may be a powerful incentive to people seeking this career. There is a personal temptation to advocate, which is constantly in conflict with the professional demand to be impartial. Because objectivity is often impossible, awareness of bias is an imperative. Students must understand the preferences and commitments of their teachers. But more important is the burden of proof professors have for their scholarly presentations and the opinions they express in public.

There is, theoretically, an elusive concept called academic freedom: the right to free expression of ideas and the unlimited right to search for truth, which is bound only by requirements of disciplinary assignment, good taste, and common decency. Conferring of tenure, in essence, licenses faculties to engage in any responsible expression of ideas they choose. There are, however, some complex legal limitations and requirements of which aspiring academics must be aware. Young faculty members should consider the history of AAUP and its policies on censure to get an idea of the volatility of this concept. Furthermore, arguments about political correctness and the rights of minority groups have led to important questions about the censorship of ideas. Questions about the ethics of new scientific advances such as genetic engineering and robotics will become more and more important as technology advances further. These issues are hard to evade. As an academic professional you will be expected to have opinions and prepared to express them.

Consider a typical issue in the communication discipline, a question posed to me by my doctoral advisor. "You know how to teach public speaking," he declared. "Would you teach what you know to a young person you knew would turn into Adolph Hitler?" This is an intriguing question. The speech arts confer considerable power on those who learn them. What is the obligation of the teacher to his or her students? What kinds of decisions are permissible to give or to withhold? And what of the right of the teacher to self-expression? A colleague commented about the perennial debate between pro-life and pro-choice advocates in her public speaking class. She had her own opinions. Was she justified in giving them? Does the principle of academic freedom entitle the faculty member to foist his or her opinions on members of the class? What of opinions outside of the purview of the course being taught? Does the faculty member have the right to express these opinions? Can he or she express them from the lectern, or does academic freedom only refer to rights of self-expression outside the formal lecture hall?

There is the issue of plagiarism. To what extent can academics share their work? There are now complex questions concerning rights to academic ideas in print raised by electronic publishing. The sale of second-hand books, the ability to scan books into computers or to make up packets of xeroxed chapters threaten to revolutionize the copyright laws. Respect for academic property is an imperative. Most universities have policies on patents and copyrights, but it is easy to "borrow" from one another for use in the classroom. Giving fair credit for ideas is an important component of collegiality. And today, more than ever, academics are faced with changes in the publishing industry that could revolutionize the requirements for tenure and promotion and which have already seriously restricted the outlets for their published work.

What of the right of dissent on matters of institutional policy? What if you oppose the president's policies or the dean's decisions? Does academic freedom entitle you to resist? If so, what are the legitimate forms of this resistance? Can you speak against administrative policies? Where? Must your speaking be confined to the legitimate forums provided by the institution, or can you take your case to your fellow faculty members? During the years when faculties were forming labor unions, several professionals, active in organization, had horror stories to tell about how their institutions took retribution against them.

There are also other major political issues embodied in academic freedom. In recent years the core of the canon of instruction has come under fire for various political and social reasons. Female activists and members of ethnic communities talk of "other voices." They are concerned that what is taught is mostly the work of "dead, white, European, men." They want a voice. They demand that works of broader scope and diverse origin be included in required courses and that special attention be paid in all courses to people outside the traditional academic mainstream. Academics are expected to take a stand on ethical questions such as diversity, "other voices," and political correctness.

But what if you dissent? Does it make you a racist if you believe that the works of Scott Fitzgerald should be included in a basic American literature course and the works of Eldridge Cleaver excluded? Does it make you a sexist if works by female authors make up only 20% of your reading list? As women make up more than 50% of the population, should readings be parceled out proportionately? What are the standards for judging whether a work should be included as required reading in any course? Are the writers of this book to be condemned by bringing up this question in such a way as to suggest that there may be arguments on both sides?

And what of the free speech aspects of those who oppose the "other" voices? What, for example, is your stand on the question of whether students should be allowed to speak openly of their opposition to homosexuals? In fact, should a faculty member be allowed to speak against feminism or African-American separatism? In a major case in Ontario, a psychology professor published an article in which he reviewed approximately 1,000 studies of racial accomplishment and "concluded" that Orientals and blacks were always on the extreme ends of the continuum, best or worst, whereas Caucasians occupied the middle position (not always, but as a rule). He published the results in a major scientific journal and received the support of a sizable minority of the members of his discipline. But the province of Ontario, through its legally designated representatives, felt he was guilty of racism. They attempted to have his tenure revoked; they tried him under a provincial statute forbidding denigration of a minority group. On the other hand, in the early months of 1992, a young, African-American columnist on the student paper of a major university wrote a column in which he called on his fellow students to buy guns to protect themselves from "the white oppressors." Many people condemned the student paper for publishing the column. The paper claimed first amendment rights and demanded that the column be published. Others pointed out, however, that the paper would not have published similar sentiments by the Ku Klux Klan advocating killing African Americans. Where would you stand on an issue like this? These kinds of arguments are becoming more and more frequent and more polarized. National organizations are forming (for example, University Center for Rational Alternatives), some made up of conservative academics who support the "canon of the dead, white, European men," and others of liberals who advocate that "other voices" be heard. They write in shibboleths and shout slogans at each other. They expect their colleagues to take sides. The academic programs of major universities have been affected by the outcome of these battles. A major southern university, for example, assembled an English Department made up mainly of deconstructionists. The 1991 meeting of the Modern Language Association was characterized by political clashes between the conservative and the politically correct. Although most academics still stand apart from the battle, the ferocity of the argument indicates that more and more professionals will be forced to take sides. And when this controversy is settled, there will be another and still another which will demand your attention and decision.

One of these is compensatory education. It seems almost obligatory at academic cocktail parties to spend a little time attacking the public schools (or preparatory schools, if you are Ivy League) for doing a poor job of preparing students for college. There is some talk about African Americans and Hispanic Americans and whether they are qualified for academic careers, or whether they need special training in reading, writing, and study skills to qualify them for academic work. Should they compete on equal terms as freshmen, or should the standards be lowered on their behalf both in admissions and in expectations of performance? These are not easy questions to answer. Alan Dershowitz, for example, points out in his book *Chutzpah* (1991) that at one time Jews were excluded from major universities by a quota system; in some cases, they were not regarded as fit for instruction. Now, he points out, schools are required by affirmative action to modify their entrance requirements in favor of ascribed minority groups. Professional publications regularly present arguments on all sides of these issues. Most recently, one contributor argued that affirmative action legislation actually works against Americans of Oriental ancestry. As a corollary, there is the issue of foreign students and how they are to be treated. One colleague, who specializes in the instruction of foreign students in English, reports that some Middle Eastern students refuse to work with her because they do not want to be taught by a woman. How much instruction in nuclear physics would you want to give a talented young scientist from a potential enemy country? Whom do you support? Do the Arabs have a right to their "cultural" norms on American campuses, or must we take a stand to protect the rights of our colleagues? Do we have the obligation to share important scientific information with everyone, regardless of the use they would have for it?

Then there is the question of the relationship of athletic programs to instruction. At many institutions, the academic disciplines are subordinated (or seem to be subordinated) to major athletic enterprises. The trustees argue that a good athletic program makes the school visible and draws students. (Are these the students you want?) On the other hand, compromises are sometimes called for in the way the athletes are treated.

There are questions of the arts and fidelity to the common culture as well. E. D. Hirsch, in his book *Cultural Literacy* (1987), raised the question of whether there was a common core of knowledge we all must have for meaningful education to occur. On the other hand, there is a clamor for "value received" in a college education. Students, often with the support of their parents, demand that college prepare them for life in the world and train them to obtain and hold jobs. Can a universal canon of literacy of any kind (with or without "other voices") hold its own in competition with a demand for trained specialists who can go into industry, draw good wages, pay taxes, and make society run. What is the purpose of a college education anyway? And does it make a difference what kind of college it is? Does the Ivy League-type school have a different responsibility from the state university? Does the community college have a mission that drastically differs from the private liberal arts college?

There is a legitimate argument between those who advocate that there is a continuity of learning from the liberal arts and those who urge that "other voices" be heard. The idea is to balance respect for the ideas of the past and the academic tradition with changes in society and the position of various people and groups in it. The academy has always changed; for example, it has accommodated to revolutions in technology. The adaptation, however, has generally been gradual. We respectfully suggest that a major obligation of academic professionals is to find and defend one's position on these and other difficult issues.

Is there a core of knowledge everyone ought to have? If so, who decides what it is? How does new "stuff" get in? What about the rights of other voices to be heard? These arguments, oddly enough, are not largely confined to the liberal arts, which are regarded as less and less important in some quarters. In other sections of the university, vocational preparation and integration of the university with industry are of paramount consideration. Professors of engineering and communications/journalism have to be sure that their students are employable.

How (if at all) should professional training in law, medicine, and theology be revised? What is the future of professional training for academics? Is the traditional core of education viable? To what extent will the university become a feeder system for industry and government? Is it the case that college is a way of keeping control over entry into the labor market? To what extent will the community college and university branch become a vocational training ground tailored to the needs of particular communities? All of these issues must be faced.

The problem is where to stand on issues that arise between general education in the liberal arts and specific professional needs in engineering or business. How are people to be prepared for such professions as law and medicine? Where do the academic's responsibilities lie? Are they to the discipline or to the students? Is there a necessary conflict between economic interests and the continuity of human knowledge? The dialectic between higher education as training for life or as preparation for a career constrains the interests and activities of academics.

The political and ethical issues you will confront have the potential to divide campuses across political lines, and they can potentially interfere with careers. Professionals often acquire potentially embarrassing information about others and must make a decision about "whistle blowing." Sometimes the exigencies of promotion and tenure present temptations to cut corners. There is no prevailing code, although professional organizations such as AAUP attempt to monitor institutional violations. Individual cases of breaches of ethics are often swept under the rug or handled "confidentially." Do you secure your rights by joining a labor union? Are the present professional organizations sufficiently powerful to protect you from encroachments by political agencies and administrators? Or, are you on your own?

Finally, there are issues relevant to funding. How can we pay the bills for higher education? Are we to depend on legislatures for funding? What about dwindling endowments? Rising costs? How are salaries to be managed to attract the "best" possible people into the profession? Should academics be responsible for funding their own work through grants? The personnel policies of the future will certainly relate to funding.

Do we need new personnel policies? Must we all assume heavier teaching loads or larger classes? Do we need to reconsider some of our provisions for tenure? Should we use more part-time faculty? What are the motivations for teaching in a university? How do they affect costs? What is the proper balance of a graduate vs. an undergraduate education? What about the proportion of teaching vs. research that should be expected? Is "publish or perish" an appropriate constraint? Does it make money for the university? Where should the financial emphasis be placed: on vocational training or on liberal education?

It is likely that funding will be seriously revised over the next decade. It would be fatuous to make predictions here about what the nature of funding will be. Universities make a major effort to obtain funding from their alumni. They engage in commercial enterprises and often find themselves in conflict with their neighbors, an economic form of the town/gown battle. The results of the funding wars will affect your future, both in deciding who will pay your salary and how large it will be. It may threaten the policy of granting tenure, for it is very costly to maintain. It may affect the quality of education, and it may produce institutions at which it is not so attractive to work.

You cannot ignore your own personal stake in the process! To review, you must:

- understand the power structure
- make allies, take sides
- develop a research and publication plan
- cultivate teaching skills
- see to the ambiance of your own lifestyle
- make moral decisions about your relationships with students and administrators
- be prepared to deal with the moral and political issues with which you are confronted.

◆ RESPONSE TO CHAPTER TWO
JULIA T. WOOD

Radio commentator Paul Harvey generally follows his first dramatic comments on a story by saying "and now for the other half of the story." In my response to Chapter 2, I wish to offer at least another part of the story, which is a different perspective on issues facing all beginning academics. Although I do not disagree with Professor Phillips's observations on campus politics, I think his presentation is somewhat misleading in presenting them out of a larger context which reveals that political activity can be constructive for and integral to academic life.

At the root of the divergence between our position are quite distinct views of the nature of political activity. He seems to view politics as an exchange: You rub my back, I'll rub yours; you grease my palm, I'll grease yours; you do me a favor, I'll owe you one and you call it in. In contrast, I see politics as a way to further causes in which individuals and groups believe. Political action is collaborative. It is a way of creating and advancing positions and enlarging one's impact. It is in this sense that academic life, and mentoring and collegiality in particular, are positively political.

Academic institutions exist to create and share knowledge. Those faculty who most enjoy an academic life are the ones who have a broad, basic love of learning and who wish to participate actively in the learning process throughout their careers. In this sense, the academic enterprise is inherently political because strong beliefs and intense arguments are the essence of engaged participation in learning. Thus, faculty have different views on issues, disagree, and try to advance what is their best understanding of knowledge and the ways to enhance its creation and promulgation. This, in fact, is one of the integral qualities of good faculty and good institutions: They allow—even encourage—disagreement and debate. In this book, we follow that model, arguing with each other's positions, offering alternative views of issues, and seeking to call readers' attention to various perspectives.

Each of the four of us argues a point of view, yet there is something larger to which all of us are committed. We think that we and those who read this book are more likely to have a holistic perspective and to understand the complexities of academic life as a result of considering different opinions than out of having any single viewpoint presented as "truth." Even though I may disagree with my co-authors on a host of issues, I realize I need to hear and consider their ideas. I need to do more than tolerate their positions or grant them polite hearing; I need to wrestle seriously with their viewpoints in order to clarify my own thinking. This is the nature of academic life at its best, and it is why the academy is and should remain politically charged. Without strong beliefs supported by impassioned arguments and without the willingness to hear and consider views different than one's own, the academy cannot evolve and change in ways that keep it and those involved in it reflective, informed, and vital.

I also wish to add my perspective to Professor Phillips's comments on mentoring and collegiality. Again, I agree with the claim that these are in part political activities, yet I do not share his view of what politics are nor his implication that they are necessarily bad. At their best, both mentoring and collegiality are richly collaborative, ongoing interactions that enhance all participants. Many have assisted me in my education, scholarly projects, and career growth, and Gerry Phillips is at the top of the list of those who have supported me. Despite his focus on tradeoffs, exchanges of favors, and balance sheets, I have known Professor Phillips to mentor and work with a variety of individuals who could in no way advance his position or directly return his support. He does so for a simple reason: He believes in certain ideas and issues, and he is willing to assist those who share his views, regardless of whether they can reciprocate in kind.

This captures much of what mentoring and collegiality mean to me. In my experience, mentoring usually is based on mutual interests and respect and a shared commitment to particular research programs, theories, and/or teaching goals and practices. Thus, people whom I mentor are the ones with whom I share important assumptions about our field and the nature of academic life. We collaborate to teach each other more about those matters and to enhance each other's ability to advance our theories in varied contexts. I expect no "payoff" from those I mentor other than seeing them continue to engage in thinking, teaching, and service that make a difference to our field and the academy. Their accomplishments are rewarding to me, as is the process of working closely in a collaborative manner.

Mentoring should involve a senior person's awareness of his or her power and the responsibilities incumbent in that. The position that I enjoy, for instance, provides me with opportunities to exercise some influence on the direction of my department, field, and campus. I did not achieve this position all by myself, although I have pulled on my own bootstraps. I was materially assisted every step of the way by people such as Professors Phillips and Gouran, as well as many others. They invested time and energy in me, and I feel grateful more than indebted, I express the gratitude not by a quid pro quo return to them, but by passing on their support to rising scholars of the next generation so that these individuals may exercise their influence in years ahead. It is this recognition of a larger community and long-term goals that informs my mentoring and my sense of the political, that is, partisan, choices to support certain individuals and ideas.

In academic institutions, the "lone warrior" is generally ineffective. There is little an individual can do to advance causes, create change, or resist what she or he considers ill-advised. More constructive is working together with others with whom one shares important premises about a discipline and the academy. By networking with others and interacting collaboratively with colleagues and junior colleagues, faculty members expand their influence and the impact of their ideas. From my perspective, politics as collaborative, collective, rhetorical activity is the lifeblood of a vigorous educational institution and an engaged academic career.

◆ RESPONSE TO CHAPTER TWO
DENNIS S. GOURAN

In his observations, Professor Phillips brings into focus numerous matters of which those new to the academic profession may not be aware—or at least not previously affected by in any significant way. In so doing, he has rendered a valuable service. The type of inoculation his remarks provide can do much to help one cope with the excesses of the political aspects of academic life that may be encountered. In certain respects, however, my colleague may have overstated his case about academic politics. At the very least, he may be guilty of focusing too much on extremes.

That there is a political dimension to the academic profession is hardly disputable. Its role and impact, however, may vary from limited to dominant. What is difficult to establish is what is normal or typical. This is understandable because, as in many other aspects of life, it is the atypical that focuses our attention. Cognitive scientists (e.g., Nisbett & Ross, 1980; Tversky & Kahneman, 1973) remind us that both perceptions and social judgments are frequently subject to the undue influence of information that is available in memory and most easily retrievable. Information exhibiting these properties is likely, moreover, to involve the novel, vivid, and infrequent components in a perceptual field. In addition, media coverage is likely to reflect what gatekeepers consider to be newsworthy. One finds few stories, for instance, about successful promotion and tenure cases, university presidents who retire without golden parachutes, grant and contract offices that deal honestly with funding agencies, and the like. News about excess, therefore, tends to shape our perceptions of life in the academy.

My point here is that much of the day-to-day business of academic life is essentially apolitical. Even those thoroughly enmeshed in academic politics, in all likelihood, spend proportionately a much greater percentage of their time performing the routine aspects of their jobs than in dealing with the sorts of issues Professor Phillips mentions (e. g., academic freedom and political correctness, in-fighting, jockeying for position, and influence peddling). This is not to imply, of course, that the percentage of time expended on political activity is inconsequential, but merely to offer an alternative and, I think, more isomorphic view of the reality of college and university teaching.

There are two aspects of professional life Professor Phillips sees as essentially political, for which different characterizations can be offered: mentoring and collegiality. I confine the remainder of my comments in this chapter to these two phenomena.

Although I cannot deny that some individuals may function as mentors out of an interest in building alliances and consolidating power, it is difficult for me to believe that most individuals who enact this role are so motivated. There are individuals who are genuinely interested in seeing colleagues succeed and who invest energy in doing what they reasonably can to assist them. I regret that my colleague has apparently never encountered such individuals. Even if one denies the possibility of genuinely altruistic impulses, however, the model of social exchange on which Professor Phillips's views rest is not the only one that can be advanced.

Individuals who serve as mentors may, in some instances, derive personal satisfactions from the successes of those to whom they have been of assistance. Still others may see their efforts as contributing to the overall strength and well-being of their departments. Even self-centered motivation, then, need not necessarily have as its focus the gain in personal power my colleague appears to feel is universal. Professor Phillips also seems to view collegiality as reflective of completely self-serving motives. Faculty new to the profession, he suggests, need to get along in order to achieve tenure and related forms of professional advancement. Again, I cannot dispute the possibility that some—perhaps many—individuals feign interest in supporting the activities of colleagues only out of a desire for personal gain. I must assume, however, that one of the attractions to a career in higher education is the subject matter one's discipline represents. That interest, moreover, in all probability, extends beyond the confines of one's own specialty. Hence, collegiality can, and properly should, be the simple manifestation of the desire a professional has in seeing the discipline survive and flourish. In my experience, the lack of collegiality professionals display toward one another more often than not reflects differences in personality rather than an unwillingness to be supportive of a department's efforts. (Both Professor Phillips and I have more to say about this topic in a later chapter.)

Although I have offered alternative views concerning mentoring and collegiality, I nevertheless feel that Professor Phillips makes an important point in respect to competitiveness—a quality that can be injurious both to genuine mentoring and collegiality. Since 1980, political and economic life in the United States has been heavily influenced by a resurgence in Social Darwinism (K. Phillips, 1991). That influence has also found its way into academic life, as colleges and universities have increasingly adopted the corporate model and are being run similar to businesses. Under conditions of uncertainty and scarcity, survival instincts are apt to be pronounced. When these are coupled with management styles reflecting adherence to the Social Darwinist ethic, the type of extreme manifestations of academic politics to which Professor Phillips alludes are matters to which those in higher education clearly need to attend, lest the academy go the way of many of the businesses on which it is very unfortunately being modeled.

◆ RESPONSE TO CHAPTER TWO
SCOTT A. KUEHN

Unlike my colleagues, I have a small repertoire of experience from which to comment on campus politics. However, my first five years as an assistant professor have provided some interesting instances. I wish to offer them from the perspective of a beginner for the benefit of others just entering academe. I do not intend these incidents to represent any sort of generalizations, nor do I claim to be a font of wisdom. Indeed, all they do show is what went through my mind as I learned to navigate through the university system.

At first I remember being befuddled by my role in the university system. I remember thinking, "Wasn't an assistant professor supposed to be able to make decisions and take responsibility?" It seemed one had to obtain permission to do practically everything. I noticed that I spent more time determining who exactly had the ability to do what than in accomplishing something. I messed up a few times and discovered the principle Professor Phillips referred to under the heading of "input," the desire of bureaucrats to act as gatekeepers. Secretaries became angry when I took red pens without asking. The computer center had to OK my request for a modem (even the brand and baud rate), the dean's office had to sign permission to enter course slips for my advisees, and requests for overhead projectors had to be made in duplicate and sent to the right department. Dialing long distance with a 9 prefix instead of an 8 meant I had to sign numerous forms claiming I was not making personal calls. These things and many others seem trivial now, but were fairly distracting to a new academic. I had to learn that if one did not receive approval in the accepted manner, things did not get done.

My first real taste of campus politics came a few weeks later. Our faculty was divided over a plan to expand our master's program. The dean placed me right in the middle. I was assigned the task of drawing up an alternative curriculum for the master's degree. I walked the fence between those who wanted no change and those who did. This was one instance in which I could have made enemies for opposing one side, but I think the type of professionalism Professor Gouran mentioned was prevalent. No one grew angry, but then no real change occurred either.

I noticed that on our small campus a new assistant professor seems to attract projects. One becomes distracted and flattered by the attention. I now regret that I did not choose to follow Professor Phillips's advice not to be an easy volunteer. When I arrived, our small university still had no institutional review board. In discussing this with the dean for graduate studies, I was asked to chair a development committee. The appeal of such responsibility was enormous, and without thinking I jumped at the chance. I was sent to seminars in Philadelphia and Phoenix, and I contacted many similar institutions in our area for human subject review documents. The committee and I spent much time putting together a policy proposal. We answered parochial questions about how this would infringe on the workings of this or that program, and so on. Suggestions were made to reword the document so that "nonresearchers" could understand it, that is, to make it easy to explain to undergraduates in research courses. This all required a lot of work.

Then, things began to stall. As we were beginning a third rewrite, the graduate dean retired. Then, the Provost left, followed by the President of the university. We were not able to find any interim official willing to make a decision on the policy for two years. I had not bargained for this type of hard work. I learned much about IRB's and the protection of human subjects and that was profitable. But I cannot help wondering about all the research I might have done in the amount of time I spent sending memos arguing why our campus needed an IRB. It was a trade-off I did not anticipate. I feel satisfaction in supporting research ethics, but that is little compensation for not having something in print.

If I had it to do over I would have spent more time considering how I was dividing my time. I believed I could do many things and began to feel that I was indispensable for some. But the rewards from departmental and university service have not been as satisfying as I had hoped (although they may have been for another person). Today, I have a better idea about how much time membership on a university committee can take and what type of effort I feel is realistic to invest. I can remember it hitting me in my the third year: "Gosh, I can't do all this!" Now my computer has a time management program, and I am learning to set priorities. Knowing what I know today, I would have paid good money for a time management seminar for new professors. It would have paid for itself by now.

3

ISSUES FACING NONTRADITIONAL MEMBERS OF ACADEME

Julia T. Wood

- At the 1990 SCA convention, I ran into someone I had not seen in several years. In the course of catching up, he asked, "Why did you switch from serious research to gender communication?"
- When I was awarded tenure in 1981, a faculty member from another department remarked, "It was a good time for you to come up since the university can't afford to deny women right now." The same day I was told, "You made it even though you're a woman." The first statement implied I received tenure because I am a woman; the second intimated I did in spite of being a woman. In highlighting gender, both dismissed the possibility that I earned tenure based on my work and my merits.
- In 1984 when I visited a colleague in his office, I noticed a calendar with the pin-up of the month clad in a g-string bikini. I told my colleague I found the photograph inappropriate in a faculty office. He responded that he was entitled to have any pictures he wanted, and I should respect his freedom of speech. I noted, "Your freedom of speech ends at the point where it infringes on me." In amazement, he asked, "How in the world does my enjoyment of a beautiful woman possibly affect you?" I explained it led me to question whether he perceived other women colleagues and students in sexual terms.

He scoffed at my "excessive sensitivity." Not long after this, an administrator suggested the pin-up calendar created an atmosphere hostile to women faculty and students. The freedom of speech defense provoked the administrator to respond, "This office belongs to the university, not you. You are allowed to use it in accord with university principles."

- To meet growing demands for classes open to working students, faculty are encouraged to teach night courses. When I was asked to offer a class from 7-8:30 p.m. two nights a week, I refused, pointing out it was unsafe for me or women students to walk on campus after dark as the university had been unresponsive to requests for more lighting and greater security. The person trying to persuade me replied with some irritation, "You women faculty seem to feel you have special entitlements." That year the number of rapes on our campus tripled. The number of lights and security personnel did not.

When I joined my university in 1975 I was surprised by incidents like these I have recounted. I had assumed—somewhat naively, I later realized—that the academy was above sexism, racism, and other forms of exclusion encrusted in the culture as a whole. I believed in the ideal of the university as a rationally ordered institution in which the quest to gain and share knowledge yielded attitudes, values, and behaviors more progressive, open-minded, and innovative than in other spheres of life.

In the 18 years since launching my career, I have discovered this ideal is only partially realized. My experiences lead me to conclude that most universities are less prone to bias and discrimination than society as a whole. At the same time, universities are not immune to profound biases and stereotypes that permeate the culture in which they are embedded. Layered, institutionalized devaluation and exclusion exist in academe, and they diminish the opportunities and comfort of nontraditional faculty.

In this chapter I describe the nature and impact of biases that intrude on nontraditional academics including women, people of color, gays and lesbians, non-Euro-Americans, disabled people, and members of minority religions. Because many obstacles and problems confronting nontraditional faculty do not affect most academics, it is unsurprising that the majority often fails to recognize the problems and their own complicity in sustaining them. Layers of prejudice, severally and in tandem, create difficulties and inequities uniquely experienced by academics who are women and/or members of minority groups.

In focusing on biases in academe, I obviously address those who are and will be most directly and deeply affected—nontraditional members of the academy. Equally important, I intend to speak to those who have always comprised the majority of faculty, many of whom are unaware of the extent to which academic life poses unnecessary and sometimes onerous dilemmas for colleagues who do not share the presumptive legitimacy inherent in certain demographic qualities. I assume traditional faculty, like those I have talked with over the years, including my co-authors, want to be aware of individual and institutionalized practices that systematically produce inequities for some of their colleagues.

THE STANDPOINT OF NONTRADITIONAL ACADEMICS

Before delving into these topics, I should introduce myself as my colleagues identified themselves in Chapter 1. Standpoint theory (e.g., Harding, 1991) argues that one's position in a social system profoundly affects perceptions, knowledge, values, and how one experiences social life. My position in Western culture and in academe is different from that of my co-authors. Because we participate in the same society, and we are all academics, we share aspects of a common heritage and many professional experiences and values. Yet, I am a white woman, and they are white men; and this makes a difference.

My gender yields a standpoint divergent from theirs in important ways. As a woman, I share with other women and members of marginalized groups the experience of being relegated to the periphery of cultural life and being regarded as out of place, unwelcome, deficient, and/or deviant from the white male standard that defines what is normative in society and the academy. Those whose presence in the ivory tower is unquestioningly accepted lead a life substantially different from those whose legitimacy must be proven continually. Common to nontraditional academics is a history of exclusion and still-tenuous status in cultural life in general and the academic profession in particular.

The fact that women and minorities are marginalized groups does not mean, however, that all women and minorities or even all women are defined by some universal set of qualities, experiences, and abilities. As recent scholarship (Irigaray, 1985; Spelman, 1988; Wood, 1993b, 1993c) has increasingly made clear, there is no generic woman any more than there is a generic person of color or, for that matter, a generic white male Protestant. Women and minorities consist of individuals, each of whom has unique experiences, values, perspectives, abilities, inclinations, and beliefs. Thus, I do not attempt to represent my experiences and perspectives as those of all nonmajority faculty members. Mine are those of a 41-year-old Caucasian, Southern woman, who is heterosexual, middle class, and not affiliated with any conventional Western religion. My perspective has been materially shaped by generous support and guidance from a number of women and men, a department actively support-ive of repressed voices, and relatively little deliberate, personal discrimina-tion, and recurring, if unintended, exclusions, slights, and disregard in professional interactions and contexts. I earned and received tenure six years after joining my faculty; I earned and received early promotion to Full Professor eight years later. Unlike many members of marginalized groups, whose circumstances have been less propitious than my own, I have few personal axes to grind.

In a single chapter I cannot elucidate the range of biases nor all of the ways they are enacted in the academy, nor can I probe how my own thinking is clouded by prejudices of which I myself remain unaware. Instead, I offer an unapologetically tendentious reading of pervasive prac-tices and attitudes that have long been inadequately recognized and indicted and which have grievously injured people outside of the stan-dard mold. Augmenting my own experiences with years of observation, conversations, and reading, I call attention to assumptions and practices that burden and sometimes sabotage individuals whose participation in academic life is still less than fully accepted or appreciated.

THE FOUNDATIONS OF EXCLUSION: LAYERS OF PREJUDICE

Discrimination is sometimes misunderstood as bad motives and behaviors in individuals. Although these exist and are deplorable, the greater prob-lem is at once less conspicuous and more pernicious than personal actions. Biases inflicted on nontraditional members of academe include not only individual attitudes and actions, but also institutional structures, policies, and practices that systematically reproduce inequities. That much of this bias may be unconscious and unintentional is beside the point. Whether intended or not, the impact is the same; whether con-scious or not, systemic sexism, racism, and other forms of discrimination distinctly disadvantage those who historically have been denied first-class membership in society and academe.

Blatant, Individual Bias: "You Aren't Wanted Here."

Conscious, explicit individual bias has considerably attenuated in recent years because many people have struggled to overcome learned preju-dices, and flagrant bigotry is no longer generally accepted, much less polit-ically correct. Yet, pockets of it persist in academic life as well as elsewhere.

Evidence of the extent to which overt and vicious prejudice still infects academic environments is unfortunately common. Outbreaks of hate crimes, usually against Jewish and black people, have plagued a number of campuses in recent years. Homophobia is still rampant as evidenced by vituperative campus graffiti and editorials maligning "queers and fags." Women continue to be harassed by lewd remarks by strangers and from male peers who hold up cards rating them on a scale from 1 to 10 on appearance. Within the last year a male professor lecturing on anatomy tweaked a female model's nipple in front of his class of women and men. Also, last year several faculty trivialized women by telling their classes jokes such as "how many co-eds does it take to change a tire?" Another professor included several slides of virtually nude women in a technical presentation, which he justified as a way to sustain students' interest. Incidents such as these pollute academic life and reflect the extent to which undisguised disdain of women and minorities is still present—and tolerated.

THE "CHILLY CLIMATE": PERVASIVE DEVALUATION

More widespread than overt, intentional bigotry is a range of behaviors and practices that do not emanate from bad motives or conscious biases, but that nonetheless marginalize and demean groups of people and areas of inquiry. It reflects a profound lack of understanding of women and minorities. During the Hill-Thomas hearings of 1991 the phrase "they just don't get it" was coined to describe male congressional representatives' inability to understand the dynamics of sexual harassment and the reasons why many victims do not respond assertively and immediately. The phrase means that someone who has not endured a particular oppression and has not been socialized to be passive really cannot comprehend the situation of someone who has.

In addition to sexual harassment, there are myriad examples of unintentional, but nonetheless noxious insensitivity to nontraditional members of the academy. Despite decades of argument and evidence of its prejudicial effects, so-called generic language is alive and well in many quarters. Linguistic exclusion renders women invisible and reminds them that their place in academe remains dubious. On my campus the administration still uses the title "chairmen" to refer to men and women. Repeated objections have been discounted as silly and trivial. Last week I was invited to attend a dinner and "bring my wife." In classrooms, women are linguistically eliminated when "he" and its variants punctuate lectures. The persistence of noninclusive language reinforces the entrenched belief that higher education is a male enterprise.

Minorities, as well as women, are victims of linguistic exclusion.

Consider, for example, the impact of interpersonal communication text-books or instructors who present "the typical family" as spouses and their children as if two-parent, intact families are the norm in our culture. Not only is divorce common throughout society, but single-parent families are especially prevalent among African Americans. This problem is com-pounded, not solved, by appending minority experiences as an after-thought in course coverage. When minority life is allotted a final few min-utes after extended discussion of white, middle-class patterns, marginal-ization is fortified, not mitigated.

"Add women and stir" is a phrase Spitzack and Carter (1987) used to describe a common and wholly inadequate means of acknowledg-ing women and their activities. It transpires when a topic is discussed assuming a white male standard and then reference to one or more women or minorities is tacked on at the end. Adding one or two members of a repressed group as an afterthought hardly achieves inclusion. There are many ways this takes place in academic life. One example is including one and only one woman or minority person in a group of candidates for an opening. Recently I participated in a search process in which all appli-cants were internal, that is, within our institution. As I and the other (all male) committee members reviewed applications, we all agreed that three white applicants were superbly qualified and included them in the five we would interview in person. Another committee member identified an Asian individual as someone we should also interview, and everyone con-curred. I then noted another minority applicant who seemed as well qual-ified as the four we had already selected and who perhaps should be our fifth. The response I got was, "Affirmative Action is satisfied as long as we include one minority." A minority has been added, so it is assumed there is equity, regardless of how qualified other female and minority candi-dates might be. Similarly, more than once I have heard members of other departments claim their faculties are integrated because they have a black scholar: Add one and stir.

Variations on this method also reinforce marginalization, and they occur with stunning frequency. For instance, not long ago at a uni-versity business meeting, a high-ranking administrator opened the session by announcing this agenda: "We have a number of issues important to faculty welfare to consider today. Then if time permits, we'll discuss mat-ters pertaining to women faculty." I was offended that he separated issues affecting women faculty from matters of "faculty welfare" and that "women faculty's issues" would receive attention only if time allowed. The import of his comment was to announce that women are regarded as "a special interest group," not regular faculty.

Consider another way in which marginalization is sustained, despite a conscious effort to be inclusive. Recently a colleague from anoth-er university informed me, "I've made my public speaking course inclusive by assigning a speech by Elizabeth Cady Stanton." Does he really believe that covering one speech by one woman renders his course inclusive? My response, appropriate though perhaps less than diplomatic, was, "Maybe I should add a speech by some man to my course on public speaking."

Related to "add women and stir" is what is termed *spotlighting* in which a woman or minority is singled out and asked, "So what do Asian people/gays/women think about this?" Many women and minority faculty report that although their ideas about issues involved in academic life are seldom sought, they often are asked to represent "the women's/blacks' perspective on X." This technique simultaneously brands those groups as deviant from "the norm" and totalizes one aspect of an individual's identity.

TRADITION: "THIS IS HOW THE ACADEMY HAS ALWAYS OPERATED"

Most pernicious and pervasive are those forms of exclusion and devaluation that stem from recalcitrant, sedimented biases. Like all institutions, universities and colleges have traditions to which they are wedded with greater fidelity than marriage itself currently enjoys. Certain modes of operation are treated as the normal, natural "way to do things." These traditions define, among other things, policies and procedures for tenure, processes for constituting committees, "appropriate" pedagogical content and methods, and the kinds of benefits offered employees. Because these practices were designed by those who originally made up academe— white, Euro-American, male, heterosexual Protestants—it is only predictable that the practices reflect their values and the conditions of their lives. It is equally predictable that this limited perspective fails to accommodate the interests, needs, and circumstances of people who do not fit the traditional profile. When minority faculty question or resist ensconced practices, they often are dismissed for wanting "special treatment" or exceptions to the rules designed to apply to everyone. This response is typical: "If you want to be part of this system, you play by the same rules as every one else." This stance is justified as treating women and minorities as equals.

If we inspect that pat rationale closely, however, it appears rather precarious. Consider, first, what "as equal" means: It is an unfinished construction, which, if completed, would read as equal to white, heterosexual men. Investigating further, we find "equal" translates functionally to "the same as." So, the goal is to treat women and minorities the same as white, heterosexual men. This linguistic exegesis discloses a number of problematical assumptions: Who decreed that middle-class, white, heterosexual men should be THE standard for all faculty? Is it appropriate to act as if women and minorities are the same as men? If they differ in important respects such as physical nature or life conditions, does insistence on rigid equality actually result in inequity? "The rules apply to everyone" presumes institutional rules are immutable, rather than responsive to the demographics of those who make them and whom they affect.

Blatant, undisguised bigotry in individuals, failure to realize how certain practices and behaviors marginalize, and institutionalized bias are foundations of prejudice that render academic environments less than hospitable to those who do not fit the traditional profile of membership. These multiple and interactive bases of prejudice promote inequities that encumber the personal and professional lives of nontraditional faculty.

MANIFESTATIONS OF INEQUITY: EXCLUSIONARY PRACTICES

Benefit Packages

Benefits are perquisites such as health care and retirement payments that institutions sponsor and sometimes subsidize in part or full. Although a standard benefit package usually exists, in many cases it does not provide equitable assistance to all faculty. Differential effects of "identical benefits" accrue from critical discrepancies between the needs and circumstances of diverse people. The differential effects reflect institutionalized bias because, once again, the male-as-standard model governs how everyone is treated, but it fits only the mythical standard male.

Disability Leave: Pregnancy and Childbirth

Institutions routinely allow faculty specified time away from work for "medical emergencies and temporary disabilities." Included are nonelective surgery, recovery from accidents, sickness, pregnancy, and maternity leave, a classification that offends many. Controversy swirls around the issue of maternity leave.

Most universities specify six weeks as the maximum amount of time that will be compensated for maternity leave. For many women this is an adequate, albeit not generous, interval to recover from labor, adjust to a baby, and make arrangements for its care when they return to work. Yet, because not all mothers and not all babies are alike, the standard disability leave fails to cover situations in which a mother and/or baby would be jeopardized by resuming academic duties in six weeks. At my university a woman in the opening week of a semester was diagnosed as having a toxic pregnancy. She was extremely ill, and her doctor advised her that working would endanger the life and health of her fetus. The university did not provide additional leave time to accommodate her medical needs. Fortunately, her colleagues were more compassionate and flexible than the institution, and they covered her classes so she could stay home while remaining on salary.

Such good fortune was not enjoyed by two other women on my campus, one of whom had a complicated pregnancy and one of whom had a child requiring extended care after birth. There were no provisions to extend their paid leaves, nor even any guarantees that if they took additional, unpaid leave their positions would be held for them. Their choice was between safeguarding their own and their babies' welfare and ensuring employment. This not uncommon choice facing women faculty almost never confronts men.

Another wrinkle compounds the controversy over benefits for pregnancy and childbirth. Some faculty feel that paid leave of any duration should not be provided, because having a child is a choice, whereas other circumstances for disability leave are not. In a recent discussion of this, a middle-aged male professor contended, "There's no reason women should get paid for staying home with a baby. They choose to have babies; let them—not the university—absorb the consequences of that choice. Besides, if they'd plan, they could deliver in summer and not miss classes." The view that as a choice pregnancy should not be covered is given more currency than warranted. Not only is pregnancy not always chosen, but other disabilities result from choices individuals make. For instance, heart attacks and emphysema, both of which qualify for disability leave, frequently are caused by smoking and/or other self-induced abuses of body and spirit. Reasonable care would preclude most accidents that cause temporary disabilities. Do we want to exclude from coverage every condition that results in some degree from careless or imprudent choices people make as well as from trusting products (from cars to contraceptives) that fail to perform as advertised?

But individual attitudes toward pregnancy are not the major source of inequity in benefits. Many institutions have a policy that makes it problematic for women to avail themselves of even the allowed leave time. Known as "the hidden penalty clause," this is an unstated practice by which a university grants disability leave to individuals, but offers departments no funds with which to hire substitute instructors to cover the absent faculty's classes. De facto colleagues volunteer or are assigned uncompensated overloads, which interfere with their own work. Not surprisingly, this can generate considerable resentment, which is typically directed toward the absent faculty member. Resentment creates more than discomfort: It can vitally affect women's academic careers. Because starting a family and a career often occur concurrently, many women needing maternity leave are untenured. Resentment from colleagues who cover classes sometimes adversely affects how those colleagues later vote on tenure.

Resentment also may be expressed by pressuring new mothers to return early and/or to manage some teaching responsibilities while on leave. For example, a colleague at my university told me that from the day she returned home from the hospital with her new baby, she was grading papers from her students at the request/demand of the person allegedly covering her classes. When is the last time you heard of someone on leave for a ruptured disk or a heart operation being expected to continue performing instructional duties?

Family Leave

Childbirth and recovery are not the only responsibilities that disproportionately affect faculty women. As life expectancies lengthen, many mid-career people find themselves caring for parents and in-laws who need help. Our country is facing a crisis generated by the simultaneous increase in elderly people requiring degrees of assistance and the decrease in full-time homemakers who historically donated that assistance (Wood, 1993d). Dual-worker families also have no intrinsic arrangement for occasions when professional help falls through, and men seldom stay home with children or elderly relatives (Hochschild with Manchung, 1989; Okin, 1989). Because women continue to perform the preponderance of society's caregiving, their professional lives are inequitably affected. Until institutions provide real benefits for care responsibilities (e.g., on-site day care), women will continue to suffer career penalties that do not routinely encumber their male colleagues.

Evaluating Productivity

Decisions about tenure, promotion, and salary typically are based on assessments of productivity in research, teaching, and service, with the weight accorded to each contingent on institutional missions and departmental philosophies. Although each of these criteria appears to pertain to all faculty, the differential circumstances of women and minority academics' lives render their generic application inequitable and inappropriate.

Evaluating Scholarship

Titling her recent book *Whose Science? Whose Knowledge?*, Harding (1991) argues that one of the most pervasive and pernicious types of institutionalized bias stems from unquestioned adherence to restrictive criteria for what counts as knowledge. She and other critics (Bleier, 1986; Haraway, 1988; Keller, 1985; Smith, 1987) claim that traditional views and practices of scholarship exclude a range of legitimate concerns and methods of inquiry.

Such challenges are not new; historically, knowledge has evolved in response to scientific revolutions, which contest contemporary orthodoxy and replace it with new assumptions, methodologies, and domains of study. What is new is the origin of challenges. Instead of issuing from accepted members of academe, many critiques today emanate from voices outside of the "sacred grove." Yet, these alternatives are routinely denigrated as "inferior." The theme is familiar: What is different (translated: different from the established white male standard) is not good, respectable, authentic, substantial, and so on.

Questions of what counts as scholarship and who decides have a disproportionate and deleterious impact on nontraditional participants in academic life. Although the pressure and desire to publish is common to all committed faculty, it entails special constraints for those using unorthodox research methods and/or studying nontraditional topics. Those who review manuscripts submitted for publication typically are individuals who have achieved stature in a field. Because it takes time to earn prestige, and because women and minorities have only recently entered the academic profession in significant numbers, it is not surprising that most editors and reviewers are male. Further, most were trained in and are committed to research traditions and methods that enjoy a long history of acceptance among members of the intellectual community. Their backgrounds often hinder their ability to understand, much less appreciate, scholarship that departs from what they deem normal (= good). Work whose merit they do not apprehend is rejected for publication.

An African-American colleague finds it unfair that she is required to explain much of African-American culture and communicative patterns every time she writes a paper. If she does not, reviewers reject her submissions because "you have not established a context for this study." My colleague argues that this response marginalizes people of color by assuming white is normative: Reviewers never consider that they have a responsibility to understand nonwhite lives. Similarly, a gay academic asks: "Why must I justify studying gays and lesbians in each article when nobody is required to justify studying heterosexuals?" Again the burden of explanation carries with it the tacit message: heterosexual = normal.

Even when nontraditional inquiry is well justified and contextualized, it may be rejected simply because it falls outside of established traditions of research. Further, if it is published in a specialized journal such as *Women's Studies in Communication,* or *Journal of Homosexuality,* unorthodox work often is discounted as "not mainstream," implying good scholarship is delimited by conventionality. Notice the circular "logic" of this reasoning: Because mainstream publications often do not appreciate research that departs from established conventions, it must be submitted elsewhere; but what is published elsewhere does not count as "real scholarship." It is an ongoing double bind for scholars who specialize in historically marginalized groups. This conundrum often leads nontraditional faculty to perceive that the only way to be accepted by the mainstream (= good) publications is to stifle personal identity and scholarly interests, a cost not incurred by academics whose identity and intellectual concerns enjoy automatic legitimacy.

A very recent case illustrates the burdens borne by faculty whose focus transcends the "mainstream." Last year a person in Speech Communication at another university phoned to inform me she had just been denied tenure because, as the official letter explained, "your focus on gender and communication does not fit within the mainstream of disciplinary scholarship, and, thus, your contributions to teaching and knowledge are not sufficient to justify permanent status on the faculty." She had published well and gotten good teaching evaluations, and a specialization in gender communication was the central qualification in the description of the position for which she was hired. That she later won her appeal of the denial does not reduce the toll the process took on her, nor does it alter the fact that what she does and who she is are tenuous in her colleagues' judgments.

Evaluating Teaching

Pedagogy poses its own set of dilemmas for nontraditional faculty. Courses in emergent intellectual areas often are deprecated simply because they depart from prevailing perspectives and represent "specialized interests." Informing that view, however, is the assumption that culture and knowledge consist exclusively of the experiences, values, and perspectives of white, Euro-American, heterosexual males. Anything outside of that narrow realm is considered specialized—an irony because males comprise less than half of the population. The myth of white male-as-standard, however, seems uninhibited by demographic realities. Faculty who teach in emergent intellectual areas report responses ranging from acceptance, curiosity, and subtle disdain, to overt ridicule. Given this, beginning nontraditional academics have to weigh the costs of repressing personal experiences and professional interests against the risk of being denied tenure. This is another strain not endured by faculty whose professional foci are granted unquestioned legitimacy.

Nontraditional course content is often disparaged and belittled. Not long ago I overheard a faculty member advising a student to "take a course in feminist scholarship if you really need to get that out of your system. Then get some substantive training in research methods." Similarly, a student informed me his advisor recommended he avoid "fluff courses" such as the ones in the African-American curriculum and instead pursue "serious study." A graduate student who proposed a thesis on mother-daughter communication was offered the unsolicited counsel to "study family communication instead," causing her to puzzle over why mothers and daughters somehow were not part of families.

Evaluating Service

Service includes activities other than research and teaching that advance departmental, disciplinary, and institutional interests. Particularly salient to women and minority faculty are disproportionate committee, advising, and mentoring responsibilities. Many institutions have policies requiring one (and often only one) woman and/or minority be on every commit-tee. Yet, because there are so few women and minorities, each one is asked to serve numerous times. The time and effort committee work requires detract from what can be invested in research and teaching, both of which generally receive more weight than service in tenure decisions, however, not to serve risks perpetuating the historical silence of marginal-ized viewpoints and issues.

Advising students is another area of service that entails particular-ly difficult choices for women and minority academics. Statistics sum up the problem: At most institutions women comprise less than 25% of all faculty and minorities less than 5%, and women students outnumber men. Because many undergraduate women and minorities intend to pur-sue careers, they seek role models and more experienced people similar to themselves with whom they can discuss career options and obstacles. Expecting a minority of the faculty to advise and mentor the majority of students is obviously unfair, especially when advising is typically accorded little value in tenure decisions. Minority and women academics experi-ence painful ambivalence when they are forced to choose between advancing their own chances for tenure and professional stature and helping younger members of disadvantaged groups.

Tenure and Promotion Schedules

One of the most fateful forms of institutionalized bias concerns tenure and promotion policies. Women and minorities frequently have noted that the procedures for obtaining tenure and promotion evolved when virtually all faculty were middle-class white men whose wives attended to family and home. This no longer typifies faculty or families as less than

7% of Americans currently fit the "standard" pattern. Nonetheless, expectations reflecting that no-longer valid model persist, usually to the disadvantage of women and minorities, who assume disproportionate responsibilities for family care.

A more equitable and no less rigorous alternative path to achieving tenure is "tolling the tenure clock." The essence of this proposal is to allow leeway in the timing of tenure decisions for men as well as women, who have or adopt a child, or have severe family crises during the early years of faculty appointments. But, in general, institutions have responded by "holding the line," insisting that women and minorities "measure up" to the same standards as all other members. Variable policies responsive to diverse circumstances are dismissed as constituting "special treatment," which administrators argue would be discriminatory.

Yet, there is another way to view orthodox traditions as well as the challenges to them. Prevailing tenure policies were created by and served a faculty that was virtually exclusively white, male, middle-class, heterosexual, Protestant, and married. That no longer describes all participants in academic life. Advocates of change point out that the purpose of policies is to reflect and support members of the academy; thus, when membership changes so that some participants' interests are neither represented nor served by existing practices, the practices—not the individuals—should adapt accordingly.

Advocates of change are not asking for less rigorous, or even different standards for judging the tenure triumvirate of research, teaching, and service. Instead, they argue that equity would be better achieved by allowing variation as to when standards are invoked, not whether or what standards apply. Medical professionals define six weeks after delivery as "the point at which one is physically able to resume former levels of activity." That calendar assumes an uncomplicated pregnancy, delivery, and recovery, as well as a healthy baby with no special needs. The standard schedule also completely ignores the fact that a new mother is supposed to resume "former levels of activity," in this case teaching and research, while simultaneously assuming the substantial new responsibilities entailed in parenting.

A year or more seems a more reasonable amount of time for new fathers and mothers to accommodate their lives to a child's presence, or for faculty to adjust to being primary caregivers for other relatives. If the purpose of tenure is to assess an individual's intellectual productivity and potential and teaching ability, then an inflexible timetable may be counterproductive to rendering informed judgments. A rigid tenure schedule pointedly disadvantages women because they are the ones who give birth, recover from pregnancy and labor, nurse, and are likely to assume primary responsibilities for caring for children and other family members. The capacities and commitments of women, then, render uniform equal tenure procedures gravely inequitable.

Issues of Identity and Allegiance

Nontraditional members of higher education constantly confront paradoxes about their identity and, relatedly, their allegiances. A number of years ago Conrad and I (Wood & Conrad, 1983) identified a basic conflict between a woman's identity as a woman and her identity as a professional. Professionalism has been defined by male norms as historically men have dominated the paid labor force. Associated with professionalism are qualities such as ambition, assertion, self-interest (although perhaps enlightened), and primary commitment to work. Traditional definitions of women center on nurturance, deference, and primary commitment to relationships. Cultural images of womanhood, thus, are in many ways at odds with established views of what it means to be a professional.

Because women academics are both professionals and women, identity conflicts sometimes arise. A common case involves relationships with students. In general, female faculty are approached considerably more often than male faculty for counseling about personal and interpersonal problems. If they enact culturally prescribed femininity by responding to students' needs for attention, they erode time needed for research, committee work, and teaching preparation, all of which affect tenure and promotion decisions as well as stature in their fields. On the other hand, if they adopt norms of professionalism and safeguard time for their own work, they may violate internalized feminine values. Further, women, more than men, are judged harshly if they are unresponsive and uncaring. This ongoing strain defies resolution and permeates the daily lives of women faculty.

Identity conflicts also arise in other arenas of professional life. I cannot count the number of times I have been the only woman on university committees. In such cases I always wonder whether I was selected because a woman—some woman, any woman—was needed, or because I was qualified on the issues and respected by my colleagues. Which identity—my gender or my professional abilities—is the basis of my appointment?

This conundrum spawns an even more disturbing one in which a woman or minority person is defined by his or her gender or race and is expected to represent all members of his or her group. During my service on a council selecting recipients for university research grants, the other (all male) members of the council turned expectantly to me when the first application from a woman was considered. They waited; so did I. Finally, the chair asked, "Julia, is this a strong proposal?" Because the proposal came from a woman, they seem to believe only a woman could judge it. Were my evaluations of male colleagues' proposals somehow invalid? Were males unable to assess women scholars' applications? Similarly, I have repeatedly been asked, "How do women at the university feel about this?" So far I have resisted the temptation to comment on the preposterous assumption that all women at my university have homogeneous responses to issues. "What's the African-American position on this?" similarly defines a person by group membership and implies all members of that group think alike. When is the last time you heard anyone ask, "How do men or whites feel about this?"

A different and equally vexing conflict in identity and allegiance arises when concerns of women or minorities are not represented—are often not recognized—by white males in a group. Should the woman or minority person be the voice for those concerns? To do so risks reinforcing others' identification of you by group membership and/or being discounted for representing "specialized interests"; not to do so betrays a group into whose interests you may have insight.

When I was a dean, I met regularly with other administrators to deal with student appeals for academic relief, for example, adjustments in requirements due to unusual circumstances. Quickly I learned that medical reasons for granting relief included physical and psychological conditions that could reasonably interfere with academic progress. We made adjustments for sprained ankles, divorces, deaths, and stress. The first time a student sought relief because she had been raped, however, the request was denied as not within the guidelines. When I questioned this, I was patronizingly assured that "we understand your special sensitivity on this topic," but was told that because the student was not in counseling, she was not psychologically stressed. I dissented, arguing rape is intrinsically and always stressful—far more so than many of the events for which the committee routinely granted relief. Eventually rape was added to the list of legitimate reasons for dispensation.

In that case I considered it necessary to accept the cost of arguing from and, therefore, highlighting my identity as a woman. The same tension accompanies writing this chapter. Even though I want all faculty to be aware of ways in which women and minorities are routinely marginalized and devalued, I dislike spotlighting myself as a woman, which risks eclipsing my identity as a scholar and teacher. In calling to my co-authors' attention their neglect of professional issues that uniquely affect nontraditional members of academe, I also risked alienating them, which fortunately did not occur. Tensions concerning identity and allegiance are a constant fact of life for women and minority faculty, one that does not complicate the daily experience of those whose personal identities are compatible with the norms and assumptions of professionalism.

Sexual Harassment

An especially injurious, despicable, and, unfortunately, common proof of persisting sexism and racism in Western society and academe is the prevalence of sexual harassment, which predominantly affects women and, particularly, minority women. Reflecting attitudes that women are sex objects and fair targets for abuse, sexual harassment on college and university campuses affects as many as 30% of women faculty (Blum, 1991; Jaschik & Frentz, 1991; McMillen, 1991). In the wake of the Hill-Thomas hearings and the Navy's Tailhook scandal and a chorus of allegations against Senator Packwood, along with recent judicial rulings that establish institutional liability for punitive and compensatory damages to victims, widespread attention finally has centered on this long-tolerated violation of human rights.

Because sexual harassment specifically within the field of Speech Communication has been discussed in detail elsewhere (Wood, 1992), I do not probe it extensively here. Nonetheless, sexual harassment must be named in any consideration of ways in which academic institutions create, tolerate, and/or enable marginalization and devaluation of women and minorities. The long silence surrounding sexual harassment (Wood, 1992, 1993a) resulted in large measure from the fact that it seldom affected and, thus, was not salient to those who have been and still are the majority members in most professions. Sexual harassment takes many forms, all disempowering, humiliating, and demeaning. It ranges from displaying sexually provocative pictures of women in workplaces, to sexist jokes, to quid pro quo demands for sexual favors in exchange for professional security and/or advancement. Compounding the abhorrence of sexual harassment itself are all-too-frequent misrepresentations, silencings, and trivializations of victims and their accounts, as well as institutional tolerations and justifications of harassers.

The cost of sexual harassment is disproportionately born by women and minority faculty, and it is a very high cost. From victims' accounts we know that the damage is not confined to the incident itself, but rather lingers even decades later. As such, the persistence of sexual harassment—and the knowledge that it disproportionately affects only certain faculty—is a brutal reminder of the peripheral placement and marginal value of women and minorities in institutional life.

Responding to Institutionalized Discrimination

My purpose in writing this chapter is not to advise beginning academics how to deal with the range of overt and subtle biases I have discussed. Instead, I intend to point out that recognizing their existence is integral (unfortunately) to understanding professional life. There are unique conflicts, issues, and institutionalized discriminations that enormously complicate the careers of women and minority faculty.

Before completing the final draft of this chapter, I asked three colleagues to read it: a white woman, an African-American woman, and a white, middle-aged, heterosexual male. One response common to all three readers was, "How do you deal with the anger and bitterness provoked by what you've written?" Oddly enough, I find I am neither angry nor embittered generally, although there are moments when one or both emotions prevail. My experience is that those responses are self-defeating as they do not direct me toward action that might alter conditions that diminish the moral, intellectual, and human integrity of the academy.

Anger tends to feed on itself and does more damage to the one who is enraged than those who merit indignation. Often it generates strident, accusatory stances and communication that sometimes provides immediate personal gratification and a sense of self-righteousness, but that is more likely to alienate than educate those whose support is needed to reform institutions. Bitterness invites passivity and/or distancing from the conditions producing it; thus, it too hampers efforts at transformation. Whether operating individually or in tandem, when anger and bitterness predominate, they distort my perspective on university life and myself. If I allow sexism to become the dominant lens through which I view life, I will overemphasize its presence and underrecognize more positive, more enlightened motives and values in individuals and institutions.

For me, coveting and cultivating anger and bitterness have proven less effective and, therefore, less gratifying than working to name inequities that degrade the academy and to promote reform. My ability to instigate change has enlarged as I have become involved in networks and have earned security, respect, and the voice to which those entitle me. Unfortunately, it remains more true than not that achieving some security and stature advance an advocate's impact: Admission to "the club" confers the privilege of participating in how the club works. During my years as a faculty member I have become more—not less—committed to the academy and to my own responsibility for helping it realize its ideal as an institution uniquely able to enhance the quality of personal and cultural life.

◆ RESPONSE TO CHAPTER THREE
DENNIS S. GOURAN

The issues Professor Wood raises in her discussion of the problems experienced by "nontraditional members" of the academic community are of considerable importance and ones about which she writes with both sensitivity and understanding. As she notes and very well illustrates, it is clearly, and unfortunately, the case that many of the difficulties women, minorities, and other groups regularly confront in the larger society are no less pervasive in higher education.

Although there are often legal remedies for more blatant forms of discrimination and personal mistreatment, the more subtle manifestations of the sorts of conditions Professor Wood describes do not admit to easy remedy, and institutional mechanisms for dealing with them have thus far proved not to be especially effective. In fact, in some instances, the measures that colleges and universities have implemented appear to be largely cosmetic. To achieve a state in which historically underrepresented and frequently disenfranchised groups can function free of the influence of others' attitudes toward their membership in such groups, feel that their performance is being judged on its merits, and not be subjected to the insensitivities and forms of outright abuse to which Professor Wood had alluded, necessitates commitment, sustained effort, and ongoing education. Her illumination of the issues is very helpful in this respect.

If there is to be meaningful progress in creating a climate in which all members of the academic community are accorded the professional respect they are due free from the personally threatening aspects of institutional environments, each of us needs to take a role. It is not my intent to suggest a specific set of solutions to the many and diverse problems Professor Wood has identified. Such an attempt would be both presumptuous and necessarily inadequate in the context of this volume, and specifically, as a comment to a chapter written by an individual far more knowledgeable on the subject than I am. I do think it appropriate to observe, however, that meaningful resolution ultimately must begin at the individual level and, in my opinion, requires self-examination, self-monitoring, and constructive action.

All of us would do well to engage in some thoughtful self-reflection about the matters Professor Wood has raised and ask ourselves about the ways in which we may directly or inadvertently contribute to the problems related to them. The consequence of such exercises, of course, is often to find ourselves free of any culpability. It is difficult to admit to insensitivity, neglect, and especially direct responsibility for harm to the well-being of others. Honest self-appraisal, however, is within our capabilities and serves to bring to light aspects of our behavior toward others of which we may not all that frequently be consciously aware.

Recognizing that we do contribute to problems and identifying the specific ways in which we do, although helpful, is not sufficient to eliminate them. A further step of self-monitoring is required. I am not using the term *self-monitoring* in Snyder's (1972) sense. Self-monitoring as an alteration based on perceptions of others' expectations regarding acceptable behavior, when dealing with the issues Professor Wood has raised, is likely to represent little more than lip service to announced institutional goals and, more often than not, hypocrisy. Some of the most outspoken champions of equitable treatment and women's and minority rights I know are also among the most disingenuous. The type of self-monitoring to which I refer involves conscious recognition of the ways in which one's behavior can be injurious to others accompanied by deliberate attempts to alter that behavior. It has much more to do with interpersonal sensitivity than accommodation, attitude change than appearance, and alterations in behavior than the verbalization of platitudes and professional fashions of the moment.

Self-monitoring, as described above, can be helpful, but there is yet another respect in which individual initiative is crucial to the eradication of the problems Professor Wood's examination encompasses. That is constructive action. Claiming exemption from responsibility on the grounds that our own professional conduct in the areas of concern is appropriate is neither a sufficient nor satisfactory response. It is also important that we support initiatives aimed at the prevention and correction of these problems at the institutional level. Contributing to a supportive environment under conditions in which substantial segments of the academic community feel alienated is no simple task, but to the extent that colleges and universities undertake actions along these lines, they are deserving of active support, not merely passive acceptance.

As a realist, I am fully aware that the issues Professor Wood has raised are not likely to disappear overnight or even in the reasonably near future. The inertia induced by general societal conditions, long-term neglect, and minimalist measures will be difficult to overcome. I am also idealistic enough, however, to reject the notion that they are beyond resolution. Whether the problems are satisfactorily addressed will depend on how substantial a commitment both those new to the profession and those who are an established part of it are willing to make. Professor Wood has identified what needs to be done. It remains for the rest of us to take the necessary steps.

◆ RESPONSE TO CHAPTER THREE
GERALD M. PHILLIPS

Standpoint theory is an interesting notion. I, too, am a minority group member. I am old, fat, baldheaded, Jewish, and disabled. I cannot climb the stairs to the department office; I am not romantic looking. I cannot attend committee meetings on Yom Kippur. However, because my publications are assessed by blind refereeing and I have my own talent in the classroom, none of that matters much. I suspect everyone is in a marginalized group when you stop to think about it.

Oddly enough, we all discriminate, too. We have our preferences, and some people do not meet our standards in appearance, wittiness, or social acceptability. It is entirely valid to be upset about being excluded for reasons you cannot control, yet it is entirely fair for each of us to make choices based on our personal preferences. No one, in short, is unbiased. There is considerable data showing that women are paid less than men in the academy and elsewhere. The question is how much of the shortfall is a result of prejudice and how much because of personal reasons and natural biases. It is unreasonable to demand the impossible, and to ask everyone to suspend prejudice is like asking the sun to stop shining.

Sexual harassment is something else again. I would argue that any male professional is absolutely obligated to keep sexual issues out of professional life. Sex in the workplace is always detrimental, unprofessional, and immoral. On that ground, I thoroughly agree with Professor Wood and probably would go much further in sanctioning and punishing anything that smacks of sexual harassment and intimidation. In fact, it is for this reason, especially, that I advocate minimizing contact between students and faculty. I would hope that adult females would have enough nerve to challenge depredations by their male colleagues.

The linguistic matter, however, presents some complicated issues. We learn from earliest childhood those labels that express status, inclusion, and exclusion. To demand that these be purged from our collective vocabularies is unreasonable and probably unconstitutional given recent Supreme Court decisions. On the other hand, there is nothing wrong with expected good manners. The question is: Would I be a bigot if I opposed hiring a candidate for a job because he or she displayed bad manners? Or, is the sanctioning of bad manners unconstitutional?

As to tokenism, what choice do you have? There really are not enough qualified African-American, Native American, and Hispanic candidates to go around, and as my colleague points out, women are sometimes overempowered because they are presumed to represent their gender. I think this kind of thinking is insidious. One may represent a company or a political party, or themselves, but it is unfair and irrational to demand that anyone represent a group that did not elect or appoint him or her to so represent them.

Homosexuality presents another kind of issue, to wit, the right to privacy. I do not believe sexual matters belong in the workplace. I do not talk about my sexual activities or lack thereof. One's sexual preference should not earn any special privilege, nor should it engender discrimination. It will not if it is considered to be a private matter.

Entitlement for natural biological infirmities is yet another matter. It seems only fair to honor motherhood and provide necessary leave time. Regarding sick parents, however, anything more than "luck of the draw" is arguable. Life, generally, is not fair, and all of us have our adversities including wild and disobedient children, bankruptcy, marital discord, interfering in-laws, and the effects of bad habits such as alcoholism, overeating, compulsive gambling, chronic overspending, and so on. We should not earn entitlements because of ordinary adversities in life. If I stub my toe, I am out of the marathon.

The academic issue of African-American and feminist scholarship is a real sticking point. It is my opinion, for what it is worth, that people who wish to do this kind of scholarship must justify it. I have always wanted to write a piece on the rhetoric of the Huns, but I have been unable to find any speeches by Attila. My national group is thus disfranchised, our voices are not heard. I am frankly annoyed with the level of brouhaha this issue has caused in the academy, and I would argue that the burden of proof is on the person who advocates change. Thus, women and minority groups are obligated to argue the merits of their genre if they wish others to accept it. Perhaps in time they can establish its viability. To date, I am not convinced and earnestly recommend to my minority students that they do research and publish in mainstream areas. When they are duly tenured and protected, they may break new ground. Oddly enough, I have wasted a lot of time trying to break new ground from which nothing grew. I have no one to blame but myself. Either my digging was not good enough, or I was wrong to begin with, and it is important that I be able to recognize it and acknowledge it.

In short, Professor Wood makes an argument worth making, much of which I disagree with, but an argument that should be taken seriously by all who enter the academy. Women and other minorities will have to chart their own ways through the political waters. Professor Wood has given them fair warning about the location of the shoals.

4

SECURING A POSITION

Scott A. Kuehn

The job candidate was a young man in his late 20s. He was finishing his doctoral program and said his dissertation was almost done. Our department was interviewing him for a position in media graphics. At first, he seemed pleasant and intelligent. But this impression began to change when he distributed materials to demonstrate his graphics proficiency. One was a family newsletter he sent to his relatives. The headline read: "John A Shoo-in for Professor Job at Clarion" (John was not his real name). Although the candidate thought this was a cute jest, I thought it was inappropriate and wanted to determine exactly what kind of "shoo-in" he was.

I asked a question about the choice of font size for the headline, and I asked how he would teach newsletter layout in a reproduction graphics course. I also wanted some specifics about teaching audience analysis. I got ambiguous answers. Someone else asked how to import photographs into a desktop publishing program. We wanted to hear about specific techniques and procedures. But again we got an ambiguous response. Later, the candidate said he would like to teach two courses that were not in the published job description. His credentials showed doctoral work in educational systems, but less background in mass communication. Because his newsletter looked amateurish, his graphics proficiency was unproved, and his teaching interests were in other courses, I concluded that the candidate's strengths did not fit the job description. I was not alone in that opinion. Later, another candidate was offered the job.

Why start a discussion of job searches with an unsuccessful episode? Because it brings out two vital criteria for assessing candidate strength: (a) the match of teaching experience and scholarship to the job description, and (b) the presentation of self that supports the general ideal of collegiality. The candidate failed in both respects. He gave the impression that his expertise was in other areas, and his sample headline gave the impression of overconfidence.

In this chapter I present a procedural framework for job applications. It can help you make your best case for matching the job description and provide you with strategies to present yourself truthfully, but still in your best light. One thing it will not do is to transform you into something you are not. An important part of this process is carefully setting out your career and personal goals. I show you how to uncover your career talents, desires, and goals to construct your unified career priorities. Next, I discuss a method for critiquing available positions to perform the best match of your career priorities to job openings. Finally, I cover some issues connected with job searches, such as dual career families, salary negotiations, and concerns with settling into a new job.

STEP ONE: DETERMINING YOUR UNIFIED CAREER PRIORITIES

Successful job applicants are able to show a prospective employer that they are a good match for an advertised position. Therefore, the most important place to start the job hunt is with yourself. You must define your goals and career priorities. As a graduate student or a beginning professional, goals are nothing new to you. It is a safe bet, however, that employment goals were not your central focus as you completed your studies. Perhaps you thought that you would someday write a book about small group dynamics, but you probably did not envision the setting in which you would write it. With the need to seek employment comes the opportunity to set out your priorities. The concept of a *unifying principle* provides a useful framework for doing this. A career-bound unifying principle is a match between your personal talents and desires and employment goals. Your first task in putting together your job case is to match career talents to career desires and goals. If talents are simply the things that you are good at, then career talents are the things you do well related to your career. For academics, they could be teaching, writing, critiquing, and so on. At the next level, career desires are broad-based ambitions that could be related to job performance, environment, or simply personal needs. Examples include growing intellectually, providing quality undergraduate instruction, or living in a big city. The last of the three, career goals, refers to specific actions and achievements, such as teaching under-graduate courses in media criticism, writing a book analyzing current trends in group discussion research, or teaching graduate-level courses in quantitative research.

It is simple to match these three categories. Take a sheet of paper and divide it into three columns. Across the top label the columns "Talent," "Desire," "Goal." Now brainstorm. Fill each column with descriptions of how you see yourself now and in the next five years. Most people find that their talents, desires, and career goals relate to the three areas of academic life—scholarship, teaching, and service to the profession. You can keep these areas in mind as you construct your columns, or you can use other areas. Later, I use these topics to discuss how to unify your talents, desires, and goals.

The next stage is important. Indicate a ranking next to each description. Rank your greatest talent number one, the second greatest number two, and so on, for each of the talents. Then move over to the Desire column and do the same thing. Finish with a ranking of the career goals. You can then clean up your table by making another copy and arranging the rankings in order with the smallest at the top and the largest at the bottom of the table.

These rankings are an important self-analysis step. Therefore, be honest. If you are not happy with the rankings, perhaps you can use pro-fessional development activities to change them in the future. But for now they are important in helping you match your career perspective to avail-able positions. Give the rankings time and your close attention. Table 1 is an example of a Career-bound Unification Chart that includes career tal-ents, desires, and goals for the mythical "John B. Academic."

John's rankings show a strong desire to pursue research and pub-lication. However, we can see two other categories of career pursuits here—teaching and professional service. He appears to desire a position in a research institution teaching graduate-level students. If John wanted to gain a quantified sense of his unification area priorities, he could take another piece of paper and divide it into columns labeled research, teach-ing, and service. These are John's unification areas. He could then tabu-late the ranks from his unification table and fit them within the unifica-tion areas. He would then find the mean rank of each of the areas. The one with the lowest mean rank would indicate his highest priority. The highest mean rank would show his lowest priority. It is no surprise that research has the highest priority for John ($M = 1.83$), followed by profes-sional service ($M = 3.5$), and then teaching ($M = 4.28$).

Your unification areas may be different. For instance, you may regard corporate consulting as a professional area. Similarly, you may not even need to tabulate the mean ranks to learn which area is your highest priority. However, the mean ranks could show divergences in your priori-ty rankings. Indeed, you could become technically extreme and do a

Table 1. Career-bound Unification Chart—John B. Academic.

Career Talent	Career Desire	Career Goal
1. trained writer	1. to write scholarship	1. to conduct research on small groups
2. proficient statistician	2. to network with other researchers	2 to publish position on small group discussion
3. knowledgeable teacher	3. to read scholarship in my field	3. to teach graduate research courses
4. competent analyst, critic	4. to work with graduate students	4. to be thesis and dissertation advisor
5. enthusiastic instructional designer	5. to provide quality undergraduate instruction	5. to be active in scholarly organizations
6. computer applications proficiency	6. to live in a warm environment	6. to teach undergraduate group class

Kruskal-Wallis test to examine the null hypothesis that your unification area rankings are not different from each other. The point here is not to convince you of false precision in this type of exercise. It is simply one way of beginning to think seriously about job hunting and to make it a little easier to separate attractive from unattractive prospects.

GATHERING YOUR MATERIALS

Knowing your career priorities will aid you in identifying appropriate positions. Next are the materials you will need to include in your applications. At the minimum these consist of a cover letter, current vita, and applicable samples of teaching data, consulting work, presentations, and publications, if any.

Although you may not believe it, you probably have many materials that can support your employment case. That is why it is important to begin this step of the job hunt process with another brainstorming session. List all of your accomplishments related to your academic work. Include everything from the different courses you taught as a graduate assistant to the most technical accomplishments you made in your course work. Do not discount anything as unimportant at this stage. Personally, I failed to note on my vitae that I taught a studies skills course one semester as a graduate assistant. I mentioned it in a job interview and found the interviewers were quite interested. What I considered a passing interest was really a job qualification in the eyes of one prospective employer.

After you have carefully considered your list of career accomplishments, have a talk with others around you. Ask them about their accomplishments. A good source would be assistant professors in your department and others who have recently been in the job market. It does not hurt to ask others what they have included in their vitae, and most will be happy to help. The best source of information here, of course, is your advisor. Advisors have a strong sense of what constitutes a good vitae for your discipline. They have been around long enough to have helped other advisees seeking jobs and have served on search committees themselves. Advisors are such an important part of the employment picture. I have more to say about them later in this chapter.

Vitae contain specific information about the applicants' education, teaching experience, and scholarship. They are formal and similar to professional resumes. Plan ahead to make your vita complete and professional looking. Although the conventional wisdom is that you should shy away from fancy paper, typefaces, and excess wordiness, you probably would do well to have a final version done by a professional print shop. This may not be necessary if you have access to a high-quality laser printer and desktop publishing equipment and if you know how to use it. Keep it simple and elegant, but include important details about your professional experiences.

Samples of your work can convey important information about your proficiency. A personal story illustrates my point. I did my graduate work at what Professor Phillips calls a "multiversity." Because I had been around graduate assistants regularly throughout my college career, I thought all those who would be reading my application would know what I meant when I said that I was a graduate assistant for two sections of fundamentals of public speaking courses. However, I was a finalist for a position at a smaller public university where the chair of the search committee was unfamiliar with the role of graduate assistants at larger institutions. At her small university, the faculty union had kept graduate assistants from having course teaching responsibilities. She assumed this was a norm. I was surprised to receive a call from her in which she questioned my role as a graduate assistant teacher. I later dispelled the confusion by compiling my syllabi and course handouts in a neat booklet and sending it along with assurances from my supervisors that I had complete responsibility for designing and teaching courses as a graduate assistant. Had I known that, I could have avoided this confusion by including such materials at the outset; I would have included them with my application.

The audience reading your employment credentials will be varied, and supporting materials documenting your work will help to make things clear. I have noticed that as a search committee member, I am more impressed with candidates who provide good examples of their work. The important word here is "good." Show your best materials. Works in progress and hastily prepared teaching aids may not portray you in your best light. Some candidates assume that if a search committee is interested, they will ask for more information. The logic here is backward, however. The best way to create interest is to demonstrate your proficiency. Materials that support your vita make you more interesting.

BEGINNING THE INTERVIEW PREPARATION

The next part of the materials preparation stage is to begin thinking about how you will conduct yourself if invited for an interview. An accepted practice for an academic job interview is to have candidates give either a presentation about their research or to present a sample course lecture. Because you believe (and rightly so) that you will be interviewing for jobs, you should begin putting together these two types of presentations. Do not take this lightly. You may be convinced that because you are so immersed in your dissertation research, it will be easy for you to explain it, or that because you have experience teaching a subject, it will be easy to work up a sample lecture. Remember, you may know your dissertation research so well you are insensitive to general points necessary for those without technical knowledge in your area to assess your proficiency. Similarly, you will need to focus a sample course lecture in which you make few assumptions about the knowledge level of the audience. Organizing your job presentation ahead of time will make you feel better about giving it. Later, when you receive specific offers to visit campuses, you will be able to tailor your presentation to the specific set of interviewers. Your goal should be to give a proficient, not merely competent, job talk.

Start early by gathering topics, exploring visual aids, and asking others to listen to you explain portions of your research. You will discover that others can help you hone your explanations for audiences unfamiliar with your research topic. Later, you can make appropriate modifications for each visitation.

PREPARING APPLICATION SUPPORT MATERIALS

Now you can begin to construct a base for your application cover letter. Similar to the vita, it too conveys information about you. You will do best by simply stating your objective in applying for the given position. Cover letters should be focused on specific job openings. They should reflect your personal attention in applying for that job by identifying correctly the job correspondent—whether a department head or a search committee chair—along with a statement about how you match the specific job criteria. Thus, you can prepare a broad-based framework ahead of time, but you must be sure to send specific, focused letters with each application. Using a word processor will save you time here.

References are another part of your application material. Ask for references early, and give reference writers sufficient time to write about you. Of course, it is obvious that you should ask for references from those with whom you have worked most closely. General references are easy to spot, especially by those who write references themselves. A good place to start is with your doctoral committee. In addition, you could include assistantship supervisors who could say something about your research capabilities or other teachers who are familiar with your work. However, be selective in gathering references. One reference for a job candidate in our department read: ". . . will prove to be a competent intellectual with time. Even though I enjoyed using _____ as a foil in my seminar on communication theory, he experienced considerable frustration in allowing others to express opinions contrary to his own." This candidate obviously had a mistaken notion of what this professor felt about him.

For the last part of your materials preparation, schedule a meeting with your advisor. Have him or her look over your materials and provide you with some feedback. Good advisors will know you better than you may know yourself. Good advisors also know how to use the job network. They talk to friends who have job openings or who have heard about job openings. They are often a first source for job placement information.

EXAMINING THE JOB MARKET

Once your self-analysis and preparation of application materials are complete, it is time to examine the job opportunities in your field. First, you will need to select colleges and universities in the job listings that fit your career priorities. Next, it is important to learn specifics about the departments you visit for interviews. You need not do all this at once. Your analysis will become more specific as you receive offers to interview.

Professor Phillips provides an excellent framework for judging college and university environments in Chapter 1. Table 2 presents a summary of these characteristics using his headings. This summary allows you to quickly match your career priorities with institution types. For instance, the mythical John B. Academic, whose unified career priorities are listed above, had research as his highest priority, followed by participation in

Table 2. Characteristics of Six Types of Higher Learning Institutions.

Multiversity

1. large, diverse student population
2. research centered
3. prestigious
4. undergraduate, graduate, and professional programs

Comprehensive University

1. large student population
2. some research
3. midlevel admission
4. many undergraduate, graduate programs

Smaller Public University

1. middle-sized student population
2. mostly teaching centered
3. low to midlevel admission requirements
4. Mostly undergraduate, some some masters programs.

Urban Centered University

1. mid- or large-sized student population, percentage of urban minority
2. teaching centered, with some research opportunity
3. low to midlevel admission requirements
4. Mostly undergraduate, graduate, perhaps even Ph.D.

Community College—Univ. Branch

1. small to midsize student population
2. teaching centered, training oriented
3. low or no admission requirements
4. 2- year undergraduate, associate degree, some 4- year programs

Graduate Emphasis Institutions

1. small, mid-, or large, depending on programs
2. research and professional
3. high admission requirements
4. graduate and professional degree programs

professional organizations and teaching graduate students. The best match with John's priorities would seemingly be the multiversity, with perhaps the comprehensive university a close second. John may also find some urban-centered universities acceptable, but would probably want to discount community colleges. This is just a framework; actual cases of job listings may be considered for individual strengths. But now John would have a sense of his criteria for rating available positions.

Job listings can be found in your professional organizations' newsletters, in the *Chronicle of Higher Education,* and in direct mail announcements to graduate departments. In the area of communication, the Speech Communication Association's newsletter, *Spectra,* regularly includes job listings, as does the International Communication

Association's *IA Newsletter*. The Association for Education in Journalism and Mass Communication has the *AEJMC News*, which also carries national job listings.

There are a few red flags you should look for in evaluating these ads. First, is the position a guaranteed opening or an anticipated opening? Many listings contain the phrase, "The Department of Communication anticipates a tenure track position in . . ." Sometimes "pending administrative approval" will appear in an ad. This may mean that there is no firm commitment that the opening will actually materialize and that the department is hedging its bets that it will be granted the permission to hire. You may want to take a chance that the position will go through and send in your application materials. But you might be well advised to ask whether a firm commitment has been given before you accept an invitation for an interview.

Another set of red flags deals with the rank and salary of the anticipated hire. Look for the words "tenure track" in the listings. If you do not find them, assume that the position is contingent on annual renewal and perhaps is temporary. You may be looking for a short-term appointment anyway, so such a situation is not necessarily a problem. Similarly, examine the rank of hire listed in the ad. Lecturers are often at the bottom of the pay scale and probably not on a tenure track. Visiting assistant professor means a temporary position, perhaps to fill a vacancy created by a sabbatical leave. Most reputable ads spell positions out. Nevertheless, it is well to resolve ambiguities.

Possibly the best prospects will come your way from your advisor. When an advisor is properly networked, he or she will have colleagues calling them for prospective applicants. Advisors often have knowledge about the story behind the ad. Another personal illustration is pertinent here. My advisor warned me against a particular job opening because he knew there was a hidden liability. It was actually a set of two jobs, both of which fit my wife's and my area of expertise (we were finishing our dissertations together). Against his wishes and my wife's better judgment, I insisted we both interview at this site (we had been offered interviews). It was a disaster. I found out later that someone else was in negotiation for one of the jobs as we were interviewing for them. I believe they thought they could get one of us on the tenure track and create a temporary position for the other. At the end of my wife's interview, the department head told her that one of the jobs had just been awarded to another candidate. He asked her if she was interested in the other position. She demanded to know why she had been put in the position of competing against her own husband for a job when she had assurances this would not happen before we came. She declined the position. The real kicker was that I thought some of the people at this job site were my friends. After defending these folks before the interview, I later had to admit that I was wrong and both my wife and advisor were right. This was very difficult.

While we are on the subject of the ethics of job searches, let's look at the other side. Should you send application materials to departments that list jobs for which you have only peripheral qualifications? That depends both on how you represent yourself and on the job itself. Sometimes job listings contain a major teaching role and then a number of subspecialties.

Perhaps you specialize in a secondary subject on the list, and the main one is a secondary area of interest for you. In this situation, you could send your materials, and perhaps the department will find that your qualifications fit. It is not advisable, however, to misrepresent yourself. It will become apparent by the end of your job interview.

Search committees carefully scrutinize applications for teaching and scholarship experience in areas outlined by the job description. The job description itself is often used as the final measure of a candidate's rank. Usually, only after failing to find the exact qualifications desired in a candidate will search committee members look for candidates who qualify in peripheral areas.

THE DUAL-CAREER SEARCH

Job searches are often made more complicated because of dual-career families. Finding a job in an area near a spouse's place of employment can seem nearly impossible, especially in university towns that are isolated and small. My wife and I were looking for jobs at the same time. Furthermore, we are in the same profession, so we examined the same listing services for job openings. We used a simple procedure of blocking regions of job openings. Although not totally effective for all regions, it was easier for urban centers. For instance, we decided that we could live with a one-way commute of a maximum of 40 miles. My wife found job listings in Chicago and Milwaukee that fit her expertise. I found one in Chicago and another west of Milwaukee.

As our options became limited, we collapsed the regions. My wife's job opportunity fell through in Milwaukee, so we concentrated on the Chicago positions. We did the same in regions elsewhere in the country. Sometimes it works out that dual-career couples live in the middle between two widely separated positions. Some dual-career families have waited years to find optimum blends of geography and job opportunities. My wife and I were lucky. Our advisor (yes, we even had the same one) helped me obtain an interview at a university at which my wife had interviewed. She was offered a position in the department of speech communication, and I was hired on the same campus in a separate mass communication department six weeks later. Since then we have helped our ex-advisor place other job candidates. Connections can be very important.

PLACEMENT SERVICES

Another source for job openings is a professional organization's placement service. Many people use placement services, which often provide an opportunity for short interviews at conventions. These are good opportunities at which to hone your interview skills and practice some of your job talk. But be aware that your interviewer may be tired after hearing the conversations of many candidates following a tight schedule of appointments. Do not be surprised if they are not all that enthusiastic and enchanted with small talk. Speaking of conventions, many people make connections through informal talks with those who are hiring. Take advantage of this opportunity if you can. Many advisors make it a point to introduce prospective employees to colleagues at conventions.

A final point about searching the job listings: Send your applications on time, preferably early. Search committees are given an arduous task of ranking many candidates, and this work is time-consuming. They like to get going, as they have hiring deadlines to meet. Assume that they will not wait for your application. Early applications often receive early rankings.

PREPARING FOR THE JOB INTERVIEW

The usual last stage in the job search process is performing effectively during the interview. It may not seem likely to an anxious applicant, but the interview invitations do roll in after a time. Once you are invited for an interview, you have a set of tasks laid before you. You must handle the visitation arrangements, prepare your job talk, and research the department you are visiting.

Let's begin with researching the department. You can start by asking for departmental brochures and catalogues when you are contacted for your interview arrangements. Try to obtain materials that show what the department has been up to. Many departments have alumni mailings. These would be a good source of information. Next, try to locate some of the work done by individuals in the department. Try to understand their research interests and positions. This information may be useful in constructing your job talk.

Be sure to obtain clear instructions about what is expected of you during the interview. Ask for an itinerary. Do not be shy. Most search committee chairs appreciate pleasant requests for specific information concerning the visit. It helps them prepare for your visit more efficiently. The more competence you demonstrate in making your visitation arrangements work smoothly, the more you communicate preparedness. Furthermore, it may be wise for you to plan ahead for the visitation by having a source of funds at your disposal. Often, you will have to be patient as you wait for reimbursement from host sites. Sometimes departments will have limited funds for your visit and may be unable to provide full reimbursement.

ACADEMIC INTERVIEWING

An interview is more than a process of judging a candidate for a position. Candidates should judge the position for its fit to career goals. Candidates need to be honest, straightforward, and have confidence both when they talk about themselves and in discussing the job position. Ask questions. What courses will be taught? How have they been taught before? What is the course load? What is the base salary and benefits? What are the requirements for tenure and promotion? How many have recently been denied tenure? Why? What resources are available for scholarly interests, including library, computer, and telecommunication resources? Be sure to communicate your needs as these things will be important to you. Make sure ahead of time that any equipment you need for your job talk is available and on hand. Practice your talk before you go and share it with your advisor and friends. Be sure your explanations fit in with general understandings of the concepts you are explaining. It probably is not wise to make overly controversial claims during your job talk, unless you have explicit data and analysis to back them up. Obviously, this is not the audience for untested speculations. If you have not analyzed your dissertation data completely (or other research relevant to the interview), demonstrate your partial analysis and discuss your procedures for data collection. Do the most you can to demonstrate your research progress.

Field questions gracefully, without rushing through your answers. It is OK to pause and examine the rationale of your answer before you give it. Be respectful, even if you are subjected to some rough treatment. Your patience communicates the ability to cope with pressure. Stick by your analysis, but acknowledge other points of view if they seem viable to you. You may even ask questioners for further clarification of their ideas as you answer questions. This communicates a willingness to learn and a focus on scholarly exchange.

Expect meetings with the department chair/head, along with the dean of the college. Smaller colleges and universities may take you to see higher level administrators. Administrators have a hand in setting salary limits, so do not be reluctant to ask them about benefits and resources. Similarly, take the opportunity to talk to students about the program.

Graduate students, if there are any, can be especially helpful in providing a sense of the learning environment. Before you leave the institution, inquire as to when you will be hearing about the hiring decision. Those responsible should have a reasonably good idea about the length of time it will take for job offers to go out. Also, be sure to find out how you will be reimbursed for your expenses, if reimbursement is to be provided.

AFTER THE INTERVIEW

The wait for a job offer can seem endless. These matters often take a good deal of time. Departments vote on candidates, send their rankings to the administration for approval, and then make offers to the top candidate. The second and third have to wait until the first candidate accepts or rejects an offer. This can take up to two or three weeks. So, it becomes a game of chance for some applicants. They may receive one offer from a school, but wait to hear from a more promising prospect. The dilemma is whether the chances of getting the second job are good enough to reject the first. Often it is better to go for the sure thing.

Some candidates are in a position to negotiate salary and benefits with a job offer. This is rarely true, however, for those starting at the assistant professor level. Indeed, in these days of state budget cuts to universities, you are not likely to have much leeway at a public university and probably little more at a private college. Again, the best strategy may be to argue for resources that aid in your professional development, rather than make demands as bargaining chips. You may find that universities will choose another, less expensive alternative.

Although it may now seem almost beyond your grasp, it will happen. You will find that job. Consider your new job as part of your commencement because as you will see in the next chapter on attaining tenure, beginning a job is just a part of the story. But it is exciting, and, yes, stressful. Taking control early can alleviate some of the stress.

ACCEPTING THE JOB

Once you have verbally accepted a position, the institution will send you a contract. Usually you have a period of time in which to sign and return it. If you have made explicit arrangements for salary level and resources, check the contract for these items. Do not hesitate to call and ask for explanations if you feel there are discrepancies or unanticipated sections of the contract. Benefit packages and scholastic resources may well be included. It is wise to check carefully to see how these sections match the expectations you got during your interview.

Once you have signed the contract, the time to prepare for your move is at hand. Many considerations come into play: What kind of office will I have? When may I move in? How do I order the books for my classes? Where do I begin to look for housing?

Those entering the job market for the first time often find they had not anticipated the difficulty they actually experience in finding a place to live. This is especially true if they are moving to a college or university town in the middle of the summer. The best housing is usually unavailable by that time, and often, beginning academics find they must make do with what is left. Planning ahead could save some anxiety later. If you plan to rent, set goals for the type of rental unit you will settle for. Often, you will find lower rentals available in areas outside college and university towns. If you do not mind commuting, these may be right for you. One of my friends made it a point to obtain a local newspaper when going on interviews. The classified ads from these newspapers enabled him to preview the housing situation in each of his visitation sites. He was able to find a rental house about 10 miles from his university that cost half the amount a similar unit in the town would have cost.

Buying a house is another story and beyond the scope of this discussion. I suggest that you obtain a detailed manual on mortgages, property assessments, and procedures for purchasing a house, especially if it is a first experience. Again, planning ahead can save time and money. Before going back to look for a house, contact the local chamber of commerce for lists of real estate brokers. They will also provide packets of information about the community which can be helpful. Similarly, check with the local Better Business Bureau or Chamber of Commerce for brokers who have good business reputations. Finally, it is wise to check local newspapers for current events in the area. You do not want to find out too late that the house you obtained for a "sweet deal" is located less than a mile downwind from a new landfill.

SUMMARY

Locating a job is work. It requires patience, and it costs applicants time and energy. One would think that with all the time and effort spent in locating a position, something should work out. Unfortunately, there can be disappointments, embarrassments, and lost opportunities. Although these can be minimized through careful planning, there are no guarantees that interviews will be pleasant or job offers will go according to your expectations. It is difficult not to be self-critical in such demanding situations. Perhaps it is best to concentrate on the things you can control and not experience anxiety about those that you cannot.

You can control the quality of your supporting materials with effective self-analysis and preparation. Similarly, proper preparation will allow you to present yourself in your best light when interviewing. Therefore, it is best to treat the job search as more than a necessary distraction from your everyday work. The chances of finding appropriate positions increase as the amount of serious effort increases.

◆ RESPONSE TO CHAPTER FOUR
Julia T. Wood

I wish I had read a chapter such as this when, as a 24-year-old with a spanking new Ph.D. in my pocket, I sought my first position. I found Professor Kuehn's observations and advice sound and very useful in suggesting how to go about the difficult and confusing task of securing an initial faculty appointment. I was equally impressed by the wisdom of the responses from Professors Gouran and Phillips. Their observations constructively augment the perspective Professor Kuehn provides. Following their lead, I try to add to what they and Professor Kuehn advised by focusing on issues that are unique to women and minorities seeking an academic position. Because their presence has not always been sought in the academy and because it still is not welcome on many campuses, they need to exercise particular caution to ensure a comfortable and effective fit between themselves and an institution.

For women and minority individuals interviewing for jobs, two issues provide the best indicators of campus climate toward historically marginalized interests. These are the presence and stature of women and minority faculty and the kinds of benefits offered. Regardless of whether you personally plan to join networks and/or avail yourself of benefits such as maternity leave, policies in these two areas are critical gauges of the extent to which an institution actively and materially supports nontraditional faculty and their concerns.

To find out how a campus regards nontraditional faculty, a bit of detective work is in order. Any candidate considering a position has the prerogative of asking the hiring department to set up appointments with the director of Women's Studies, African-American Studies, and so on. Even if you do not choose to affiliate directly (e.g., through cross-listing courses in communication with these curricula) with these programs, people in them are valuable sources of information. Typically, faculty in these areas have considerably more information about women and minorities than do faculty in a specific department. While there, you might also ask whether the university provides grants, research leaves, and other forms of research support specifically for work in nontraditional areas. Also ask about the proportion of women and minority faculty and how it has changed in the past 3, 5, and 10 years. Institutions that have a real commitment to diversity manage to hire and retain increasing numbers of nontraditional faculty. Salary equity is another key issue. Usually faculty in Women's Studies and African-American Studies know whether nontraditional faculty have equitable salaries. If they do not, contact the local AAUP chapter. Salaries are the most clear indicator of the relative value an institution places on traditional and nontraditional faculty.

While interviewing on a campus, also make time to stop by the benefits office (called Faculty and Staff Benefits, Human Resources, etc.). Find out what benefits are available for pregnancy and family leave. Even if you plan not to have children, the nature of these policies tells you something about an institution's awareness of and responsiveness to non-traditional faculty. It is also worthwhile to peruse a list of what is and is not covered under the standard health and hospitalization policy an institution provides to faculty. Some insurance companies are more progressive than others in the coverage they furnish for various kinds of prenatal, pediatric, and gynecological health needs. An institution really committed to women faculty will have secured insurance coverage that addresses the needs of women and minorities.

Hiring women and minorities is more common than retaining them, so the ongoing support an institution provides should figure prominently in assessments of institutions you might join. Does a university have a flexible schedule for tenuring so that faculty who have or adopt children or take on other primary care responsibilities are given additional time to demonstrate professional merit? Are there provisions for compensating departments so that substitute faculty can be hired when family leaves are taken, or does an institution foster resentment toward women by expecting colleagues to cover classes as uncompensated overloads? All of these issues reflect an institution's commitment to nontraditional faculty.

It is also worthwhile to ask about "the revolving door," which is a term used to describe the common institutional practice of hiring women and minorities, keeping them for 4-6 years when their energy and ambition enable them to make major contributions to universities, and then not tenuring them. Thus, women and minorities often pass through the revolving door. If you are a female or minority person, ask others in the programs I have mentioned and/or local AAUP chapters about an institution's history of tenuring—not just hiring—women and minorities.

Finally, I wish to add my support to the point Professor Gouran makes regarding malcontents and gossips. My experience, like his, is that at least one of these characters resides in most departments. They are the naysayers, the prophets of gloom and doom, the people whose preoccupation with what is wrong blinds them to all that is right. The danger of malcontents is not so much that their criticisms are erroneous, but rather that their perspectives are imbalanced yet regarded and presented as the whole truth. Their complement, also found in most departments, is the inveterate optimist who has nothing but positive views and good words for a department, faculty, and campus. Neither presents a complete picture, and in their partiality each misleads. Prudent candidates will, therefore, seek conversations with as many faculty, staff, and students as possible in an effort to gain a perspective as multifaceted as institutional life.

In my last sentence I alluded to one source of information not noted in Professor Kuehn's discussion of how to evaluate different institutions. That source is students, and they usually offer important perspectives, ones that reflect viewpoints and insights often unavailable to faculty. When we invite candidates to our campus, we routinely schedule time for them to meet with graduate students without any faculty presence. We do this for two reasons. First, we value our graduate students' perspectives on candidates, so we want them to get to know and assess individuals we are considering for positions. Second, we think candidates should have access to the kinds of insights that nonfaculty can provide. If time with students, graduates and undergraduates, is not scheduled for you by a hiring institution, it is to your advantage either to request or arrange for it yourself.

Finally, I would add a word of advice regarding women and minority candidates' presentation of self. During the interview process you may be asked in subtle or overt ways to explain the extent of your allegiance to women and/or minorities. Faculty may ask whether you consider yourself a feminist, whether you plan to conduct feminist and/or gender and/or minority research, and whether you want to teach "specialized courses." The goal of securing a position may tempt individuals holding strong stances to attenuate their positions, but this is generally unwise. If you declare you do not wish to teach courses in gender or the oral traditions of minority populations, then you may have ensured that you will not be able to teach them. Faculty hire people to teach and conduct research in particular areas, so what you announce as your focus becomes part of at least the informal contract that governs your employment and, later, decisions on tenure and promotion. In short, it seems unwise to commit yourself to any positions with which you would be unwilling to live. Also, if you are hired to teach and conduct research in nontraditional areas, make sure that understanding is on the record in writing.

In sum, in the search for a position, the goal is to find a fit between you and an institution. This is unlikely to be accomplished if you overlook important information about campus climate, fail to put extreme positions (whether positive or negative) in a larger perspective, and/or misrepresent yourself. Decisions based on incomplete or distorted perspectives are usually not the best, so getting information from diverse sources is any candidate's best insurance for making informed choices. Similarly, hiring that grows out of misrepresentation of interests and allegiances tends to result in disillusionment in all or some of the people who have to live with the hires. A less than candid explanation of your interests invariably leads either to entrapping you in the restrictions you declared and/or incurring resentment from colleagues who were misled by your statements during the hiring interview. Neither makes for congenial, collegial life.

◆ RESPONSE TO CHAPTER FOUR
GERALD M. PHILLIPS

I placed my first Ph.D. in a good job in 1966. He later became a department head. Since then I have placed approximately 75 students. There are 2 college presidents, 1 vice president, 3 deans, 3 endowed chairs, 19 full professors, and about 6 I have lost touch with entirely. I have 2 entrepreneurs that outearn me by $100,000 a year. I can testify that job hunting is not a "crap shoot." It is a manipulative, meticulous process of making connections, exchanging favors, and making sure you have a good product to trade.

It helps if your candidate has a good vita. As an advisor, you can facilitate this by making sure your candidate buys a good computer, turns out some acceptable papers, presents at conventions, and meets the people in your network. It also helps if the candidate finishes on time. There were a few instances when a candidate made a liar out of me by not finishing by the time I promised in my reference letter. This makes me angry, and I do not usually give another reference.

I know that every candidate I place carries my name. They are known as "Phillips's people" whether they like it or not and whether I like it or not. So, I know I must do my job as advisor, and they must measure up as students, or it will be very difficult for the next candidate. Every student who does not meet the expectations I create with my reference letter makes it difficult for the next student because it cheapens my word. By the same token, I dare not exaggerate in my reference letters. I must praise a flawed human being, and we are all flawed, but I must be careful to avoid damning with faint praise.

In short, candidate and advisor must collude to make a good placement.

But let us note that the picture is changing. For one thing, affirmative action requires at least the appearance of a fair search. I know that some schools have found ways to get around affirmative action. And there are the charges: "Black females get all the breaks while males take it on the chin." Actually, affirmative action makes very little difference. Good people get good jobs, and occasionally a deserving candidate gets a boost he or she might not have otherwise gotten.

What makes the real difference are the economic changes in the academy. For one thing, many states are cutting budgets and laying people off. There are assaults on tenure; many schools are cutting the number of tenure-track positions. A large number of schools (at least as of this writing) have job freezes, and there is little chance of them being lifted in the near future. The boom days of academia are over.

It is hard to find jobs these days. Very often you will have to take a job at a school you think is beneath you. (Most graduate students have a notion about the "high class" school at which they will work.) Newly minted Ph.D.s must, these days, choose from among the offers they can get and resolve to make their career at that school by doing good work, publishing, teaching well, and serving their institution. In short, a tight market makes professionalism very important.

Economic changes are important once you get a job offer. Be sure to find out about the medical plan. Private policies are very expensive, and medical insurance is very necessary. Find out about the pension plan and whether there are special plans that reserve funds so you are not taxed until you withdraw them. Find out if your pension is transferable, and if you have a choice of plans, check the companies carefully.

It is possible that by the time this book comes out everything I said above may be wrong, but I do not think that will happen.

I add another piece of advice from the point of view of a long-time member of search committees: Try for an authentic vita. So many candidates have one heading called "works in progress" and another called "works submitted." Often, these are identical. We notice that. Many candidates work in continuing education and do "gigs." They list these jobs on their vitae as "seminar on oral presentations sponsored by a major manufacturer." We know this means they taught a session on public speaking to the Weeble Widget Company. What search committees look for are bona fide publications, bona fide documentation of teaching skill, and evidence of activity in professional organizations. They look for references from people they know and trust. Dr. Kuehn commented on how important it is to be sure of the reliability of your referees. Members of search committees also look for references from people with whom they have experience. Consider that a bad reference from an enemy of someone on the search committee may be more valuable than a good reference from a person unknown. It is all very subtle and very unpredictable.

In the 1970s, a great many more Ph.D.s were produced than the country needed. These aspiring professors became part-time teachers. My son-in-law fell into this notch. Recently, now over 40, he got a starting job at a small college and is going through the stress of seeking tenure. We may be in these perilous times again. Not all of the new Ph.D.s will get jobs in academic professions, and of those who get starting jobs, many will not achieve tenure—anywhere.

You seek a professorship because of your love of learning and your desire to contribute to the advancement of knowledge. This sounds very idealistic, but these days, these are the only reasons to do it. It surely is not for the money or job security anymore.

◆ RESPONSE TO CHAPTER FOUR
DENNIS S. GOURAN

I have no real disagreements with Professor Kuehn's suggestions as to how to go about the process of securing an academic position. On the whole, I find his discussion to be both constructive and useful. There are some aspects of interviewing that he does not mention, however, for which it is worth being prepared. These fall into the "things no one ever told me, but I wish they had" category. Two, in particular, can make the experience of interviewing less than pleasant and leave candidates for positions in doubt about how best to respond.

Nearly every faculty has at least one malcontent or inveterate gossip in its midst. Encounters with such individuals may take one or both of two directions. In the first instance, the individual will regale an interviewee about the department's "dirty linen." In the second, he or she may seek verification in the form of "Is it really true about. . . .?" questions relating to the interviewee's current institutional affiliation. Although exchanges involving such topics are often innocuous, at times they can make an interviewee quite uncomfortable. Because they do, it is good to have some sense of how to respond, should such difficult moments arise.

The occasion of an interview gives those at the host institution the opportunity to offer an interviewee some insights into what professional life at that institution may be like for him or her. There is nothing wrong with this. In fact, it can be helpful to a candidate in deciding whether he or she would want to accept an offer, should one be extended. It is valuable, therefore, when members of the faculty speak honestly about such matters as support for research, teaching loads, governance, availability of equipment, and institutional expectations concerning professional performance. The problem for the interviewee is that he or she is not always able to discern the accuracy of the information. There are some signs, however, by which one can begin to gauge it. If the source prefaces revelations about the department and institution frequently with such openings as, "Please don't quote me," "I would not want it to be generally known that I said this, but . . .," "Nobody else would probably admit to this; however, . . . ," or "I may be speaking out of place; nevertheless, I feel obliged to tell you that . . . ," there is an excellent chance that you are being misinformed. Another sign is the absence of any unsolicited corroboration by others. In a genuinely troubled department, there are few individuals who pledge an interviewee to silence or who feel a need to acknowledge that others are afraid to be open.

If you encounter this type of individual, it is probably best to listen politely and respond as little as possible. You need not be concerned about your lack of responsiveness because the malcontent has a story to tell, and to that person, it is much more important to complete it than it is for him or her to win a possible ally. You should remember that the person unloading on you probably has little interest in having you as a colleague in the first place. After all, your visit is the product of decisions and actions by individuals about whom the complainant is expressing his or her considerable disapproval.

You might think of the type of person whom I just described as a "dirt dispenser." The other type to whom I alluded falls more into the category of "dirt gatherer." Some individuals in the profession take delight in others' misfortunes. Whether true or not, they appear to have an almost insatiable appetite for stories about departments in decline, individuals being sued, faculty members whose futures are in jeopardy, breakups of marriages, removals from office, and the like. In an interview, these types of participants are apt to put candidates in the awkward position of having to respond to direct questions about people and departments at the institutions they are representing. Awkward though it may be, in my opinion, the best responses to such inquiries are direct ones. To the extent that you may be in possession of accurate information, you are in a position to offer correctives on what it is that your inquisitor has "heard about X." Rest assured that what the person "has heard" is very likely to be erroneous in significant respects. If you have no information relevant to the question, you should say so.

Some individuals do not make it quite so easy to respond as my comments above would seem to suggest. Such may be the case because imbedded in their queries are also characterizations, which are typically unflattering. For example, "Is it true that. . . . is as big a tyrant as everybody seems to believe?" Sometimes one can dismiss a question of this type with an observation, such as "I wasn't aware that everyone believed that." Responses such as this make it clear that the interviewee would prefer not to engage in conversations of a personal nature, and most reasonably intelligent people, even if they have a malicious streak, are able to read the message.

You should also be aware that by indulging in gossip of the more personal variety, you probably will not do anything to make yourself more attractive to those whose curiosity you are gratifying. More than one person who has succumbed to pressures to confirm others' impressions of what is happening at a candidate's home institution has later become an object of unfavorable reaction by those very same individuals. Having acquired the desired input, they may then turn around and say something such as, "If there is anything I can't stand, it's a person who bites the hand that feeds him."

Awkwardness in response to the kind of situation in which malcontents and gossips sometimes place an interviewee is understandable because they so often appear to be "in the know" and imply that they have high standing, if not within the department, then either in the college/university, or the profession at the very least. In dealing with such individuals, however, you might do well to ask yourself whether or not a person who feels compelled to seek out someone new to the profession for the purpose of either dispensing or acquiring "dirt" is likely to have much clout. If the person is as influential as he or she would have you believe, it seems reasonable to assume that he or she would not require your assistance to effect some desired change or to acquire information of interest about what is occurring elsewhere in the profession.

Should you have the misfortune of interviewing at an institution in which the faculty appears to have an inordinately high proportion of malcontents and gossips, you may wish to pass on a job offer. Life on such a faculty is not apt to be very fulfilling unless one has an extraordinary facility for dealing with problematic individuals. The good news, however, is that this type of department is the exception rather than the rule. In my experience, most of those at host institutions who participate in the interview process do attempt to look for qualities in prospective colleagues that make them attractive. When they are critical of their own departments, moreover, the motivation is more often than not benign. They want the candidate to know that he or she will face problems, both of an interpersonal and professional nature. To conceal those realities is to be irresponsible. Still, there are those whose motivations are directed toward other ends, and this is something with which you simply have to learn to live.

5

STARTING OUT

Scott A. Kuehn

It always happens in such a way so that I'm walking down corridors that look like weird combinations of the halls where I spent my undergraduate and graduate days. I see a familiar face or two, sometimes they nod identification, at others they seem to ignore me. There are faculty offices and classrooms mixed together in a whirl of passing backdrops, like a cheap action sequence from a "B" movie. Nothing appears especially wrong or out of place, but then nothing really seems "right." I know I am supposed to find a classroom with my students, but I never seem to get there. I ask my colleagues who happen by, but their directions are unintelligible or lead to the wrong place. In a strange way I feel that what I am doing is ordinary, that I do this all the time. But then I feel frightened by the prospect of finding the classroom.

One of my old friends laughed: "That is pretty strange. In yours you can't get to a classroom, in mine, computer keyboards and diskettes melt in my hands like M & M's." We laughed again, the three of us—close friends from graduate school—sharing recurrent dreams. It is a national convention in November, a time to renew friendships and rub elbows. We had been out in academe about five years or so, and we were catching up. Two of us sitting at the table had been working for about five years. We were coming up for tenure. The other was still searching for his ideal tenure-track position.

Someone once said that college professors are not made overnight; they reach the height of their profession by degrees. Witticism aside, I think there is some irony in that statement. You are probably reading this having earned a brand new formal degree of some sort. But that is just the beginning. As you begin your professorial career, you enter a unique sociocultural system called the *tenure track*. This track is designed to display your fitness for running. And, the spectators can get in your way. Runners on this track need to know the fast and slow lanes to construct their strategies for the race.

THE NATURE OF TENURE

Tenure began as an informal process of seniority. When a teacher reached the "10-year" mark, he or she was accepted as a peer by colleagues. This system was adapted by land grant institutions in the United States in the late 1800s. Eventually, the expectation of tenure became a probationary period. The junior faculty were to be watched, mentored, and either accepted or rejected for the particular organization. The system evolved to the point at which supposedly "teaching, scholarship, and service" were the criteria for judging tenurees. However, research institutions based their decisions mostly on scholarly productivity and teaching colleges mostly on student learning and satisfaction.

Today, tenure is a legally recognized system of due process protection for faculty. Tenured faculty have the right of hearing in first amendment cases involving classroom and scholarly discourse and teaching methods. The same is true for firing decisions. Nontenured faculty may have similar rights or protections, but only if specified in their contracts. Tenure and academic freedom are thus closely tied together. Universities cannot suddenly fire tenured faculty without providing reasons or charges answerable by the faculty. However, the Roth (*Board of Regents* v. *Roth*, 92 S.Ct. 2701 1972) and Sindermann (*Perry* v. *Sindermann*, 92 S.Ct. 2717 1972) cases, decided by the U.S. Supreme Court, show that nontenured faculty can have their contracts unrenewed without reason, and the courts will not consider this a violation of academic freedom (Hemmer, 1986).

Beyond the legality of tenure is the emotional state connected with it. Tenured faculty feel accepted, more at ease, and thus more able to concentrate on their career goals. Tenure is desirable for all these reasons. Some hot shots are offered tenure as part of job packages, but most of us go through a probationary period leading to tenure. Crafted legally, these probationary periods offer some protections to tenurees, but they seem to be inadequate to dispel much of the anxiety connected with the process of getting tenure.

BEGINNING TENURE: THE FRANTIC CYCLE

Catching one's breath after finishing a dissertation and chasing down a job is hard. We are often faced with the prospect of teaching new courses. Added to that is the sense of "well, now what?" that comes with any type of matriculation. The first semester in a new job often becomes a frantic cycle. Part of this is dealing with new teaching duties, but another part is often self-exploration. The role of assistant professor may be so new that hearing "Dr. _____" initially seems strange. Some former graduate students have told me that they felt unsure about how to begin. One even wished to contact his doctoral committee for a list of books, a sort of professorial reading list. Such role ambiguity is more common than we believed as graduate students. Of course, we saw how professors acted, and we certainly had role models. But that did little to settle the newness, the feeling of ambiguity that went with being, not just acting like, a professor.

Now let's add a few more items to the frenetic cycle of being a new professor. First, consider the newness of working as an identifiable entity to the administration. As graduate students we were purely numbers to deans and provosts. We may have even taught courses as teaching assistants, but deans and provosts were not part of our organizational network. Now, we have performance reviews with administrators. How do you treat these folks? How will they treat you? Your experience as a graduate student will probably not prepare you for this interaction. A personal story provides a good example. I attended a large university for my doctoral program. The dean was not part of my life there (although he signed the contracts). However, I learned from my teachers that deans controlled the fate of faculty and should not be regarded frivolously. Thus, I stereotyped the dean as an ivory tower official. I got a job at a medium-sized state university. The dean was a man in his late 50s, and he seemed very authoritative in my job interview. The next time I saw him, he looked completely different. I checked in the week before the beginning of the semester and found him on his back on the floor of the office constructing a desk for a secretary. I helped him (but still let him decide where and when to put the screws in the wood). Looking back, I am glad this experience did not totally disarm my caution when dealing with administration.

Next, consider dealing with your colleagues. There are many issues here ranging from what to say at faculty meetings (or even how to look involved and interested) to whether to engage in controversy to the choice of friends. Not only do you have connections with faculty in your department or unit, you must deal with committee meetings and groups of faculty across the campus. We discuss this in more depth later.

So, those who jump into the professorate, publish their dissertation and a series of articles in their first semester, and do not seem to sweat it, must come from the planet Krypton. Yes, but who would expect to do that? I have found that the frantic atmosphere for new professors is largely unexpected. Friends have echoed my experience of believing that once the dissertation was done and the job was in hand, life would slow down automatically; like moving the weight up on the arm of a metronome. If it has not happened to you, take my word for it, that weight is moving downward.

DEALING WITH THE FRANTIC CYCLE

In this chapter we are going to discuss ways of dealing with the frantic cycle of getting tenure. There are three things that are important in achieving stress management: (a) know the rules for tenure, (b) know the people who will vote on your tenure, and (c) know exactly what to do to get tenure.

Actually, the very first decision a tenure-track appointee must make is whether or not they really want to stay at their institution. Many accept positions as stepping stones to others and stay only a few years. However, some accept jobs that do not really suit their strong points. Think of the wonderful teacher in the prestigious land grant university. He has student accomplishments to brag about, but a very short list of publications. Disappointment comes heavy when the realization sets in: no publications, no tenure. On the other hand, what about the research hotshot who takes a position at a teaching-centered, unionized institution where the pay is high and the benefits are good? Teaching four courses a semester with three preps means less time devoted to writing, but more contact with students. Frustration sets in when he or she realizes that the tenure committee weighs heavily peer and student evaluations in his or her tenure evaluation. In either example, knowing ones' professional strengths meant as much as simply knowing the rules.

There is also another situation. What if you have to stay? We looked at the problem of finding a job in a dual-career family in an earlier chapter. Sometimes we are faced with making a career at a place that is not wholly suited to our ideal. In this circumstance we must adapt to the rules. The point is, no matter what the situation, once you decide to seek tenure at an institution, your judgment should be based on matching your abilities and goals to the rules and procedures of getting tenure.

There are two types of rules for getting tenure. Explicit rules are in your contract and faculty handbook. Almost all colleges and universities have explicit rules that say you have to teach well, pursue scholarly activity, and perform service to the institution and the community. Sometimes there are specifics, but often the language is ambiguous. This is when the unwritten expectations come out. The implicit rules can be explained by those who have recently obtained tenure. They are among the most important to know.

Let's go back to the written rules. Most universities list teaching as the most important function of the university in their mission statements and faculty contracts. It is well known, however, that many research institutions prize a publication record more than teaching excellence. Publications are quantifiable evidence that the researcher is adding to the prestige of his or her particular institution. Here, tenurees need to get the low down on what type of publication record is necessary for tenure. Often it takes one journal article in a national publication during each year of the probationary contract, plus convention appearances and regional publications. To find out the specifics, the tenuree must ask someone with the information: successful tenure applicants, the department head, or the dean.

A friend of mine found out "inside" information from one of the dean's secretaries. She had seen most of the application files as her duties involved maintaining faculty records. She provided a wealth of information about how to structure a folder of supporting documents and the aspects of the successful vita. This enabled my friend to make tangible publication, service, and teaching goals consistent with the expectations for tenure at his university. Having this information by the second year reduced the pressure.

Knowing the tenure rules helps the tenuree divide his or her time fruitfully. If you are expected to teach proficiently, you know that you need the extra time to prepare courses, review potential texts, and meet with students. If expectations point to service to the institution, one takes the time to get involved in university committees. Time management is essential in any profession, but it really works when fortified by tangible goals. Time management also reduces stress. The point is to know the rules so you can plan a successful tenure case. This relates to knowing what to do to get tenure, which is covered later in this chapter.

MANAGING RELATIONSHIPS

The scariest part of the tenure process is unpredictability. Any social scientist will tell you that individuals are among the most unpredictable entities in the universe. So you can handle the writing and the class preparations, but what do you do about that old curmudgeon whose office is down the hall? Should you stop your lecture and rip the newspaper out of the hands of that obnoxious student or put up with the indignity?

There is another set of unspoken rules that goes along with managing your relationships with colleagues and students. A friend suggested that a good metaphor for these rules is a fraternity "rush" (or substitute sorority if you are so inclined). The underlying connection seems to be that tenurees are tested for devotion, skill, and fortitude. And, it helps to be skilled in the social graces. What I like about this metaphor is that it places a nonrational schema over a nonrational situation. People do not treat each other rationally on a day-to-day basis in the academic organization.

A popular organizational communication text states that all interactions between people working together should be based on "trust," defined in the vernacular sense of the word (Haney, 1992). I have doubts about its application in business organizations, but I am sure that this is bad advice for anyone approaching tenure in a college or university. Academic departments have self-sufficient entrepreneurs known as tenured, full professors. They do not have to follow a company line. They can function as they please and are required only to meet classes and give grades if that is all they want to do. The point is they can (and do) act irrationally at times and still not hurt themselves. But, they also have the ability to zing others.

Tenurees get caught up in the emotional morass of pleasing self and/or pleasing others. We never really know what is a test of ability or a test of fortitude. One day we see a tenured colleague and share the hassles of dealing with "a problem student," and on another day the same colleague will ask us why we were abrupt with his advisee. One day the course we teach "is a good grade inflation fighter," on another day it is "we shouldn't scare our freshmen into a tizzy." This type of Doolittlian "pushme-pullyou" activity can seem so unintentional as it unfolds. Perhaps this is the only difference between a real fraternal hazing and the academic style. Academe is much more subtle.

That is, sometimes it is much more subtle. Tenurees can actually incur the wrath of tenured faculty. We hear stories about how the tenuree is perceived as doing a better job than an old curmudgeon who has not kept up in the discipline. After a while the jealousy becomes overt, perhaps in the form of a negative peer review of a class visitation or bullying in a faculty meeting. Now, try to achieve a climate of "trust" with this person. Sometimes you cannot avoid making enemies. But you can make allies and friends.

A network of allies makes things less unsettling. Realize, however, that allies will sometimes haze. But these instances are often private, mostly subtle, and rarely harmful. You know you are in a network of allies when you can express your opinion and you get a respectful answer when it really counts. Of course, there is the saying, "just because you're paranoid, it doesn't mean they're not out to get you." Know your friends, and enemies will diminish in stature and importance. But they do not disappear.

Not everyone will take advantage of academic hazing opportunities. The most secure persons, or those who suffered brutal hazings of their own, will not do it. Sometimes you have a person who takes an interest in lessening the frenetic pace of your tenure cycle. Mentoring comes in many forms, with many degrees of helpful and harmful results. Finding a tenure mentor, however, really does take the stress down a degree. These mentors provide the inside information about who thinks what about what, and so on. All mentoring relationships are two-way, however. What do you do in the situation in which someone wants to mentor you and you do not want it? One friend described a situation in which he was the first of a younger generation to be appointed on the faculty. There were full professors lined up for the mentor job. The association was to make them more powerful, he thought. He ended up as a friend to all, but rarely saw any of them socially. He said that walking the line between being mentored by any of them was difficult the first three years. Then another new faculty member was hired.

This illustrates a good principle for dealing with this uncertainty. Learn about the people in the department. Study their interactions. Try to anticipate behavior, but realize that you will have a low probability of success most of the time.

Before we leave the topic of managing relationships, let's pull out a subject that is constantly on the mind of tenurees: How much should I stand up for myself? I believe, now that I am at the end of a tenure probationary period myself, that the question is better phrased: How well can I control my emotions and still deal assertively to express my needs? Conflict will occur naturally, one way or another, and more than once. If you roll over, you will be trampled (and some good ideas may have no effect), but if you "bite back" too swiftly and too hard, you may make enemies needlessly.

The need to assert oneself will come up. It is how you do it that will make the difference. First, try to disconnect your emotions from your response. Count to 10 (or 10,000, whatever it takes) to calm down. Wait a day or two before you act. Let reason and evidence, not passion, guide your behavior. I wish this were my advice, but a colleague whom I regard as wise filled me in. It has worked. Find someone to talk to. My wife over lunch or after work has been an immeasurable help in diffusing anger.

A second point: When you act, do so in an accepted channel and in an appropriate way. Department heads and chairpersons are always a starting point for the resolution of cross-faculty conflict. The failure to observe accepted channels can have embarrassing consequences. A disgruntled tenuree in a university near mine complained directly to his provost of being passed over for a new computer. He found out about it and in anger fired off a memo. It seems he got a used model that was slow and cumbersome, whereas the tenured professor down the hall, who had no computer skills, got a fast, sleek new one. The tenuree reasoned that he should get the new machine so that he could do all the statistical analysis he needed effortlessly, whereas the tenured professor should have the slower computer with which to learn. A week later he got the computer he wanted, then found out his dean blocked the purchase of all software for his department to pay for his new computer. Needless to say, he made few positive impressions with his rash behavior.

Sometimes we find ourselves in situations in which rash emotional responses are hard to avoid. Again, the best advice is to keep under control. Remember, all your colleagues work under the same pressures that you do. Teaching, advising, writing deadlines, grading, committee meetings—all these things tend to make tension. Yelling back at someone yelling already really accomplishes little. However, consolation can be seen in the understanding of colleagues that see you are under pressure too. If you express anger, you may not have to worry too much about it. It's likely that the next day you will be able to say, "hey, sorry about that. I guess it will happen from time to time."

DEALING WITH ADMINISTRATION

Someone should write a book titled "Dealing with Administration: How to Get What You Want Without Selling Your Soul." I am sure it would sell as well as any book on obtaining grants and probably better. Deans, provosts, directors, vice presidents, presidents, and department heads all have an enormous amount of influence over your tenure case. Incredibly, many of these people rarely know you, probably never see you teach, or never read one of your articles or manuscripts in its entirety. But they often judge your tenure application. Your tenure case will probably gain its most support from your department, but there is a signature trail leading all the way up to the president's office. As Yogi Berra said and any Cubs fan could tell you: "It ain't over till it's over."

Find out what type of influence certain administrators have on your tenure case. In some universities the academic dean makes the final decision on tenure, based on the departmental recommendation. In others, mostly unionized colleges and universities, a university-wide tenure committee may be responsible for the thumbs up or thumbs down. In the first case, it would make a great deal of sense to understand your dean's position on tenure. What does the dean view as adequate scholarly development? Get him or her to quantify or otherwise operationalize his or her definition when you begin your tenure position. The last thing you want to discover is the dean's notion of how many publications it takes to be tenured the year you are coming up for tenure. Planning is essential in this regard.

An earlier chapter pointed out that deans and other administrators are not simply faculty who have keys to executive washrooms. They do an entirely different job, with an entirely different career focus. It is important for you to realize this when you begin your tenure track. Friends have pointed out that administrators often look for new faculty with whom to work. Why? First, new faculty are often hungry to prove themselves, and good administrators know that if they are effective coaches, they will build strong departments (and strong cases for their own promotions). You can bring well-reasoned cases for developing programs and research to your department head or dean and often they will grant aid. Remember, however, that you lose credibility if you are perceived as a grabber. Making a case for a 50mhz 486 computer with a 3 gigabyte hard drive and 16meg of ram just because you do multivariate statistics will prompt questions about why the mainframe isn't sufficient. Ask for exactly what you need with a detailed justification. Administrators deal in paper. Show them on paper a good case that will bring a return to the college (such as an eventual grant, series of articles, and other publicity) and you will get serious consideration, even in these days of budget cuts.

A second reason administrators often look to new faculty is because most of the established ones they deal with are pains in the neck. New faculty are somewhat controllable, as contrasted with an entrenched full professor. Tenured faculty are less accountable to deans, but often demand perks ranging from graduate assistants to office space, furniture, and parking spaces. Someone has to pay, and often there are other priorities. Deans and department heads spend much of their time saying no. Sometimes they enjoy it, but not all the time. They will jump at an opportunity to work with someone they perceive as agreeable.

Although you will deal with your department head and dean the most, you will encounter other administrators. At our medium-sized university of about 385 faculty, the president and vice president know us fairly well. Social functions provide a forum for chit-chat (or other memorable occasions, such as the time our 2-year-old knocked a glass ornament off the president's Christmas tree onto her foot. She still laughs at our embarrassment). Sometimes, however, the forum is not so agreeable. There is, for example, the recent instance of how an interim administration at the University of Nebraska, following the advice of some seemingly nameless and innocuous accountant, decided to close down the department of Speech Communication to save money. Situations in which financial and physical plant directors wield influence are common, but not as graphic as this. Even though we can happily report that the department was not closed, many of your colleagues are sure to have stories about parking spaces, offices, and budgets disappearing at their institutions.

MAKING ALLIES

Much of the activity at a university is committee centered. You will encounter many fellow faculty members from a variety of disciplines. I have a friend at my university who was taken aback by the behavior of some of his colleagues. He was a professional in industry for many years, went back to school, and began a career in academe. Call it a stereotype or unfounded ideal, but my friend really believed that college professors interacted "at a higher level than name calling, defensiveness, and accusations." He was certainly surprised.

Many of us from large graduate programs know better. We have seen our advisors duke it out. We have seen the spoils that go to the victors and the agony of defeat. We know that interaction within academe is not purely academic. But it really does not hit home until one becomes involved. Keep in mind that your goal is to build allies. The advice about counting to 10 applies to colleagues outside your department: You never know what type of role they may play in your life in the future. One semester's nemesis may be next semester's source for grant opportunities. Do not make needless enemies, even if you are a target. Forget about the unpleasant and move on to what is important.

Whether it be subtle hazing or overt manipulation, remember that dealing with your colleagues will be part of your academic life. Many of the indignities suffered during the tenuring process will pass, but some will remain. A friend of mine said she got through it all with the thought: "Do I want to be like THAT?" She now helps others through their tenuring relationships in their departments.

SUCCESSFUL TENURE PERFORMANCE

The last part of this chapter focuses on doing what is necessary to gain tenure at your institution. It is not enough to know the rules and navigate your way through relationships. In the end, it is your performance that will be judged. Performance is behavior. You need to understand what you must do to become successfully tenured and how to do it.

How do you know what you need to do? Start by being briefed on the rules. Know how to put together a tenure file long before it is due in the dean's office. Find out from others how to put it together. Know the decision process. Know the expectations of those making the decisions.

Tenure standards differ widely. You have read in this chapter and in others about how these standards differ. Making a choice whether or not to stay on for tenure depends on whether or not you fit in with the standards at your institution. Those who focus on research will prefer to be judged on the number and quality of their publications. Those who focus on teaching want to be judged on instructional development talents. A teacher probably will not be tenured at a research institution, and a researcher will have a rough go of it at a teaching institution.

Let's assume you have made your choice of institution based on an assessment of your career goals and interests. Next, you research the rules and guidelines for obtaining tenure at your institution. You have operationalized all the definitions like a good scientist: To be tenured, you find you need teaching evaluations with better than average scores, you must publish at least one article or book chapter a year and present papers at major conventions, and you must participate in at least two areas of university governance. Your sources are your department head, your dean, the secretaries, and your colleagues who have been through the process. You examine the procedures and make a checklist of all the important things you need to do to build your tenure file.

I have talked to successfully tenured colleagues who have learned something more: Prepare a plan. One colleague had a folder for each of the things he knew was necessary for promotion and tenure. He worked steadily to fill each section of the folder to build his tenure case. Another colleague constructed a detailed PERT chart (an algorithmic breakdown of steps needed to accomplish a task placed on a grid) outlining each item he needed to achieve tenure and promotion. His PERT chart was broken down into specific behaviors and time periods. He knew exactly what he wanted to accomplish in each semester of his tenure probationary period. He said his focus was strong, and he would turn down opportunities that did not lead to his goal. Others may argue that such a myopic approach is overdoing it a bit, but he seemed less stressful than the rest of us. I notice he has plenty of opportunities now.

THE DECISION

There is light at the end of the tunnel. While I have been writing this I have been in my last semester of my probationary period. At this time my tenure case has moved successfully through the department committee to the university-wide tenure committee. I am told the president notifies applicants at the end of the semester about her decision on tenure. My nerves are calming.

Sometimes, however, things do not work out as we had hoped. One of my friends lost a tenure case this semester at another university. The process begins all over now—the job search, the tenure decisions, and so on. The worst of it is having to deal with the frantic pace for another five or six years. However, some good can come out of this. Many universities pick up bright assistant professors who failed in their tenure bids at "name" universities. These places can be excellent environments in which to begin again.

Throughout this chapter we have asked the question: Is tenure worth it? Perhaps we should have asked: Is academic freedom worth it? It is naive to assume that no one will bother you once you get tenure. It is equally naive to assume that you can do anything you want and not get fired. However, the professorate is dependent on tenure. Without it we would have George Orwell's *1984* in the classroom and in our offices. Today, more than ever, students need to be exposed to and stimulated to think about a variety of views. Just think what would happen to the political correctness debate if faculty could be laid off like autoworkers. There would be no debate at all.

Perhaps that is why tenure has become an institution. Similar to having a baby, we suffer, grunt, groan, and sweat when we are in the midst of it, but we forget much of that once birthing is over. We have a baby to nurture and play with. We sympathize with those in the process, but the process will continue.

◆ RESPONSE TO CHAPTER FIVE
DENNIS S. GOURAN

As a recently tenured professor, our colleague Scott Kuehn is much closer to the experience of being reviewed, with all of its attendant anxieties, than Professor Phillips, Professor Wood, or I. As we regularly participate in the review process, however, we can appreciate the concerns Professor Kuehn has enumerated and illustrated. His portrayal of the process as essentially a rite of passage—hazing in his terms—is one with which I have some difficulty, at least in respect to the generalized way in which he describes it. Missing from the discussion, moreover, are some considerations I personally believe give a more balanced portrait of the process. I attempt to deal with these matters in the remarks that follow.

I am certainly in no position to dispute another person's perceptions of a process he or she has experienced; however, I do question the extent to which the events typically involved in assessments of untenured professors' professional experience constitute a form of academic hazing. To be sure, there are despicable individuals in higher education (as there are in every profession), and a certain percentage of them will find their way onto promotion and tenure committees and into positions in which they may be able to affect the fate of newer members of the faculty who have not as yet established credentials sufficient to warrant the type of long-term commitment tenure represents. That they exist in the numbers Professor Kuehn's observations would seem to imply, however, is doubtful.

In my experience, control freaks are relatively few, and most members of the tenured faculty are genuinely interested in seeing colleagues succeed, not fail. In fact, one of the reasons for multiple layers of review in the process is the concern that at the departmental level, faculty committees may not be sufficiently rigorous in their application of tenure criteria. If one encounters difficulty, it is more likely to occur at the college or university level, where those involved may not be especially appreciative of a candidate's discipline or feel that the individual's record is on a par with those of representatives of other disciplines at the same level of experience.

Professor Kuehn also tends to portray departments as being divided into camps and argues that it is therefore important to form alliances with those who have the most power. His views in this respect are certainly consistent with those I have heard expressed by many individuals in the ranks of the untenured. The question, however, is whether such a judgment is warranted by the facts. I am not convinced that it is in most instances.

Even if I accept the basic premise that most academic departments are divided along political lines and that faculty members harbor considerable animosity toward one another, most institutions require some type of input from external reviewers in the tenure process. This input has substantial weight in the decision reached. A consensus suggesting inadequacy will most likely not result in a favorable tenure decision, no matter with whom the person being considered is allied. In addition, favorable external assessments cannot simply be dismissed. Departmental committees are not free to ignore the input they solicit, and even if they were to, the denial of tenure is typically a dean's decision, not a departmental committee's, or even a chair's. Conferral ultimately is in the hands of a higher authority—the president and board of trustees.

If a departmental committee or chair's recommendation is inconsistent with the evidence assembled in a candidate's dossier, a dean's committee or the dean him- or herself is free to recommend action different from that coming from the lower level. I hasten to add that a departmental recommendation would have to show considerable evidence of serious misjudgment in the case of a negative recommendation for those higher in the authority structure to overturn that recommendation. The same does not appear to apply in the case of positive recommendations. College committees and deans, for some reason, do not show the same degree of concurrence with positive recommendations of departments as they do with negative recommendations. Still, there are protections at this level of review for dealing with precipitous and arbitrary action.

As I mentioned in an earlier response to Professor Phillips's observations, when properly viewed, tenure is not a goal one attempts to achieve. I recognize, of course, that it would be the extreme in naiveté not to acknowledge that a very high percentage of college and university faculty members conceive of it in precisely this way. Still, in essence, tenure is a form of recognition of a level of achievement that leads those in positions of authority to conclude that one's contributions are sufficiently promising to justify long-term association with the institution.

The view of tenure as some sort of prize unfortunately leads to actions excessively, if not exclusively, focused on winning. As Professor Kuehn notes, nontenured faculty start wanting to know exactly how many articles they must publish, what is the acceptable minimum average for student ratings, what committee assignments do and do not count, what conferences will be viewed favorably, and the like. One begins to wonder in time whether individuals so obsessed can do anything professional independently of how it conceivably affects their prospects for achieving tenure.

An undesirable consequence of achieving tenure under conditions in which the goal itself is the only incentive for professional activity is that victory leads to letdown and performance may diminish. The individual has survived, but at what price to any genuine sense of professional commitment? A good friend of mine once observed, "If you want to know who the real scholars in the field are, look at what people do after tenure." Those who have invested all of their energy in achieving it may have achieved nothing else in the process.

Because tenure decisions, of necessity, have a subjective component, it is highly unfortunate when a person whose record should have led to favorable action does not receive tenure. It would be nice if completely objective means for assessing accomplishment and promise existed. They do not; therefore, in addition to cases in which favorable action was not taken when it should have been, there are also instances in which favorable action has been taken when perhaps it should not have been. We hear relatively little about the latter type of situation.

The decision to grant tenure is an important one, and I recognize that faculty facing the decision cannot afford to be cavalier about it. On the other hand, it can become so much a concern that it interferes with the most effective utilization of one's talents. Unfavorable decisions are not the end of the world, even though they admittedly complicate people's lives. In the end, however, quality will out, and those who have the ability to contribute, in the vast majority of cases, will find the opportunity to do so at one or another institution over the life of their academic career.

◆ RESPONSE TO CHAPTER FIVE
JULIA WOOD

The process of being considered for tenure is inherently stressful. Professor Kuehn's account of his situation seems, however, to include a series of stresses that I have found to be neither inherent nor common to tenure as it works at most institutions. In responding to this chapter, I wish to recount my own experience as an illustration of alternative ways the process may work. In doing this I simultaneously advance a view of the tenure process and decision that diverges from Professor Kuehn's image of hazing. Yet, I also note one type of misunderstanding that I think does inappropriately affect tenure decisions.

When I was considered for tenure after five years at the university I found the process very stressful; it could not be otherwise given what was at stake. I also found it extremely thorough, fair, and constructed in ways that mitigated the potential for abuse or disproportionate influence by any single individual. I was informed from the day I joined the faculty that research, teaching, and service were the criteria for achieving tenure, and I met with my chair each year to receive feedback on my record. Thus, through my initiatives and my department's willingness to provide guidance, I was informed of what was expected and told whether I was perceived to be on the right track.

During the time prior to receiving tenure I engaged in some research and testing outside of the mainstream. Some of my courses and publications focused on gender and feminist issues, which were even less well accepted in 1980 than they are today. So, my work was not entirely consistent with prevailing views of "serious scholarship." I also did a good deal of writing and teaching in established areas such as interpersonal and group communication. Thus, my record could be read as indicating both that I was able to teach and conduct research on conventional topics and that I was likely to depart in some ways from convention.

When the time arrived for my tenure evaluation, I was invited to submit names of people in the field who would write letters evaluating my achievements and promise, and some of these individuals were asked by my department to render assessments that were part of a formal file. In addition, outside reviewers not on my list were also asked to review my work. Along with these letters, I submitted my vita, copies of a number of my publications, and summaries of my teaching evaluations.

My institution, like most, requires multiple levels of review for all tenure decisions. My department made the first vote, the College of Arts and Sciences passed the second judgment, and the University Board of Trustees and Chancellor made the final decision. In my case, the judgment at all three levels were positive, yet I realized that the multilevel process ensured a check against any undue influence by an individual judgment that was not fair or well considered. That I received tenure and was kept informed about progress toward it does not, however, mean some of the issues raised by Professor Kuehn were not present. There was one individual who did not support me because I had refused to follow his advice as to how to focus my research. His lack of support seems to me particularly strong evidence that one individual cannot disproportionately affect such a momentous decision.

Since receiving tenure I have found myself on the other side of the process—my role now is to participate in making decisions about tenuring and promoting younger colleagues. What I have come to realize that is not evident in Professor Kuehn's discussion is that tenuring is anxiety producing for those making judgments as well as those being judged. It is so because it is a very serious issue both for the individual and the institution. A positive tenure decision represents an enormous financial and personal commitment from an institution—a guarantee to provide salary and conditions for working for the rest of that person's 30- to 40-year career. Such a decision cannot be made lightly, nor should it be. Also, it cannot weigh personal ties and compassion to the disregard of other criteria relevant to departmental and institutional needs and mission. A positive tenure decision should grow out of the related judgment that an individual has earned permanent standing on a faculty, and she or he will advance and enhance the institution in the years ahead.

Neither can a negative tenure decision be lightly made, and I have never seen any faculty committee vote against tenure without extended reflection on the candidate's record and their perspectives on her or him. Faculty realize that the denial of tenure has both personal and professional impact. It can be devastating to an individual to be told he or she is not good enough, not valued by colleagues, not welcome at an institution. This seldom, if ever, happens without considerable anguish and a serious search for alternative ways to assess a record.

So far, I have argued that the vast majority of those making tenure judgments tend to take their responsibilities seriously. For the most part, they strive to be fair, and they tend to be self-reflective about their own personal and scholarly biases so that these do not inappropriately affect decisions. Yet good intentions and an effort to be fair do not invariably yield equitable decisions.

Despite their best efforts, some established faculty seem unable to appreciate the value of pedagogical and research commitments outside of the traditions in which they themselves were trained. In my earlier chapter I pointed out a number of ways in which unintentional biases and blind spots affect judgments of women and minorities and their work in these areas. These biases have perhaps their most obvious and distorting impact in the tenuring process, in which a failure to appreciate research that is different and legitimate can lead to a misjudgment that it is not good. Although narrow and rigid views of what counts as superior scholarship and teaching are diminishing, they are still prevalent and this does not bode well for ideally fair evaluations of faculty. This points to an area for continued thinking and work to educate all participants in academe about diverse foci and methodologies that have validity.

The value of disparate kinds of scholarship and teaching also leads me to comment on a final matter in Professor Kuehn's discussion of tenure. He implies it is a hazing process in which candidates jump through arbitrary hoops to prove their loyalty and merit. I disagree with this view of the process as well as with the changes that Professor Kuehn suggests to lessen the subjectivity of tenuring. Specifically, although I do understand why he and others coming up for tenure decisions feel uncomfortable with less than totally explicit definitions of what is expected, I do not support an effort to devise absolutely clearcut guidelines.

The nature of what counts as good scholarship and good teaching defies absolute specification, and such specification would invite far more problems than it might solve. Consider the pragmatic consequences of Professor Kuehn's call for clearly defined requirements for tenure. Suppose an institution stipulates tenure will be granted to those candidates who have teaching evaluations in the top 40% of those at the university, one article per year in a national, refereed journal, and one scholarly book published during their first five years. A candidate could meet these requirements by courting students' favor to gain strong evaluations of teaching and by doing research within safe, orthodox areas. Although her or his work might seldom be read or cited by others, if the candidate meets the point-by-point requirements, tenure is given.

Now consider a second case. Here we have a young faculty member who teaches material that challenges what students think and pushes them to reflect further and to write more than they are accustomed to doing. This person may have lower student evaluations than the former candidate, but be a better educator in the long term. If this person also does research that stretches the definitions of scholarly areas of inquiry, then she or he is less likely to have work readily accepted by major journals and university presses. So, perhaps at tenure time this second candidate has only 4 articles in 5 years and has a book under contract, but not yet completed. Yet, one article that she or he wrote received a research award and was widely cited by others in her or his area. Clearly this person has made a substantial impact on thinking in her or his field, yet the a priori and universal requirements for tenure are not met. Case denied.

As I hope these examples indicate, an effort to define absolutely and concretely exactly what earns tenure creates greater potential for misjudgments and unfair decisions than does the current practice of having guidelines that attempt to define broad expectations without delimiting them so narrowly that there is no room left for judgment. Judgment is perhaps what tenure is all about. Judgment—at least good judgment—is not something that can be reduced to a formula. Although there are, of course, some abuses of the tenure process and some individuals who attempt to misuse their power, the process itself is constructed so that checks and balances exist. Further, it is a process, which means it is open to change as the understandings of what comprises teaching and scholarship are refined. Any effort to rule judgment out of the process distorts it into a mechanical implementation of preset and global criteria which cannot possibly be mindful of the specificities of individual faculty's careers. To disallow judgment, then, runs the risk of excluding reflection, fair consideration of individual cases, and the diverse ways that faculty may contribute to their fields and institutions.

◆ RESPONSE TO CHAPTER FIVE
GERALD M. PHILLIPS

My answer to Scott Kuehn is short and sweet. As a member of a college fraternity, it is easy to apply the metaphor of pledge duties and hazing to the quest for tenure. I always had the feeling that I was never rewarded for anything I did; I also felt I was punished because of who I was. The point is the quest for tenure can easily make you a little paranoid.

During my first years at the institution at which I obtained tenure, I wrote nine articles and three books. But I got tenure when I was off campus. A friend asked me to be a visiting teacher at his elite institution. I asked him to send a letter appointing me as "distinguished visiting professor." He did it. I gave it to my chairman. I returned to discover that I was promoted to full professor with tenure. It only took four years. I had the feeling that very little attention was paid to my scholarship and to my high student ratings as a teacher.

I was denied tenure three times previously, twice at one institution. The first time I was explicitly told it was because I was a sloppy dresser and talked too much in faculty meetings. The engineering school at this institution had been disaccredited for having too few Ph.D.s. They decided they would beat the rap by setting up a Ph.D. program, have professors study with each other, and award the Ph.D.s. I protested at a meeting of the graduate faculty. It was then that I got the word from my chairman. "Cool it kid. Stay away from faculty meetings. We'll keep you on probation and you'll get tenure next year." I found out that the school was on the AAUP censured list, and I got out quickly. I scurried about, found another job, quit in the middle of July, took a $5,000 loss on my house, and said farewell.

The other denials were much more complicated. I spent the requisite time in rank at my new institution. I also was an active participant in the ACLU. This was not smart during the McCarthy Era. My first tenure hearing led to a verdict of "delayed." My chairman explained that my colleagues on the faculty thought I was too "volatile." Understand, I was the only member of that faculty, aside from the chairman, who was on the graduate faculty. I published more than the whole department combined. This was irrelevant. I was volatile. I belonged to the ACLU, AAUP, and worked with the local ministerium, which was also regarded as "volatile." We were all censured by the "Christian anti-Communist Crusade," an organization which was very active in a nearby city.

My second denial was permanent. My department head told me that my colleagues voted against me. I polled my colleagues and found no one that was willing to swear he (there were no females on the faculty at that time) had voted against me. I protested to the dean. I retained a lawyer. I contacted the press. I got involved in a protest against the administration excusing swastika painting by one of the fraternities. I wrote a book and three articles. I threatened to go to court. The dean held a hearing. The dean overruled the department head and granted me tenure. Then I quit.

I learned, through those experiences, that life was not always fair. When I later served on promotion and tenure committees, I discovered how hard it was to make an objective judgment. When I was a candidate for tenure, it was mostly an authoritarian process. Today, most schools have carefully codified regulations, ostensibly specifying objective criteria on which decisions must be made. There are appellate jurisdictions, and in unionized schools, the tenure and promotion regulations are usually a major part of the union contract.

Eventually, I despaired of trying to make sense out of the piles of documents one had to evaluate in order to make a decision. I did what I could to avoid serving. I developed a philosophy, a notion that in some cases tenure was awarded on personality and justified after the fact, and in some cases tenure was hard won and given despite personal antipathies.

Conclusion: It is a very good idea for the candidate for tenure to do everything possible to understand the criteria, how they are applied, and by whom. You choose an academic career because of a love of teaching and learning. You do research because you are driven by curiosity, and you publish because you have something worthwhile to tell the world. You serve your institution in various capacities because it is the right thing to do. Yet, all of this does not protect you from the caprice of economic exigency and personal vendetta. With all the responsibilities of a new professor, you must still pay attention to the "regulations."

6

PROFESSIONALISM

Gerald M. Phillips

This chapter is adapted from one by Gerald M. Phillips and Mary-Linda Merriam published in *Teaching Communication,* edited by John Daly, Gustav W. Friedrich, and Anita L. Vangelisti (1990). It was the 35th and final chapter in that book, which purported to comprehensively cover the field of speech communication. The other chapters dealt with the nature of the discipline and the preparation of syllabuses for the important courses in the discipline including public speaking, interpersonal and small group communication, rhetorical studies, persuasion, organizational communication, nonverbal communication, intercultural communication, interviewing, mass communication, telecommunication, and research methods. In addition, extensive information was provided on instructional models, instructional tools, lecturing, interacting in instructional settings, individual instruction, and evaluation. One excellent chapter by Ann Q. Staton was devoted to consideration of the academic profession as a whole. We recommend this book to communication professionals.

We also recommend Thomas Benson's *Speech Communication in the 20th Century* (1985) and *Essays to Commemorate the 75th Anniversary of the Speech Communication Association,* edited by Gerald M. Phillips and Julia T. Wood (1990). Both of these books, although recent, are already out of date, but they are instructive in providing guidance in the content of the profession, and as such, they contribute to the general literacy. This chapter is devoted to a consideration of your professional life in general, and your commitment to the communication discipline in particular.

The world has changed considerably in the 10 years that covered the span of the writing of the three books to which we have referred. Communication curricula have changed; much of what is covered now would appear esoteric to professionals of a decade ago, but it will be the mundane matter of the 21st century. Computer-mediated communication, public relations, broadcasting, and film have all taken their place in the curriculum, whereas the traditional courses such as public speaking have been modified into organizational speaking in its various forms. Whereas some schools remain loyal to older divisions such as informative speaking, persuasion, and argumentation, others have modernized their curricula to include coursework in presentational speaking and such specific areas as training in the use of the teleprompter.

There is less and less emphasis on performance and intensive concentration on research and its findings. More and more, there is pressure on young academics to imitate the social sciences and humanities by filling more journals, writing more scholarly books, and presenting an increasing number of papers at professional meetings. The old, traditional courses, public speaking and group discussion, have been eliminated in many schools.

Professor Herman Cohen, in his yet unpublished history of ideas in the communication profession, points out that most of the scholarly work that has been done in the communication disciplines has been derivative and imitative. Often, communication scholars attach themselves to outmoded ideas from other disciplines, giving them one more try before they are laid to rest. Cohen deplores the loss of the unique identity of the communication field: its concern with performance. More than that, he ruminates on the perilous position of communication in the last decade of the century. The new intellectual pseudopods push off into other disciplines and are absorbed. The field of communications (note the "s") subsumes most of the modern technology, whereas the discipline of dramatic arts has absorbed the performance aspects of media. Sociologists and political scientists have made public address and media part of their canon, and they approach it using their own principles and methods. The proliferation of books on rhetoric under the sponsorship of the Modern Language Association indicates that even that ancient discipline is possibly being preempted by scholars of writing. It is a struggle for pure-form speech departments to stay alive and vital given the current political climate and economic threat that prevails in universities today. Sometimes, speech communication is a luxury an institution feels it cannot afford.

But our rationale for this chapter is that in most of its aspects, what it takes to succeed as a speech communication professional is the same as in any other discipline. The one thing that can provide security for a professor and for a discipline is professionalism. In the original chapter on which this is based, the authors attempted to examine six obligations of professionalism

1. to be culturally literate by keeping in tune with the proliferation of knowledge in general;
2. to be sophisticated in one's specialty. This includes not only innovations in your area of specialty but trends in the discipline at large;
3. to do research and disseminate the results. We have already pointed out the importance of your personal addition to the sum total of knowledge in the profession;
4. to teach well. You cannot teach well, unless you have satisfied the other three requirements;
5. to serve the academic community. This may mean politics, but these days it means pulling your oar in a boat that is about to be swamped by waves of financial catastrophe; and
6. to make sensible decisions about one's career. Your personal life is important to your professional life. The way you pilot yourself through present and future challenges to the profession could contribute to shaping the discipline of the future.

We have added two more obligations for the professional academic:

7. to maintain collegiality and mutual respect for your associates; and
8. to play a realistic role in the world at large.

Carroll Arnold once remarked that once you receive a Ph.D., you are permanently changed. You cannot go "home." The academic professional occupies a special place in society. He or she is charged with the responsibility to consume, create, disseminate, and criticize knowledge; to separate the wise from the foolish, the frivolous from the consequential, and to sustain the connection from generation to generation.

The job sometimes looks a good deal more trivial. The semester you are saddled with four sections of the basic course and 52 undergraduate advisees and your dean is pressuring you to publish, the job looks very much like a *fin de siècle* sweat shop. You take the heat and you do your job. You do it because at other times there is no profession that gives you more opportunity to be yourself and to contribute to the world at large. In part, it is luck of the draw, but mostly it is the way you shape your own life. Professionalism is adaptation.

POLICIES AND REGULATIONS

An institution of higher education is not a military institution, but it is hierarchical. Furthermore, it operates with a highly diffuse administration.

In our chapter on politics, we offered a cynical view of administration and how it deals with things that matter. To be quite honest, in most cases, "it," the abstract administration, does the best it can under the circumstances. What "it" consists of, however, is often not clear. Administrators sometimes have strange notions. For example, in 1991, a year of financial attrition, a major university spent $87,000 remodeling the president's office and over $100,000 on a presidential inaugural ceremony, much to the consternation of the legislature. Administrators see the world through the eyes of voters, alumni, parents, and potential donors. Occasionally, the students and faculty capture their attention. But they can no more be aware of what goes on in the classroom than a general can be aware of what a particular company is doing in the course of a battle.

The point is, wherever you are employed, you have to hit the ground running. The first thing you have to find out is who will judge you and how. It is suspenseful enough trying to survive the early years. If you are operating blind, you may be in trouble. A few institutions make it clear for you because they are unionized and things occur predictably. In a time of retrenchment, there could be a clarification of criteria, perhaps as a growth of the union movement.

Most institutions publish policies and regulations on tenure and promotion. These are usually found in personnel manuals, along with a listing of employee benefits. We have already taken note of the importance of having a sense of institutional politics. For your own personal advancement, it is important to understand as much as possible how the merit system works. In some cases it is capricious, depending on the whims of individuals. In some cases it is autocratic, presided over by a dean or a chancellor trying to mesh the gears in a particular plan of operation. Much of the time, it will be implemented by a series of committees, each of which passes on the candidate by comparing him or her with the criteria.

The aspiring academic must learn to understand how universities are run and how the chain of command works. More importantly, each individual must develop a working attitude toward university politics. It is, for example, possible to make a career out of serving the university but only in institutions that respect this track. The lure of participating in campus politics can sometimes be irresistible. Beginners often spread themselves very thin, accepting every committee appointment and volunteering for every task without realizing how time-consuming committee service can be. A great many young academics become so heavily involved in politics that they forget that university service is only one of several standard criteria for advancement at most universities. Moreover, sometimes their older and wiser colleagues take advantage of their eagerness by foisting off obligations on them.

Very often, university politics are left to those who do not quite make it to the top. The committee system, because it is sometimes practically irrelevant, is often dominated by permanent associate professors. The administrative design is often to provide the semblance of democracy in decision making, whereas the major decisions are reserved for the high-ranking administrators. Successful academics, those with reputations as teachers and scholars, often avoid political distractions. On the other hand, academic institutions are often beset by crises that demand that the best minds commit to finding solutions.

Being an academic professional means more than just teaching students or getting articles in print. Teaching is crucial to society and must never be demeaned, and publishing is the substance of the teaching of the future. But institutions survive only as long as the people they support provide support in return. Without the institution, the academic professional has no identity at all. The job of a professor may be "to profess," to pursue (but never find) truth, and to call the shots as he or she sees them, but this must be done within institutional boundaries. There is no such thing as a freelance professor, at least not since Socrates.

In the early 1950s, the academic world was a bit shaken by Eric Hoffer, a longshoreman who wrote a popular book of philosophy. Later, in the ferment of the 1960s, scholars without portfolios (or degrees), such as Paul Goodman, Anthony Wilden, and Ernest Becker appeared on the scene, but as they achieved credibility, they were preempted by universities. The location of a professor is very important. He or she cannot stand alone.

Communication professors have a unique responsibility in the academy for they are the guardians of the process by which knowledge is shared. Their field includes the most powerful human abilities: to voice ideas, to make collective decisions, and to share the company of other human beings. Communication professors also confront the most serious human problems: misunderstanding, conflict, exploitation, and social combat. No wonder that rhetoric was referred to as the "queen of all the sciences," and the world's first universities were devoted to its study. An examination of the obligations cited above represents the prototypical obligations of all academics.

THE OBLIGATION OF CULTURAL LITERACY

E.D. Hirsch (1987) introduced the concept of *cultural literacy*. Hirsch argued that there is a body of knowledge for which all educated humans are responsible. It includes the concepts that unite all people in our culture. Recently, the concept has been challenged by those who argue that our culture has changed materially, and ideas once regarded as common intellectual currency have represented only a small portion of the people who participate. These revisionists have argued for the inclusion of "other voices," including African Americans, women, Hispanics, homosexuals, and other groups allegedly kept out of the mainstream by political, social, and gender bias and economic exclusion.

College professors are the conservators of the common wisdom. Through their teaching and research they link past and present to influence the future. This requires more from them than a specialized knowledge of their particular discipline. They have the power to define what are the great ideas of the arts and sciences. They choose from the wisdom of the eastern and western worlds, the rhetoric of men and women, the creativity of those who are otherwise voiceless. By including it in the canon of instruction, they create a context in which students can learn specialties. In fact, they define the nature of the intellectual world. This is not a trivial responsibility.

There is no academic discipline that can exist outside the context of common wisdom. The academic professional must have a good sense not only of the context for ideas, but of where his or her discipline fits within the intellectual community. As C. P. Snow pointed out, a great many academics fall short on this count. When he wrote *Cultures and the Scientific Revolution* (1959), Snow excoriated humanists and social scientists for their ignorance of the hard sciences. Sir Peter Medawar, in some of his later essays (cf. *Pluto's Republic*), offered the same commentary. Both of these eminent scientists noted that their colleagues often were quite literate in the arts and humanities. The dialogue existing today is an extension of their critique. Women argue that men do not adequately recognize the quality of their work. African Americans contend that the work of their great writers and artists is not shared.

To an extent, the argument is excessively polarized. We cannot be like the educated person in Cicero's day, knowing everything there is to be known. The basic textbooks in some scientific disciplines are over 2,000 pages long. A great many curricula are like menus from which students can only make a limited selection. Even in required courses there are few givens. But there is a question of perception and dignity that must be answered. Some scholars argue that the ideas of the western world, whatever their origin, are noble and of high quality in and of themselves, and it is on those ideas that our nationhood and mainstream culture are based. Therefore, they conclude those ideas should be emphasized in a university education. But, argue the newcomers, the culmination of those ideas has been the admission of more people of various types to full participation in the culture, and what has been unique for them must now be shared by all. It is impossible for an academic professional to escape participation in this argument.

Communication professionals have a special obligation in this exchange. For one thing, their custodianship of the practical art of speaking mandates that they empower others to make their voices heard in the debate. In order to do this competently, they must be literate, not only regarding traditional wisdom, but the new contributions as well. The study of human discourse, by its very nature, is interdisciplinary. It is not possible to study or teach it without understanding the substantive ideas about which people communicate. It is no accident that communication is not studied in totalitarian societies. Rulers who would hold their people prisoner must control their communication. In contemporary society, the groups once excluded note that part of the technique by which they were excluded was the silencing of their voices.

Furthermore, in democratic societies, communication is the medium for the political process. Issues are not decided by force of arms. In contrast to totalitarian societies, the army and police are not inartistic proofs for the dictator's rhetoric. Issues are resolved in legislatures and at the ballot box, and those who bear arms are controlled by duly constituted authorities. Communication scholars mediate the democratic process through their analysis of old ideas and the forging of new ones about how people live and work with one another. Regardless of their specific area of specialization, communication scholars must be sufficiently well read to understand the ideas about which people speak and write.

The study and teaching of communication represent the prototypical synthesis of cultural literacy and specialized knowledge. Professional growth demands constant attention to both scholarship and current events. This includes knowledge of both historical and popular culture as well as the fundamentals of the arts, sciences, and humanities. Equally important is an understanding of the daily life of ordinary people and sensitivity to the public issues and social concerns that confront them.

Above all, the study and teaching of human communication constrains professionals to be willing and able to revise ideas when new information or refined analysis justifies it. There is no academic so stunted as one who reflexively defends ideas that have lost both their grace and utility. Professional growth means not only possessing the means of inventing rhetoric but the will to revise it when necessary in both teaching and research.

Thus, cultural literacy, however it is defined, and including the controversy about what it is, constitutes the basis of the communication professional's rhetoric. We know this includes the ability to write and speak well, to listen attentively, and to read critically. These are the culminations of education, the results of the synthesis of knowledge and experience. The communication modalities (speaking, listening, reading, writing) combine to bridge the academic cultures. As communication scholars range from phonologists to philosophers, they recapitulate the arts and sciences. Communication is the only means by which knowledge can be unified into a common wisdom. It is the duty of the communication discipline to study and teach not only how to communicate but why and how people communicate. The collective wisdom of the profession depends on sound knowledge of process combined with experience at performing it.

THE OBLIGATION OF CONTENT SOPHISTICATION

To avoid growing old and intellectually decadent requires content sophistication. Crackling and yellowed notes go hand in hand with intellectual stultification and error. There is, perhaps, no greater crime against the human mind than the teaching of error. So often, we cling to what we have learned and require others to learn despite its obsolescence. Often, we do not even question what we have been taught. Those who taught us were our masters and mentors. They must be honored, and to deny their ideas is to turn our back on our heritage. Moreover, it is often inconvenient to stay up to date. To be a mature academic professional means being intellectually contemporaneous. To sustain currency in wisdom takes a great deal of time and effort. When the blandishments of hobbies or the summer vacation and the emotional tugs of home and family supersede the demands of the intellectual discipline, the academic begins his or her decline. Failure to grow is equivalent to decline. Growth as a communication professional requires maintaining one's status as an "expert."

An expert is a person who has specialized skill or knowledge. The professional academic is expected to be an expert on something of suitable worth. Mature professionals must keep up with new information to avoid being fooled by fads. They must avoid blind alleys and be able to discard ideas when they become obsolete or are proven false. One can choose to be a generalist or a specialist. The generalist is horizontal, specializing in the overview of a field. The specialist is vertical, with in-depth knowledge of an often minute detail within that field. A great scholar once commented that it is possible for a skilled mind to succeed in any field by reading a general textbook in its discipline. To be acceptable to physicists, he argued, use the general knowledge of optics when talking to a specialist in acoustics and the wisdom of mechanics when talking to an electronics wizard.

Perhaps this is another way to look at careers. Those who compete in so-called major institutions must be in-depth experts, in something. Those who choose small and more intimate institutions, can be generalists. This exempts neither from being experts in the common wisdom. Is also confronts them with the necessity to maintain the subtle balance between revisionism and commitment.

In the hard sciences, all conclusions must be tested. Once a discovery is made, it is challenged. The experiment that produced it is repeated. Only when there have been sufficient replications (and there is no agreement on how many this is) is a proposition accepted as fundamental (but never as true). This kind of challenge is not possible in the social sciences. On the other hand, academics can profit from the life work of Sigmund Freud, which was characterized by his constant questioning of his own results. The mature academic professional must constantly question his or her own propositions even while sustaining dedication to their careful dissemination.

Academics are evaluated on their status as experts, however. Cultural literacy is assumed. The requirement of expertise carries considerable responsibility to have more valid information on a particular topic than others. What academics know is judged on four criteria: Information must be cogent, current, useful, and communicable. Their knowledge must be increased regularly and steadily through a program of reading professional journals and scholarly books, meeting regularly with other professionals, conducting serious inquiry and investigation, and by submitting their thinking to public scrutiny and critique via publication.

Cogent means that information an academic acquires is detailed and complex. It must transcend the mundane and have an original twist and a personal stamp so that it can qualify its possessor as an expert. The mature academic must be willing to credit others for ideas that have been shared. The true expert is not afraid to modify or recant, nor is timid about attempting new ideas.

Current means that information is up to date and supported by an extensive bibliography and database. This criterion carries with it the burden of knowing what others in the area have to say about the subject. The real professional must run as fast as possible, often just to stay even with the pack.

It is *useful* when the thinking of others is helped by the knowledge or it generates viable technology. There is a great deal of information that is irrelevant. But the claim that academics seek knowledge for its own sake is an empty excuse. There is a lot of knowledge that is lying around and gathering dust because there are no "implications" for it. It has no utility. The privilege of pursuing truth is hedged by the responsibility the academic has to his or her community. This implies that every effort must be made to apply knowledge to other theory or to generate technology from it.

Knowledge is *communicable* when its owner has thought about it sufficiently to speak or write about it in a fashion that is intelligible and helpful to students, colleagues, or any other interested parties. The professional must have thought about it long and hard and be able to support assertions with arguments and principles with examples. Each utterance an academic makes, whether orally or in writing, should represent the most accurate and current statement possible.

AREAS OF COMMUNICATION EXPERTISE

Speech communication, we have pointed out, is an important discipline because it functions as an equalizer. We teach the just and the unjust, the wise and the foolish. Speech is a basic skill, the substance of social life, intrinsic to decent social living and decision making. Furthermore, orality is more vital to human intimacy than literacy. Humans influence each other on a daily basis through face-to-face discourse. They also use the media; they are subject to its influence. Communication is pervasive.

Most people are not skillful at oral discourse. They may also be inept at writing, but they can easily avoid it. Their skill at oral communication is requisite to success in society. As custodians of the performance, theory, and criticism of speech, the discipline is its arbiter. It should set the standards of quality and work to ensure that people can meet them. By bringing everyone up to standard, the mission of service to a democratic society is fulfilled.

Among other things, the mission of speech communication includes training people to do mandated social tasks well so they can assume their appropriate place in their society, which in turn enables them to contribute and work to meet their needs. This means teaching them to meet others, make requests, give simple instructions, ask questions, negotiate and bargain in order to resolve disputes, state their case, advocate for their point of view, defend themselves at law, and share their wisdom with others. The mission also involves understanding and training performance in public and in media, as well as finding and teaching the standards of criticism of such performance.

It does not necessarily mean learning abstruse theory, for the discipline is weak on theory. We must understand our tradition of the canon of Aristotle, Cicero, and Quintilian as well as appreciate the influence of the social sciences in shaping our contemporary ideas. We must also understand the role of the mass media in society, perhaps through the eyes of historians and political scientists. Because of this eclectic mission, speech communication professionals must be broadly educated and sensitive to the world around them.

These are the imperatives of the discipline, and if they are not accomplished our democratic societies could well be doomed. There is nothing so dangerous to democracy as a silent electorate. The possibilities for instruction include performance, theory, and criticism of public speaking, interpersonal communication, group discussion, communication in organizations, communication in mass media, and the scientific bases of communication. Each of these components plays a role in the discipline and combines to give it a unique mission. The idea of scholasticism dividing the discipline could well spell its demise because at a time of economic attrition in education, speech communication rarely holds a favored position. Unity of concept and action is important to survival.

We must advise future scholars that their obligation is to change performance, and there is no necessary connection between learning *about* and learning *how to.* Understanding how discourse is carried on and its place in society is an important backdrop, but it plays little role in the actual modification of performance behavior. On the other hand, success at training performance depends on the discoveries of scientific research and literary criticism. Thus, speech communication functions as a union of the social sciences and humanities in both abstract and utilitarian ways.

Communication professors have a special obligation to be culturally literate. Their studies, by their very nature, are interdisciplinary. It is not possible to study communication without understanding the substantive ideas about which people communicate. Above all, the study and teaching of human communication constrains the mature academic professional to be willing and able to revise ideas when new information or refined analysis justifies it. There is no academic so stunted as one who defends reflexively ideas that have lost both their grace and utility. Professional growth means not only possessing the means of inventing rhetoric but the will to revise it when necessary in both teaching and research.

There are a great many areas in which communication scholars can be expert. I list them here, with a line or two about each, as to describe each completely would require a book in itself. This, however, will give you an idea of the depth and breadth of the field.

Rhetorical theory addresses the nature of the persuasive interaction of humans with each other. It attempts to explain how and why people are influenced by the speech of others. It has classical and philosophical foundations and is instructed by the principles of sociology and social psychology. In its most modern garb it includes the study of advertising and public relations.

History and criticism of public address is the study of presentations, usually of one person to an audience, in person or on media. It combines the methods of the historian with those of the literary critic to assess the nature of the influence speakers exert on their audiences, usually at crucial moments.

Communication theory is the broad study of human oral interaction. It ranges from the consideration of digital communication through machinery to the highly intimate connections people make with friends and lovers. It is customarily divided into components including:

Organizational communication: the study of how complex organizations function, how they are led, and how the people in them carry on various communication tasks.

Small group communication: the study of face-to-face discourse among people for the purpose of problem solving, decision making, and performing therapeutic tasks.

Interpersonal communication: the study of various forms of purposive and social intimacy ranging from the talk between lovers to the relationship of salesman and customer and therapist and patient.

Intrapersonal communication: loosely defined as the talk one carries on with oneself; in essence, thinking aloud.

Nonverbal communication: the study of the unspoken components of oral communication such as gesture, facial expression, posture, juxtaposition of person and environment, and visuals used to assist the communication process. It deals with the silent metalanguage people use to add dimension to what they say.

Performance includes training in various types of public communication including lecturing, political speaking, inspirational speaking, ceremonial speaking, preaching, presentational speaking, oral reading, and, in some cases, acting. This component of the discipline includes the design of instructional techniques, administration of criticism, supervision of rehearsal, provision of feedback, and remediation of deficiencies and incompetencies. The field of dramatic arts has taken on its own identity and deals with all aspects of theater (and often film).

Intercultural communication is the rapidly expanding study of the nature of the social encounter between people of different linguistic backgrounds and national origins. It includes the complex discipline of comparative linguistics and the mundane but essential consideration of training people to speak English as a second language. It has its roots in practical linguistics, and it is applied to the fundamentals of speech production and use.

Speech science bridges the study between speech communication and the discipline of communication disorders. This area is devoted to consideration of the physical features of speech and includes such intriguing considerations as forensic linguistics, voice stress analysis, and anatomical studies of the vocal mechanism.

Communication disorders now stands on its own, but this discipline was once an intrinsic component of speech communication. It deals with the identification, explanation, and remediation of physical defects that cause distorted speech, retraining those who learned deficiencies in speaking, and people who are disqualified from social participation because of disorders in voice quality, lack of fluency, and poor diction.

Telecommunication is a discipline that may well represent the wave of the future. It has also become a separate area of study. It includes the technology of broadcasting through radio and television, the consideration of the use of film, the budding new technology of computer-mediated communication, and various aspects of journalism that are facilitated through technology.

Freedom of speech is an offshoot of the discipline that is also essential to its survival. Specialists in this area study the whole gamut of human rights including free expression, academic freedom, the rights of minorities to be heard, and the history of human freedoms in society.

In addition to all these divisions of the discipline, communication specialists can examine the special requirements for communication such as medical and legal communication, specific business applications (such as teleconferencing, quality circles, etc.), and the applications of any feature of the discipline to a particular task or social requirement.

There is no limit to the research tools available to facilitate these studies. Each of these areas can be approached through various forms and theories of research: behaviorism, experimental studies, social theory, case history, field study, philosophy, hermeneutics and exegesis, demographics, experimental studies, historiography, and so on. Communication specialists must be sufficiently well informed to talk to their colleagues, whatever their field of specialization. When academics split off and talk only to their own kind, the whole discipline suffers from casuistry and scholasticism.

THE OBLIGATION OF "PUBLISH OR PERISH"

To begin on a facetious note, no matter how much we publish, we will all perish in the end. Still, the obligation to publish the results of individual research is shared by most academic professionals. Sharing information is a prime objective of academics. In this and the following section we discuss what we believe to be the crucial dialectic in the life of an academic professional: the balance between research and teaching. We have discussed both teaching and research in detail in previous chapters. We have also noted that they represent by far the most important criteria of evaluation for your progress as a professional.

What is at stake in the decision you make about how to balance the two is personal satisfaction with your career and the promise of being a truly professional academic. Your preferences are important and so are the demands of your institution. Wherever you are, you will find that the time you spend on teaching interferes with research and vice versa.

Few academic professionals receive formal job descriptions, but virtually all receive some sort of "faculty handbook" which explains what their institutions expect of them. We have noted the consensus that academics are evaluated on their research, teaching, professional activity, and service with each institution imposing its own balance of the four. We have noted how hard it is to evaluate teaching. Institutions vary widely in their expectations. Research, however, can be evaluated by its public results, that is, by publication.

"Publish or perish" is not a canard for the mature academic professional. He or she must know how to do research and write up the results with sufficient quality as to qualify them for publication. In addition, he or she must be able to integrate research into the teaching process. Not-so-successful professionals may regard publication as an onerous chore and take refuge in claims about the quality of their teaching and the demands it makes on their professional life. But, it is clear that research and teaching are counterparts, and both are essential to professional growth.

But, it takes time to acquire a mature conception of the relationship between research and teaching. A recent Ph.D. was interviewing at a small state college that emphasized teaching. They had a modest M.A. program, and the job for which she was a candidate called for her to teach "research methods." On returning home from the interview, she commented that she did not think she would take the job because the students were so hostile to the course. They were not required to write a thesis for their M.A. They simply could not understand why professional teachers would need to know research methods.

The learning experiences required to earn a Ph.D. are rehearsals for the life experience of the professor. Each bit of research that results in publication recapitulates the dissertation. Publication is evidence of work done. Thus, institutions justifiably require their professionals to produce such evidence. For each individual, this imposes a different kind of angst. Some are deeply committed to research and resent the way students cut in on their time. Others had enough at dissertation time and want to give themselves entirely to teaching or managing the institution. They often console themselves with excuses about an "old boy" network that controls publication, or the lack of potential outlets.

At the start of the 1990s, publication outlets were virtually limitless. The only excuses for not publishing were failure to do research and the inability to write. Neither was valid. On the other hand, the cutback in funding for institutions of higher education that started in 1992 also led to a cutback in the number of academic journals and books that were published. The issue is now in some doubt; opportunities for publication are beginning to dry up. To confuse the issue even more, institutions are examining themselves and revising criteria. Some are differentiating between teaching specialists and researchers. In a decade or so, the situation may crystallize and the requirements for professional survival may become more clear. At the moment, however, everyone is caught in the tug between the two.

At present, according to *The Almanac of the Chronicle of Higher Education* (1991), there are some 260,000 full-time academics in the United States and nearly 100,000 journals providing about 500,000 publishing opportunities per year. These journals accept monographs, articles, reviews, research reports, commentary, history, results of experiments, think pieces, philosophical essays, and reports of classroom innovations. In addition, more than 4,000 scholarly books are published each year, in addition to texts and popular articles on scholarly topics. Yet, the median number of publications for full-time academics is zero. Less than 25% of all full-time academics account for 90% of what is published. One third of all academics do not publish a single line during their entire careers.

Many academics resist the obligation to publish on the grounds that it interferes with their main mission, teaching. They argue that academic institutions should place more emphasis on teaching, or that their teaching is so good that it alone should be taken into account in tenure and promotion decisions. However, the public dissemination of ideas in some form is the only measure available of whether an academic is keeping literate. The criticism of peers is essential to informing promotion and tenure decisions. Research is a teaching/learning process for the professional. It sets the model for "do as I do" rather than simply "do as I say." Certainly any academic who deals with graduate students ought to be proficient at research and publication. The claim that research interferes with teaching may only be an excuse for taking the easy way out. In the final crunch, the act of teaching itself is a legitimate object of applied research.

Administrators of major research universities argue that the best teaching is done by alert scholars who are able to bring the most current and exciting ideas to the classroom. Furthermore, remedial programs notwithstanding, the mission of colleges and universities is more than simply educating the young. They are repositories of knowledge and charged with the responsibility of conserving and adding to that repository. Research and teaching must be, at the least, co-equal. Institutions in which faculties are primarily involved in research give more than lip service to quality teaching; community colleges encourage their faculties to do research to improve the quality of their teaching. In fact, the act of teaching itself provides an arena for interesting and productive research.

THE OBLIGATION TO THE TEACHING MISSION

In the chapter on teaching we point out that teaching is an art form, and as such, is extraordinarily difficult to evaluate. Should evaluation be done based on how popular a teacher is with his or her students? Should subsequent accomplishments by students (e.g., grades in other courses or acceptance to graduate schools) be the main criterion?

Some academics use teaching as a synonym for socialization with their students (as they use research as a synonym for pleasure reading). Still others use teaching as a way of winning admiration. The specialist in research has the advantage of more precise criteria at decision-making time, for the submission of published material for public scrutiny generates tangible evidence on which judgments can be made. The act of teaching generally does not produce evidence with this objective quality.

We do not really know what makes a good teacher, although there is consensus that it is some combination of information, communication skill, and sensitivity to students' needs. Good teachers not only are appealing to students, but sufficiently rigorous to hold students to the highest standards of knowledge. Clearly it is more than charm or charisma. Students are entitled to more from a teacher than entertainment or demands for personal loyalty. Teaching that is based on out-of-date information or on ideology is not appropriate for mature academic professionals. Neither is ego-centered teaching. In fact, the quality of the content taught is the major criterion for evaluation of effective teaching along with the quality of presentation to the students.

Academic freedom makes teaching a relatively private matter between teacher and students. It normally receives outside evaluation only at times when decisions about retention or advancement must be made. Research, however, is always done in the public view and is subject to continuing evaluation. Thus, the teacher who is engaged in research and publication, in addition to teaching, is best able to maintain the balance between content and presentational style. The detachment that comes from serious concern for research responsibilities can also help to keep a perspective and balance in relationships with students.

There is a crucial point here. A high school teacher who was about to receive his Ph.D. was discussing his future career. He had won statewide awards for his classroom teaching in high school. He raised the question of why academics sometimes protested so much about the obligation to do research versus their desire to teach. He said, "If they really want to be teachers, they should go into the public school where the teachers are." He pointed out that he pursued his Ph.D. because he knew that higher education was something different (not better—just different) from basic education in the schools. That difference was the requirement to do research and publish it.

We also make some dangerous assumptions about what students in colleges and universities want and need. We surmise that they need some sort of attention. They do. They need their self-esteem strengthened; they need encouragement; they need advice. But whether the typical professor can provide these is questionable. In a large lecture hall, there is little presumption. Students come and are instructed or entertained. They bone up for exams, pass or fail them, and go on their way. The speech classroom is often very different. The performance nature of the discipline engenders a kind of closeness not found in other courses. This raises some cautions about the nature of the classroom in speech performance courses. The closeness inherent in the relationship of the performance teacher and his or her students can lead to relationships that can alter the careers of both parties. Because of the intrinsic attraction communication teachers have for students, they get closer to their students than teachers in almost any other discipline. This is true of teachers of composition as well.

During the first half of this century, the concept of *in loco parentis* helped academic institutions keep teachers and students from infringing on each others' personal rights. Today, however, it is the teacher's responsibility to maintain the proper distance from his or her students. Relationships between them can be productive or threatening depending on the perspective of the teacher. Young students are often very vulnerable to the influence of adults whom they admire. Mature academic professionals must be careful to manage the teaching process so that it impairs neither the students' lives nor the professionals' careers.

Personal relationships between teachers and students are not unusual nor are they always dangerous, but they must be thoughtfully and judiciously managed. The 1984 Carnegie Report (Jacobson, 1985) states that more than 90% of faculty members enjoy contact with students outside of class. Only 24% believe contact should be restricted to classrooms and formal office hours. Teachers have a responsibility to confine their encounters to discussions of subject and not to place themselves in positions that suggest they can do more for the student than they can deliver.

When this happens, the teacher assumes unnecessary responsibility for what happens. When teachers define themselves as counselors or comrades they face the possibility that students may take the advice they are given. They then become responsible for the consequences of it. Because most teachers are not trained in counseling, this is more responsibility than they should have. Good sense would seem to decree that teachers be very cautious about what they advise students to do—beyond the range of courses to take and how to fulfill the obligations of the syllabus.

It is difficult to draw the line between supportive contact and pathological transference. However, the mature academic professional must be careful to protect the integrity and individuality of students and to avoid relationships that go beyond what is required to teach well. Whether the teacher's goal is to guide learning activity, provoke curiosity, stimulate originality, encourage those who fail to try again, or motivate them to aspire to greater efforts at exploration and inquiry, his or her activity must be carefully modulated to protect the privacy and integrity of everyone involved.

In situations in which students have the power to evaluate their teachers, the pressure for good evaluations can create difficult problems for both. In attempting to please the students, teachers can dilute subject matter or mollify their evaluations in order to cultivate goodwill. This confronts most teachers with another dialectical tug: the desire to be liked and appreciated versus their obligation to deliver quality subject matter. There are often compromises possible; usually they are made in the direction of the students' concerns. Each professional must establish his or her own criteria for level of complexity and quality of instruction.

Some teachers are tempted by the emotions generated from the transference that takes place naturally between them and their students. If they make themselves too accessible, students may look to them for services they cannot deliver. Furthermore, excessive contact with students may cause a decline in the impetus to scholarly activity. It is also important for teachers to avoid exceeding their competence. The temptation to counsel students about personal matters is very strong, but the mature academic professional knows when to defer to others with better credentials and experience.

For those who deal with graduate students, the mission is a bit more complex. Graduate study is built on intimacy (Phillips, 1979). Graduate students are actually junior colleagues. They represent the interface at which collegiality grows. The relationship between graduate students and their mentors is necessarily close because it involves collaboration in both teaching and research. (Medical and law students also serve apprenticeships, but they are designed as a collective experience and students rarely attach themselves to one influential instructor.) The relationship presents serious moral questions about responsibility for research, supervision of teaching, joint authorship, and the maintenance of continued contact. The mature academic professional is able to enjoy the closeness of graduate study as well as use it to push forward the frontiers of knowledge through a serious and productive collaboration.

There is one other important issue to keep in mind about your teaching. That is the need to "stay loose." Simply speaking, the state of knowledge in your discipline is likely to change radically during your career. In 1945, there were courses called "social conversation." They almost died out completely before "interpersonal communication" sprang from social psychology in the 1960s. Organizational communication was unheard of before the 1970s. Business and professional speaking was left to Dale Carnegie and his imitators. The rise of technological considerations did not have real momentum until almost the 1980s, although departments did play with radio performance as early as the 1930s. In short, you will likely change your teaching specialty and your research emphasis two or three times during your career.

You will hear the phrases "cutting edge" and "mainstream." One can get hurt badly by being on the cutting edge as there are cutting edges that rapidly become blunt. You will have to rely on your own critical sense to tell you when a "bold new approach" becomes a fad and when it changes to a superstition. You can get insight into this by following the history of general semantics and its relationship with speech communication. Many approaches that predominated in the field and became known as mainstream have dried up entirely or have become underground trickles. To be dedicated to an approach when it is no longer warranted means to put your career in jeopardy. There are, for example, those who still use the Palo Alto group's explanation of schizophrenia and the work of Gregory Bateson as bases for a communication theory, although they have long been discredited by psychiatric professionals. One older professor used to warn his graduate students not to agree with him too much because he did not want them to carry the burden of abandoning him when he changed his mind.

To sum up, whatever institution most of you serve, in some way, your main mission will be teaching. Even those who labor full time in the classroom fuel the teaching process. The proper synthesis of teaching and research is difficult to find, but the balance you discover will sustain the satisfaction you get from your career.

THE OBLIGATION TO SERVE
THE ACADEMIC COMMUNITY

The academic community consists of faculty, administrators, and ancillary personnel working together. They serve the populations of students to whom they have made commitments, but they are responsible to society as well. Each academic community is unique, each has a mission and an obligation. In some cases, these are explicit, as, for example, in the case of a church-related institution or one supported by state or local taxes. In some cases, they are implicit and subtle, as in the case of a private liberal arts college or a graduate university.

Each professional has an individual role to play. He or she must, in some way, contribute to the accomplishment of institutional objectives. This is most often done through good research and teaching, but in many cases there is an additional duty to serve in decision making, student advising, community relations, and sometimes fund raising. The academic professional who cannot find some way to associate with the mission of his or her institution and work to implement it is obligated to work through legitimate channels for change or to move to another institution with whose goals they are more compatible.

In addition to the local community at the particular college or university, the academic belongs to a larger community of scholars in his or her discipline, as well as to the community of scholarly professionals in general. There are obligations on every level. This means not only maintaining intellectual literacy, but rendering service through professional organizations. One of the most important ways information is exchanged is through state, regional, and national meetings of professionals at which papers are presented and shop talk exchanged. There is a role for everyone who wants to serve in these organizations.

The professional associations need the help of scholar-members to plan meetings, administer journals, and staff editorial boards. They need the membership dues to keep these institutions alive. Without them, academics would have no outlet for their work. They need journals in order to publish the results of their research, but without the money that comes from membership, those journals simply cannot exist. One old scholar commented that when making hiring decisions, the first thing he looked at was the applicant's pattern of memberships in professional organizations. If the applicant was not a member of his or her national, regional, or state association, he or she was rejected regardless of anything else in the resume. Without the cross-fertilization of ideas that takes place through professional organizations, academic disciplines do not thrive and often they do not survive. By observing the pattern of growth and decline in organizations, it is possible to read a history of the content of the academy. The recent split in the American Psychological Association into clinical and academic camps culminates a long story of turf wars. The inception of the International Communication Association in competition with the Speech Communication Association signaled the split between theory and research on the one hand and a pedagogy and performance emphasis on the other.

Furthermore, professionals are responsible for the acculturation of younger faculty members by providing advice, encouragement, and collaboration when possible. The mentor relationship (by whatever name you care to refer to it) between old and young faculty is an effective way of building lasting academic enterprises. However, it is equally important to remember that relationships in the academy are often temporary. Young faculty are free to follow their own muses. The academy does not thrive on sectarianism and disciplehood. Even in the most rigid of denominational institutions, academics must remember that their mission is the effective pursuit of truth and that their colleagues are entitled to pursue it in their own fashion. The prize and privilege of academic freedom is the banner around which collegiality is organized.

To serve these ends, academics must be "citizen soldiers." Academics cherish self-governance, but it can only be achieved and maintained when scholars work for the common good. This means committee service, supervision of programs, design of syllabuses, and responsibility for minor housekeeping and administrative chores. Without active faculty participation in governance, colleges and universities can become administrative fiefdoms in which inquiry is stifled and controversy suppressed. Faculty service to the institution is in an academic's own interest for they can only flourish in flourishing institutions.

Let's consider some of the possibilities for this kind of service. Courses often must be added to the curriculum. Each time a course is added, the choices students could make becomes complicated. Furthermore, each faculty member has a vested interest in his or her own course. Consequently, the process of generating new courses is often complicated by political and personal considerations. On the other hand, failure to update the curriculum by taking obsolete courses out of the catalogue and adding new ones can sound the death knell for a discipline.

The same holds true for the process of generating a major within a department or the requirements within a college. Regarding the latter, departments have their vested interests, and the conflict over what is included and what is left out can get intense. Often, those involved will temporarily forget the mission they are to serve as they get caught up in the political combat. Furthermore, the issues that plague sustaining literacy come to a practical focus in designing requirements and majors. Political correctness versus the canon is a major divisive debate in virtually every academic institution these days, and it is an issue that promises to divide colleagues for years to come. There is no way for an academic to function professionally and avoid taking a stand on complex institutional issues and participating in emotional professional controversies.

Even mundane issues such as grading and advising are not immune to conflict. One soft grader in an otherwise rigorous department can wreck havoc with equity. Students will flock to his or her class once the word gets around. Students are not immune to a little bribery, and they see "cake courses" as absolutely essential in achieving a satisfactory transcript. Aspirants to professional schools will be especially sensitive to the nature of the grading system.

It is even more fundamental to establish gradable objectives for courses and to operate a grading system that will withstand scrutiny as students examine it for equity. These decisions are sometimes made in a patchwork sort of way by each faculty member doing his or her own thing, but often they are the result of a carefully considered set of issues, a veritable rulebook of decisions made collectively by faculty colleagues.

Finally, the issue of advising is a potent interface between students and faculty. What advice do students need and want? What advice is faculty competent to give? Good advising means student retention, and it is not an issue to be taken lightly.

THE OBLIGATION TO BE TRUE TO YOURSELF

We have discussed at length how important it is to find a workplace that suits your interests and abilities. Given that the two most important issues for academic professionals are developing a research interest and growing with it and finding an appropriate teaching style and becoming better at it, the institution at which they do this is extraordinarily important to their success or failure. The best professionals have chosen their workplace with care (or have been lucky enough to stumble into one that suits them).

Choices are often difficult to make, especially in these days of fiscal attrition. The right job is often not available. Moreover, a newly minted Ph.D. does not always know what kind of job is best. Most academic professionals move once or twice before they make a permanent affiliation. Financial considerations are always important in job choice, but all things being equal, they are not necessarily the main consideration. If money is the sole goal, it is best sought outside the university.

Very often professionals are corrupted by their own success at private consulting and entrepreneurship. They may also be distracted by the blandishments of service to the employer. It is flattering to be asked to serve on important committees, and it is gratifying to get an additional paycheck. But, the early days of a career are best spent mastering the art of teaching and demonstrating the ability to do productive research.

Young Ph.D.s are often tempted by jobs at major research institutions. Many of them discover (usually after five years) that they are not willing or able to assume the burden of research and publication imposed. Either they leave and literally begin a new career at another type of institution, or they are denied tenure and face even more difficulties in locating a new job. It is important to make major career decisions early enough so that there is an opportunity to try and revise your goals and emphases without feeling a sense of failure.

In general, selection of a job depends on eight major considerations:

1. Is it possible to live decently on the salary offered? Are the salary and benefits comparable to those at other similar institutions? What is the policy on pay increases?
2. What are the requirements for promotion and tenure?
3. What are the policies on sabbaticals, obtaining research grants, and participating in university governance?
4. What obligations for advising and counseling are imposed on faculty?
5. What are the expectations for research, publication, professional contact, membership in professional organizations, commu-

nity service, and consulting? Does the university support these expectations with funding or grants-in-aid?

6. What are the expectations for teaching evaluations, office hours, and the advising/counseling of students?
7. Do the library and computer facilities meet your research needs?
8. Are colleagues compatible with your needs and interests?

It is possible to get direct information about these matters by asking interviewers or consulting local contacts and friends. Documents such as the faculty handbook, books describing benefits, catalogues, and other official publications should be consulted, and ambiguities should be resolved during the interview process. Accurate information is essential to an intelligent choice.

Most beginning faculty members have a choice of at least two or three positions. After that, moves depend on strategic job hunting combined with reputation, references, and the support of mentors. A great deal of useful information about open positions and the state of affairs at various institutions can be gained through participation in professional meetings.

There is another issue as well, that is, when or whether to leave the professorate and enter administration. A great many talented academics are tempted to move into administration. Their professional success brings them to the attention of administrators who offer them opportunities for department headships or deanships.

But make no mistake about it. The rank of professor is the highest academic rank attainable. There is no next rung on the ladder. The job of dean or department head requires a major change both in mind set and pattern of life. Regardless of high hopes and plans, most administrators must sacrifice both research time and student contact. If you receive gratification from interacting with students or engaging in research, you probably will have to give these up in order to fulfill the obligations of an administrative position.

Administration is attractive, interesting, exciting, and it usually pays more than professors receive. However, the issues are very different from those in teaching, and the schedule demands are considerably more rigorous. Administrators spend a great deal of time budgeting, attending meetings, planning, and dealing with personnel issues. Academics exploring potential careers in administration must consider carefully their interest in dealing with such issues.

In the medieval university, the faculty took responsibility for administrative work. In the American university, however, the career paths have diverged. In a few major research universities, both department headships and deanships are regarded as temporary obligations to be assumed by senior faculty members for short, specifically defined terms. In those institutions, the faculty has full authority over academic business. In most institutions, however, department headships and deanships are part of middle management. These positions are not elected; they are selected by higher administrators, and individuals remain in their position at the pleasure of their superiors.

Administration as a career may look good to faculty members who are depressed by their declining standard of living and increasing work loads, but it may not be the answer. If money is the issue, it may make more sense to seek a job in industry.

It is useful at this point to recap some of the professional issues confronting today's academics:

- There is no real prospect for major increases in salary for professors. Furthermore, the promotion and tenure requirements are likely to become more stringent. In fact, some institutions are attempting to do away with tenure altogether.
- Student bodies are becoming more diverse. Professors are becoming more responsible for various forms of compensatory instruction. The pressure to spend time with students is increasing without mitigating the pressure to produce research. Moreover, faculty members are required to be sensitive to the needs of diverse populations of students who have not, heretofore, been adequately served.
- Research funds are drying up. Major grants are usually available only to professors of high reputation. On the other hand, there are a great many small grants available for research initiation. There are also grants available that permit faculty members to experiment for a year or so as an administrator to test their aptitude and proclivity for an administrative career.
- Demographic information indicates that the number of available academic positions will be gradually increasing and hitting a peak around the turn of the century. Many of the professors who started their jobs during the baby boom years are nearing retirement age. There is a small increase in the birth rate accompanied by pressure for more people to attend college. These factors will combine to increase opportunities. On the other hand, recent events indicate that these opportunities may be casualties of the recession. Opportunities are limited when finances are tight.

To be a mature academic professional, you must make the right choice of a position that will enable you to use your talents and fulfill your goals for personal accomplishment. Those who do not find the position that suits them burn out. Those that do experience the richness of one of the most rewarding careers available in our society.

THE OBLIGATION TO COLLEGIALITY

Collegiality is a major issue. Relationships in the academy are often closer than they appear. Colleagues can be helpful or harmful. In departments divided by blood feuds and parochialism, running afoul of the wrong person can ruin a career. On the other hand, an alert and helpful mentor can help a career advance. The young academic must be able to manipulate relationships effectively along with the challenges presented by the criteria for advancement. The issue is how to combine example and precept to learn about what is to come. A subsidiary issue is to learn whom to trust. The sensible selection of informants can be very helpful in guiding a career. Young academics must be able to observe and confirm their observations with other professionals. Of special importance is our explanation of how an administrative officer evaluates faculty performance and how this figures in decisions about pay, promotion, and tenure.

Most of the important decisions about your career will be done by peer review. In some cases, popularity with your colleagues is enough for advancement. In others—mostly unionized institutions—the criteria are sufficiently explicit to minimize the role colleagues play in decision making. But, in most cases, decisions about your professional advancement are made initially by colleagues. This is why the idea of collegiality is very important to consider. The aspiring academic must understand what role colleagues play in evaluation (actually the subtext is the aspiring academic must learn who must be impressed and how to do it). A certain amount of toadying and conforming is required for minimal advancement. How much of this a young academic wants to do is a moral decision.

An important argument for collegiality is that colleagues can provide invaluable support and encouragement. On the other hand, they can also present serious obstacles to a successful career. The ability to collaborate and find colleagues willing to collaborate is an important consideration. Furthermore, people tend to see things in different ways. How people evaluate quality can range from the number of publications produced to how many times one publication is cited. There are standard strategies academics use to succeed in meeting the criteria for promotion and tenure. There are also legal protections to cover the tenure process, but for the most part, such decisions are reserved for the institution.

THE OBLIGATION TO THE COMMUNITY AT LARGE

The academic institution is part of a larger community. It serves the people. The land grant mandate, for example, fixed the responsibility of major universities to well-configured constituencies. No academic can exist apart from life in the broader universe. It is as though there is a black velvet backdrop on which the jewel of the institution is displayed. The setting and the contrast are essential to the welfare of both communities.

Events in the community often cause major problems in academic institutions. A decline in funding means fewer jobs, smaller raises, and slower advancement. Technological changes impose obligations for instruction on the colleges. The birth rate, the political climate, the position of minorities in the social hierarchy, and the dialectic between female and male all play some role in presenting challenges to academics and the institutions they serve.

Major problems in the contemporary university that will become important in the foreseeable future are dropping enrollments, vacancies caused by large-scale retirements, limitations on public funding, political moves to remove tenure as a privilege, the increase in the use of adjunct (nontenured) faculty, the use of technology in instruction, funding of research, and modification of employee benefits. New faculty members will have difficulty in selecting career paths. They will also have difficulty selecting disciplines. There are major changes and realignments in disciplines in the offing. Computers, cognitive science, and various business-oriented specialties will receive increasing emphasis, whereas traditional disciplines (e.g., classics) will decline. Academics will have to stay fast on their feet to keep up with the changing academic map. Continuing education in the form of postdoctoral study and intensive reading will be a minimum requirement for survival.

Virtually all academics will have some opportunity to apply their discipline practically in the so-called "real world." Consultancies are regularly available. Industries count on the contributions of academics to advise and assist in the development of products as well as the training and governance of their employees.

By the same token, local communities and political parties will look to academics for participation and advice. The idea of the ivory tower is long gone. No faculty member can remain isolated from the community in which he or she lives. Even the arts will look to academics for support and encouragement.

The mature academic professional regards his or her career as a learning experience. By raising hypotheses and testing them within the realm of possibilities, it is possible to achieve the balance of interests and skills necessary for professional success and satisfaction. Communication professors have special responsibilities because their discipline involves close contact with students in an interdisciplinary context. This simply is not possible to achieve without personal growth. The question is one of managing growth to the benefit of the discipline and one's own personal and professional life.

◆ RESPONSE TO CHAPTER SIX
DENNIS S. GOURAN

Anyone with more than a modicum of experience in higher education would find it difficult to disagree with very much of what Professor Phillips identifies as aspects of professionalism or the issues they pose for those involved. His views concerning collegiality, however, strike me as insufficiently expansive and far too centered on its importance to self-promotion. Displaying a lack of collegiality, to be sure, does little for one's ability to earn the respect of colleagues or to work effectively with them. I find it bothersome, however, that the importance my colleague attaches to being collegial is portrayed primarily as a means of avoiding the potentially punishing consequences of disfavor. In fact, what he appears to recommend is not collegiality, so much as tactics aimed at the creation of its appearance.

The academic world Professor Phillips implies is one in which most, if not all, people dislike one another, and those most senior continuously attempt to induce obeisance in others or otherwise control their fate. At stake is one's survival. There are such individuals, of course, but Professor Phillips sees them in far greater number and as having considerably more influence than I do. Advising newcomers to ingratiate themselves with the sorts of people populating the Phillips-constructed academic world, moreover, is not very likely to result in such reprehensible individuals having much use for those they succeed in intimidating and in whom they create an unhealthy dependence. Under circumstances in which an individual feels that, despite personal dislike and antipathy, he or she must "butter up" colleagues in the interest of gaining their support, that person would probably be better advised to seek another position.

Genuine collegiality is important to the successful operation of both one's department and the institution of which it is a part. The very nature of organized education requires a substantial degree of collaborative effort. However independent one may believe him- or herself to be, what Deutsch (1973) describes as "promotive interdependence" tends to be the norm. In a state of promotive interdependence, an individual cannot succeed in a task unless the others with whom he or she is performing it also succeed. Much of what we do in higher education is of this character. Tasks that most often induce promotive interdependence are what Steiner (1972) refers to as "conjunctive." For such tasks, successful completion depends on the performance of the least effective participant. Coordination and cooperation requirements, therefore, are high. Anyone who has ever participated in or observed a crew team will appreciate this point.

When one thinks of such aspects of academic life as the prepara-

tion of students, the frequent need to justify a department's work to higher authority, having to continue functioning in the face of unanticipated
reductions in personnel and resources, assisting graduate students in
developing defensible research projects, assessing achievement for promotion and tenure, adding coursework to the curriculum, maintaining
and enhancing a department's reputation in the interest of making it
more attractive to prospective students, and the like, collegiality becomes
an important consideration. Its absence contributes to a climate in which
the accomplishment of the kinds of tasks mentioned above can be difficult at best and perhaps even virtually impossible.

Ultimately, it is in the individual's best interest to be supportive
of the work of others because his or her successes in many instances are
likely to be a function of those of the collectivity as a whole.
Unfortunately, people in a society that historically has attached value to
competition see themselves, in Deutsch's terms, as "contriently interdependent"—in short, as believing that their successes depend on others'
failures. This mentality fosters perceptions of inequity in many instances.
A competitive orientation frequently induces misperceptions of others. (I
have never encountered a student or faculty member who confesses to
being less than average in comparison to others in the same group.) If
faculty members feel they are achieving less for what they believe to be
the same or greater effort than others—what Homans (1974) calls violations of the principle of "distributive justice"—they are much less given to
cooperative effort.

What those who dwell on inequity often fail to recognize, in addition to the possibility that their perceptions may be in error, is that others' achievements may affect their own well-being in a positive manner. In
institutions having merit systems, for instance, the amounts allocated for
salary increases are based on the performance of the department as a
whole. To the extent that the collectivity performs well, the rewards accruing to the individual are greater than they would be if overall performance was evaluated unfavorably.

In offering these observations about collegiality, I am not so naive
as to fail to acknowledge that some individuals in institutions can and do
make life miserable for others and appear to take pleasure in that activity.
Even in these cases, however, it is possible for one to maintain at least a
civil, working relationship. Doing so admittedly is not easy, but is
nonetheless necessary. Being continually at war with such individuals is
more emotionally draining on you than it is on them and, in a perverse
way, does more to assure their success than your own. If you keep your
attention focused on the larger interests of your immediate reference
group (that is, the department faculty), contending with problematic
individuals can be far less personally and professionally debilitating.

◆ RESPONSE TO CHAPTER SIX
SCOTT A. KUEHN

I find the professionalism themes expressed in this particular chapter a common current throughout this book, so I would like to limit my short comments to an area I find intriguing in this context: cultural literacy. As a beginning academic I found that the devotion to cultural literacy among professors and colleagues at my graduate institution was not present to the same extent at the university of my employment. This may have been due to the fact that I was now noticing all those professors who failed to update their notes, who failed to read in their disciplines, and who seemed to barely go through the motions of teaching. As a graduate student, I had little contact with such types. But now many were my colleagues, and some even sat on my promotion and tenure evaluation committee.

I have heard similar impressions from other beginning academics. Sometimes one finds oneself in a "vast cultural literacy wasteland" (to borrow a phrase from a past FCC chairman). What can one do? First and foremost, maintain your own notion of what professionalism means to you. Keep up with your reading and try to find colleagues on campus with similar ties to scholarship. You may have to look into different disciplines, but these connections can add perspective and interest to discussion. Second, make time to talk about scholarship and current events. The computer networks provide forums for those that can reach them. Third, push yourself to maintain your commitment to talk to your colleagues and keep posted on what they are doing. They can help you and you can help them. You cannot read everything or learn everything, but you can share what you have.

◆ RESPONSE TO CHAPTER SIX
JULIA T. WOOD

My colleague and friend Professor Phillips sees the world in general and the academy in particular as more combative and more governed by Darwinian law than I do. I assume that his experiences have influenced his perspective on professionalism and his relationships with colleagues, and that his viewpoint is reflected in the tone and emphasis of his chapter. I use my responses to his chapter as an opportunity to supplement and, in some cases, to qualify the portrait he paints.

Primary to my understanding of professional life is collegiality, and by that term I mean something other than Professor Phillips's view of mean-spirited, power-mongering Machiavellians, who dislike one another and interact only to preserve their places in the hierarchy and/or to ensure individual survival. Although I cannot say I know of no colleagues who might fit this description, in my experience they are rare indeed. I have been impressed by the consistent generosity, cooperativeness, and genuine interest in working together that is characteristic of proximate colleagues in my department and those comprising my larger network of professional associates around my campus and the nation.

I view relationships among colleagues as emanating from respect, including respect for differences, a shared commitment to collective goals, and an awareness of interdependence among individuals. It is these values that I share with my near and far associates, who, like me, believe that more constructive things tend to happen when people pool their resources and work together whenever possible and disagree respectfully at other times. Most faculty realize that collective welfare depends on the success and commitment of each individual. Given this, one person's accomplishments assist, rather than detract from those of colleagues. Consider a few examples of how a strong whole enables individual members. Deans recognize those departments that engage in cutting edge scholarship and rigorous teaching, and deans reward these departments with resources and support. Because the achievements of each faculty member contribute to creating a department that is strong, it is in the interest of each faculty member and the unit to foster and root for her or his colleague's successes.

Professor Phillips and I also differ on our views of power. His discussions suggest that he views power as a finite resource such that whatever amount one person commands is that much less anyone else has—a win-lose orientation. In contrast, I view power as not finite and, in fact, as expanding mutually when people work together in good faith. There is enough for everyone, and each person's ability to influence and make things happen can enlarge others' capacities to do likewise. A couple of years ago a colleague read a paper of mine and offered very detailed and helpful commentary on it. I revised the paper substantially based on her suggestions, and it was later published. In the process I also learned more about writing well and about clarifying complex ideas. This enabled me to be a better critic for her and other colleagues when I read their papers. In addition, the publication that resulted from our working together contributed to the department's scholarly profile. Did her investment in me and my resulting growth diminish her power? Or did it enlarge her power simultaneous with expanding my own? Similarly, when I assist a junior colleague in applying for research grants and he or she gets one, my own influence is not lessened. To the extent that he or she becomes stronger, our community is stronger and that helps us all.

The views of collegiality that I have expressed and the examples I have cited do not mean that I have not encountered individuals whom I find mean-spirited and difficult—people who covet power and who like to make others, invariably people with less status, jump to their bidding. Yet they tend to be the exceptions, not the rule, in my experience. Most faculty, like most members of other professions, are more helpful than not and more interested in cooperating than in competing against one another.

A particularly telling point about collegiality is that the extent to which it exists in any given department grows out of the nature of interaction among faculty. It's one of those cases in which the "law of reciprocity" seems to hold with greater consistency than is typical in social science research. Some faculty are generous in offering to read colleagues' papers, help them learn new computer systems, coach them on how to get through various bureaucratic mazes, and confer with them about teaching; these faculty tend to find others have generous attitudes toward them and are willing to lend time and expertise. On the other hand, faculty who are uncooperative and selfish in their efforts toward colleagues seldom find others very willing to help or support them. Your attitude toward others and the degree to which you extend yourself for them will be a primary influence on how they, in turn, treat you.

Let me touch more briefly on two other points in Professor Phillips's chapter. I agree with his comments on the interaction among cultural literacy, scholarship, teaching, and citizenry. These four broad arenas of professional life are mutually supportive. I would underscore the importance of citizenship, or service, which is typically less highly regarded by administrators than teaching and research. Yet, it is through participating on committees that individuals are able to effect the life of departments and institutions. Universities and colleges reflect the values of those who actively participate in creating rules, procedures, and policies. More than in almost any other profession, faculty are self-governing; those willing to become involved can change institutional policies and procedures, revise curricula, and redirect missions. Thus, service is both a responsibility and an opportunity of membership in academe.

I would also like to supplement Professor Phillips's listing of areas of communication expertise. Those he named are major and important emphases within the field. In addition, there are growing numbers of courses in gender and communication, traditional and nontraditional research methodologies in communication research, rhetorical practices of minority and/or marginalized cultures, and oral history, which entails both a theoretical and performative focus. To overlook areas such as these in describing our field is to ignore significant domains of study and teaching.

Finally, I underline the multiplicity of commitments entailed in professionalism as Professor Phillips has instructively presented them. A professional in academe really does wear many hats, sometimes simultaneously, and engages in a wide range of activities from conceptual to pragmatic, from individual to collaborative. The most satisfied faculty tend to enjoy the different fit, feeling, and requirements of various roles they are called upon to enact. They enjoy university and college life for the opportunities it provides to learn continually about national and international issues in a range of fields and to explore what this knowledge implies for teaching, research, interaction with colleagues, and participation in public life. It's a good career for those who find gratification in the multidimensional process of creating knowledge and in being part of institutions that support it.

7

TEACHING IN THE COLLEGE AND UNIVERSITY

Gerald M. Phillips

This is a chapter about an art. It is the basic chapter for all who seek a career in higher education. It is the point to it all. It may well be that research and publication have assumed ascendancy over teaching in the criteria for advancement, at least in some larger institutions. However, to the people of this country, the university is an institution devoted to education. It focuses on the young, but more and more the mission of higher education has been extended to lifetime learning. For those who seek an academic career, teaching is where it all begins.

WHAT IS TEACHING?

Teaching is an active process. Most of us remember having a teacher who was essentially a funnel. He or she sat at the head of the class and absorbed facts from notes or a book and spoke these facts to us as we sat at rigid attention. At periodic intervals, we were given a test, not of our knowledge, but of what we remembered from that human funnel. That is not teaching.

In elementary school, virtually all teaching is participatory. Elementary teachers are "right in there" with the little ones. They patiently lead young eyes across the pages of books and get down on the floor to direct creative activity. They ask questions, they listen, they give answers. Once, not so long ago, I had the opportunity to guide some Irish visitors around the campus where I was employed. They had just visited an elementary school. One of them asked, "What happens to these bright youngsters we saw in the elementary schools from the time they get out until they become the weary people we see on this campus." It made me think. Here I was, in the middle of America on a campus where the students were the sons and daughters of the working class. It was a traditional land grant school. The young men and women who registered did so with high hopes. Their education was to be their ticket to the middle class or better. It was a sacrifice for most of their parents for them to attend. Most of them worked part time, and school let out for a week to coincide with the planting season. The answer, of course, to the question asked by our foreign visitors was simply, "They grew up."

They left the elementary school with great disparities. Some were bright-eyed and bushy-tailed, ready to meet any challenge from the secondary system. Some were quite literate and went on to elite preparatory schools. Many, however, were children of poverty. Their elementary education had not prepared them for the educational challenges to come. The hardship of their lives made them more concerned about simple survival. The idea of pulling themselves out of their plight through education had not penetrated.

Education has always been the hope of our society. The immigrants who flooded to this country around the turn of the century came to escape the grinding poverty of Europe. Education was their ticket up and out. The situation today is no different. The United States is now multiracial and multilingual. The land is filled with newcomers, pursuing the same dream. Education is their ticket up and out, also.

The secondary schools have become the crisis area. Special programs for young children have helped the elementary schools keep pace with demands. Secondary schools face their own crisis; urban schools are in decay, handicapped by a lack of adequate local funding as central cities decay. Some of the students are lost to crime and drugs, and many who go on are not prepared to handle college work. Most institutions of higher education today are curious blends of students who need remedial training, those with ordinary education and ordinary interests, and young prodigies ready for careers in medicine, science, engineering, and law. Colleges and related institutions must meet the needs of all of them. It is clearly not the same as it was before the G.I. Bill, nor the same as it was 10 years ago. If our foreign visitors were to look today, they would find even more difference between the youngsters in elementary school and those they see before them.

Diversity is the order of the day; diversity in students, diversity in options. And it is not easy for anyone. The students and their families have trouble paying the bills. Their teachers have trouble meeting the wide range of needs with which they are confronted. They do not have the resources to individualize instruction; they cannot continue in the traditional formats that characterized higher education from colonial times almost to the present day. This is the world in which you will participate as a teacher. You may find yourself in situations for which you are not prepared. You may be required to teach students who are equally unprepared, or who cannot speak the language, or to teach returning adults who have years of experience to set against your recently acquired "book learning."

There have never been normal schools for higher education. College teachers have never been formally trained for their tasks. Even as many colleges and departments of education go out of business, there are demands for formal training for college teachers. The future is uncertain. It depends on financing, on who wins the battle about whether subject matter or methodology is more important, and on the commitment of the women and men who enter the profession.

There are many points of view on teaching and no real agreement on how it's done or how to measure who is good at it. But it will be the focus of your career. Your research will spin off from it and feed information back into the process. Only a very few of you will be full-time researchers, and it is probably all to the good. Being sequestered from others is not all that much fun, and teaching can be exciting, challenging, and most of all, productive. You can see the results of your handiwork.

Education is the vital center of our whole society, and those who engage in it are major players. However small the school, a typical teacher can, over the course of a career, influence hundreds of lives. The question is "how?" This chapter is about your participation. It is complicated, speculative, and philosophical; it offers more questions than answers. We offer it in the hope that it will help you understand the nature and sensitivity of the career you have chosen.

WHAT TEACHING INCLUDES

Teaching is the guidance of learning activity. Around the turn of the century, a number of authorities began to examine traditional notions about the teaching process. Prior to that time, teaching had mostly consisted of a standard pattern that included lecture, drill, recitation, memorization of passages, and tests. These methods went all the way back to the medieval universities at which lecturing was critical because there were no books. The professor would lecture, and the students would copy or make notes as best they could. Recitation and drill harkened back to the Socratic model and can be seen today in the kind of instruction given at many law schools. The teacher questions students individually; students may be asked to give reports on which they are examined. Readings are assigned, and students held responsible for acquiring whatever the teacher believes is important.

There is nothing particularly wrong with this kind of teaching. It requires a great deal of preparation and planning on the part of the teacher. Traditionally, in the grade schools, teachers were urged to make lesson plans so that they could account for each block of time during a teaching day. However, this kind of teaching demands motivated learners. Students who are not interested in participating are bored at best and alienated from the process at worst.

Participating is the key word. In medical and law school, there is little difficulty obtaining complete commitment from the students. They are there out of choice. They know that their professions are demanding and highly competitive; consequently, they do the work demanded of them, however fatiguing.

With the advent of compulsory education and the broadening of enrollments at colleges and universities, however, a large number of reluctant students entered the system. Teachers, already pressured by the need to prepare lectures and plan recitations and drills, were now presented with the problem of motivation. The relatively passive learners had to be involved in the process. Educational philosophers, such as John Dewey, began to involve themselves in the question of how to involve students more actively in the process and to discover ways of personal motivation.

The effect of these ideas was to advocate training teachers to devise assignments that required problem solving on the part of the students. Rote memorization and recitation were not regarded as sufficient to indicate subject matter mastery. The Dewey formulations demanded that students be able to apply what they learned to practical problems in their own life in the real world.

On a very primitive level, this means you learn to read so that you can choose what you want to read. You learn to write so you can handle required correspondence. You learn to speak to communicate the ordinary tasks you must perform in society. Performance courses in speech are generally outgrowths of this philosophy of education and are often sold to administrators on the grounds that they teach students to cope with ordinary life problems.

Teaching is the direction of performance behavior. In disciplines that have as their goal the modification of performance, a degree of formal direction of behavior is required. Most of the communication disciplines have a performance component. We learn about and we learn how, and we do not necessarily know the relationship between the two. There are great orators who never studied communication theory, yet they are able to speak well and, in fact, become objects of study themselves.

On the most fundamental level, small children must learn to perform specific routines. They must control their body processes, tie their shoes, climb in and out of chairs, and so on. As they get older, they must learn to read and write. We assume that they learn to speak and listen by imitation, but more recently it has become clear that formal instruction in speaking and listening is valuable. Furthermore, we have had available, for half a century, methods of retraining incompetent speech and overcoming impairments in hearing.

The teacher's role in these cases is that of diagnostician and director of therapy. In essence, the teacher trains the student to perform techniques that overcome inadequacies or incompetencies and in so doing, brings performance into conformance with acceptable social levels. This presumes that the teacher must (a) know what acceptable levels are and (b) know what an individual must be able to do in order to attain them. The teacher must be an expert in theory and technique, although the student (trainee) need only know the technique. Often teachers make the error of believing that learning about how something is done will facilitate doing it. However, modification of performance behavior calls for the ability to discover flaws and present remedies. Some students may require the additional motivation derived from learning the connection between exercises and results, but in most cases, by directing behavior through assignments, a vicarious kind of learning can be acquired. Whether this can be carried over into life activity is another difficult question.

Teaching is the uncomplicated presentation of information. For most college teachers, this process represents the modality. Most teachers lecture. Teachers mostly lecture. In educational periodicals attention is usually given to teachers who have "discovered" alternatives to lecturing. Formal instruction implies that the teacher talks and the students listen.

Implicit in this process are the various activities associated with the delivery of formal lectures. This includes the "Socratic" approach of question and answer; that is, the teacher assumes the student has or has not learned and attempts to ascertain this publicly by asking questions and prodding the student for correct answers. Teachers can also use this technique to carry on dialogue, that is, to push a student to express and defend a point of view. Professor Kingsfield in the *Paper Chase* exemplifies this method. The mighty professor gives his lectures, assigns readings, and assumes the student will take notes and learn, in some form, the material (ideas, facts, citations) that the professor deems desirable. During subsequent class periods, the professor tests the student by asking for a public recitation. Combined with the first option, the teacher may assign the student to make a formal presentation and submit to questions. The teacher may also ask the student to write papers, presumably to demonstrate how well he or she has learned.

All of this, however, centers on lecturing. At its simplest level, the lecture is a compendium of information. The professor divides the subject matter into categories of facts and presents the facts orally to the class. In most cases, this oral presentation is supported by the assignment of textbook and ancillary readings. Often the lecturer assumes that the student has done the reading and uses the lecture for explanation, amplification, and application of what was read.

In essence, a lecturer gives a public speech. Often it is a speech to inform. Sometimes it is a speech to persuade. Teachers have points of view, and they are often tempted to use their position as a "bully pulpit." Teachers often indoctrinate students, not only with general values about life in society, but with their positions on the various issues contained in the subject matter. For example, does a rhetorical or a communication point of view provide a more useful explanation of human interpersonal relationships? That is not a question of fact. The teacher may explain, by lecturing, what the rhetorical view is and contrast it with the communication view. This can hardly be done without sometimes making invidious comparisons as a result of which some issues receive an advantage in presentation.

We discuss the ramifications of this aspect of lecturing in detail in a later chapter. For now, we only offer an admonition that lecturing, as an instructional modality, is presumed to be a neutral presentation of information. The teacher who uses the lectern for indoctrination runs the risk of alienating both students and colleagues. Even worse, to make the teaching process into a catechism destroys the concept of academic freedom that has sustained the independence of the academy since time immemorial.

College professors are entitled to profess; indeed, they are encouraged to take a stand and defend a point of view. The entire system is mobilized to protect this privilege for them, for only through the exchange of informed and responsible opinion can our knowledge advance. Conversely, it requires independent minds to address the scholarly issues relevant in the academy, which means that students must be trained so they do not enter the research process with irreconcilable biases. There are any number of ways teachers can indoctrinate their students, but the lecture, because it is most frequently used, can be most frequently used to persuade.

Teaching is provocation of ideas and creative expression. There are a number of academic areas that do not deal with fact or opinion, but rather relate to artistic expression. The arts are an odd combination of skill and inspiration. They require training in technique and opportunities for the student to test his or her strength. The skills that are taught in the arts are offered for the express purpose of carryover. The student artist learns to make brush strokes that eventually will be used in a painting. The student actor learns to use his or her voice well to enhance a later performance in a play before an audience. A student of writing must produce text addressed to an audience and be provided with an opportunity for feedback.

Those who teach in the arts must inspire and model as well as instruct, and they must be imaginative enough to provide opportunities for students to test their acquired learning under criticism. The old adage, "those who can do, and those who can't teach," does not apply in this area of instruction. The ability to draw, act, or write does not automatically make a person into a good teacher, but it is essential to their teaching to have some direct contact with the performance aspects of their art. Learning literary criticism does not help a student learn to write, but practice at writing literary criticism enables the student to test essential skills.

All of this is especially true in the communication disciplines. Although the communication studies have drifted far from performance in recent years, performance is what they study. Despite the years of effort devoted to approaching the study of oral performance through rhetorical and communication theory and with the assistance of social psychology and philosophy, the academy looks to the communication disciplines primarily to produce performers. Detached experimentation and abstruse philosophy contribute little to the improvement of performance within the Ciceronian Canons.

This view of teaching, however, raises some genuine issues for professional advancement. Does artistic production deserve equal status with scholarly publication in assessing an academic professional for tenure and promotion? This is a matter of serious concern for professionals in many disciplines who are directly concerned with performance. Even engineers are not exempt from this paradox. If they deal with how to perform operations, is their legitimate object of research the operations or techniques of teaching how to perform those operations? Is their area of research engineering or engineering pedagogy?

Those in "mainstream" disciplines who can do the bulk of their teaching through lecturing and the design of learning activities can legitimately split their time between teaching and formal research. They may be experts on some minute detail of the discipline, but so long as they keep up generally with progress in the field, they are qualified to do their work. Those in performance disciplines must add competent performance to the requirements for general literacy and training of performance to their teaching obligations. Consequently, their task is considerably more complex.

There are some complex and abstract qualities associated with all teaching. In a sense, all teachers connect the past and the future. The vital role they play is characterized by the control of organized and systematic knowledge. Everyone learns; we learn by example, trial and error, trial and reward, or accidental association. We learn intuitively from our own observations. Theoretically, we could learn all there is to know; but theoretically, if all the monkeys in the world worked forever on all the word processors, they could produce all of the world's literature. The problem is, they would not know it.

The job of the teacher is to distinguish what is worth learning from error and irrelevancy. Each student should embark on a personal quest that goes a step beyond the teacher. In every teacher's lifetime, some knowledge is discredited, some superseded, and new knowledge discovered. The teacher's job is to keep abreast of these changes and keep his or her instruction attuned to them.

Thus, the teacher must inspire. It is not the inspiration involved with evangelism, but the inspiration that comes from unlocking and releasing the natural curiosity of the learner and guiding him or her in constructive paths. Of course, teachers make errors. Whatever is later proved wrong was error when it was taught, but the teacher must stay on the cutting edge and teach what is demonstrated, what is new, and what is relevant to the students' lives.

This means that the teacher has the responsibility of cultivating general literacy. On most campuses, at least as this is being written, this is one of the most important issues you will have to face in your career. Is there a canon worth transmitting from generation to generation, or do we have options about what should be taught? Do we agree that there is a mainstream of knowledge that must be available to all of us (with, of course, the freedom to explore tributaries and branches as we choose), or can the common wisdom be anything the authorities or experts say it is? Who is in charge?

There are several arguments being offered about the issue of common literacy. One point of view argues that the curriculum is heavily weighted toward material authored or discovered by white males of Western European origins. Those who advocate for this point of view want to open the curriculum to works from alternative sources. These include more works from Oriental, female, African, Eastern European, Native American, and homosexual sources. Those who oppose this point of view argue that there is a standard of merit a literary work or scientific contribution should meet and think such material should only be studied if it meets those standards, regardless of its source.

Concurrent with this is the argument about whether courses should be adapted so that material is consciously added that takes into account the contributions and needs of alternative groups. This issue becomes very complex when we consider the relative anonymity of scientific contributions. But those who advocate for this view will sometimes declare that the job can be done by showing women and African Americans, for example, doing work usually associated with white men. The underlying point is that people of alternative groups need the inspiration that only comes from seeing role models performing "virtuous" tasks.

The issue extends to the way material is managed in textbooks. You will notice that throughout this book we have been using "he or she" each time we need a third-person singular pronoun. Advocates of broadening the sources of information declare that this form will indicate relative parity between males and females.

Finally, there are those who advocate "political correctness." This means that invidious statements and derogatory comments made by members of one group about members of another are now off limits. Members of the academic community, including both students and teachers, are expected to refrain from any remarks that could be construed as giving any group advantage in quality over another. In Canada, this has been enacted into law, and there are complicated legal controversies raging, for example, over the work of a psychologist who specializes in studying the characteristics of racial groups. Each of his publications has been challenged under the law on the grounds that, without considering its merit and quality as research, the conclusions amount to invidious comparisons. (See *London Free Press,* October 12, 1991, E2 for a discussion of Matthew Adie et. al. and University of Western Ontario, File #20-618S.)

Attendance at college was, at one time, confined largely to white males. As more and more diverse groups are admitted to the mainstream of higher education, their accommodation becomes a matter of professional concern. There are legitimate arguments offered by those who claim the canon of instruction must remain constant and changed only when new works merit attention. Equally legitimate are the arguments of those who advocate inclusion of "other voices" regardless of merit to demonstrate equity on the grounds that it will set the model for inclusion and provide incentive to members of those groups.

As a professional teacher responsible for what you teach and how you teach it, you will have to adjudicate carefully what you say in your lectures, what you ask your students to read, and how you deal with members of various groups in class. You must learn what is expected by your employer, consider what your own professional conscience tells you is right, and act accordingly. Of course, either way, you are responsible for the consequences.

Teaching involves setting a worthy model to imitate. Initially all teaching is done by imitation. Infants do not have to attend class. They notice, listen, watch, and try. Eventually they learn to walk, talk, to be toilet-trained, and to stay out of trouble through a combination of imitation and admonition. The parents behave normally and their children learn to behave in ways that are surprisingly similar. Parents also impose their standards of morality onto their children. These moral strictures range from "don't play with matches" to "let us say grace before we eat." By the time children attend their first day of school, they are fully programmed. Their behavior patterns are cast. The seeds of genius and of future psychological problems are planted.

Teachers cannot escape the fact that they are relevant authority figures to students. They are parent surrogates. Children who have good relationships with their parents and who have learned to see them as authorities may come to accept the teacher in the same fashion. Children who are rebellious and truculent at home may well behave the same way in class. But teachers also teach by imitation and admonition. Their admonitions range from "do not put commas in the wrong place" to "do not bring firearms to class."

Imitation is a much more complex issue. To understand it, we have to look at the baffling concept of *role model*. The word has taken on multiple meanings that make it seem more important than it really is. It means, merely, that people will identify themselves for some arcane psychological reason with other people and will consciously or unconsciously try to imitate their behavior. Presumably, the people selected as role models must be plausible, that is, the way they behave should be within the range of the person who wants to imitate them. A 5-foot, 100-pound woman might admire the lifting ability of Arnold Schwarzenegger, but she would not be able to press iron the way he does. On the other hand, she might decide to try lifting weights anyway. Arnold, of course, has no idea he is so influential. He merely goes on about his business.

Sometimes the imitation is conscious. A student decides he wants to speak like a favorite professor; or a young scientist is heavily influenced by Enrico Fermi or Nils Bohr and begins trying to take on what he or she sees to be characteristic of these heroes. The role model need not even be present in order to be an object of imitation. But, teachers are present and they often become objects of imitation. In fact, the earliest pedagogical theory, that of Quintilian in *Institutes of Oratory* (Thonnsen & Baird, 1948), proclaimed that students always learn by imitation, and, therefore, the teacher must perform as a worthy model at all times. This advice is not far from the mark, although it is an onerous burden to impose. On the other hand, it is not unreasonable to expect a speech teacher to speak well and a composition teacher to write well. A history teacher should have some sense of the connection between the past and the present. A science teacher should know his or her way around a laboratory.

Teachers are, of course, free to live their private lives as they choose, but those parts of their private lives they share with students should be reasonably virtuous. Again, this is a moralistic statement, but it is not unreasonable to expect a teacher to modulate his social acts in regard to students so that he or she does not take advantage of position to exert excessive influence. During the days of protest that accompanied the Cambodian intervention in the late 1960s and early 1970s, a great many teachers were charged with exerting undue influence through their radical activity. A noted researcher at a famous Ivy League university was dismissed for exposing his students to mind-altering drugs. Today, teachers may function as advocates and influence the behavior of their students. The film, *Dead Poets Society*, depicts a teacher who harangues his students to "seize the day." In a sense, he was advocating rebellion, and the denouement of the film came with the suicide of one of the students he had influenced with his passion and his habitual flaunting of authority.

The line between a relationship and the influence of a mature professional with his or her students and the corruption of that relationship into charismatic control is a fine one. Often, the teacher does not know when the line has been crossed because it happens in the student's head. It is not overt. The obvious conclusion is that every teacher should be aware of their potential influence and consider carefully all relationships with students, including the formal relationship in the classroom and any social relationship that might result from their contact.

A president of a small woman's college once remarked that if she saw a male faculty member in a cafe drinking coffee with a student, she would be tempted to dismiss the faculty member at once. This may be a bit drastic in a multiversity, but the message is quite clear. There is a degree of circumspection required of a teacher. Younger teachers who might be less than half a decade older than their students need to show considerable caution about fraternization. There are two potential problems. One is the obvious temptation to fall into relationships that are irregular and dangerous. The other is the more subtle temptation to obtain a disciple by exerting undue influence on the student.

Teaching includes special relationships between faculty and students. There is an explicit assumption that teachers have some responsibility for helping to shape the entire academic life of their students and a tacit assumption that the contact between student and teacher is generally desirable. For this reason, most institutions require a certain amount of out-of-class contact that includes advising individuals and participation in student activities in an advisory manner. It is assumed that the student derives benefit from knowing the teacher as "a person."

It is not altogether clear that there is such an advantage. We have discussed above some of the perils of close contact, especially in the form of teachers taking advantage of their position to advocate for political or religious ideas. Although these issues sometimes can come into conflict with the principle of academic freedom, in general, such advantage should be avoided.

A more serious kind of contact comes in the form of fraternization and harassment. This issue became explicit and prominent during the Hill-Thomas hearings of 1991, but it had been lurking on the fringes of the academy for many years before. Every so often, the professional periodicals, for example, raise the question of sexual intercourse between teachers and their students. They consider it in the same terms as they regard doctor/patient or clinician/client intimacy. Without going into detail, we can offer the generalization that it is wise to avoid such contact.

This becomes very difficult, however, when dealing with graduate students. The relationship a professor has with his or her graduate student is intense and close. For a period of 3 to 10 years, they work side by side on a common project. They often seize the opportunity to cross the line from the teacher-student relationship to a collegial relationship. The distance from there to taking advantage is not great. Many of the relationships are quite successful, but in recent years female graduate students have become more and more vocal about their faculty advisors and directors pressing their relationship to achieve a sexual advantage. Graduate students seek "mentors" wherever they can find them. An influential professor can do a lot for a beginner, and beginners sometimes subvert their own cause by submitting to unreasonable requests (or demands).

The problem is not easy to resolve, and each professor must make his or her own decision about how far to go in relationships with graduate students. One of the authors of this book reports his own experiences as spanning the range from "fatal attraction" to easy collegiality. He currently works as an equal partner with more than a dozen former students. They have become very close. Others have drifted away with no rancor. But some relationships ended in flames, sometimes because of an inadvertent bridging of the gap, sometimes because of expected favors not done, and sometimes because of inadequate performance by the students.

In general, the risks of graduate instruction are very high. The situation is very different for those who teach in medical and law schools. Professional instruction is very formal; a rigid caste system prevails throughout, and although students are intellectually harassed and overworked, they rarely form attachments like those typical of the professor/graduate student relationship.

Consider, again, the concept of mentoring. Graduate students do not want mentors so much as they want protectors and patrons. They receive instruction as their right, not from a single person, but from a veritable battalion of senior professors. But among those senior professors, most graduate students identify one who could be "blocking back" for their touchdown run. This is the professor who they believe will write the letter that will get them that choice job.

It is mostly mythology. There may have been a time, half a century ago, when the word of a powerful professor would get another employed. These days, however, in an era of affirmative action, there are complex hiring rules in place at virtually all institutions of higher education. No one person has the authority to hire, and one intervention is not sufficient to guarantee employment. Gradually, the face of instruction in graduate school is changing. By the time those of you who are just beginning careers attain positions on the graduate faculty, the pattern may be completely different, and the kinds of stress so frequently encountered in graduate education today may be fading memories.

The topoi of the teaching relationship are various and complex. Whatever else is true of teaching in a college or university, the one universal generalization is that it is not easy. In addition to being sufficiently well informed to be regarded as an expert, the teacher in an institution of higher education is responsible for delivering the most challenging and complicated subject matter encountered anywhere in the curriculum. And it is not offered to excited children and inquiring minds. In the elementary school, students have a quality of eagerness and a respect for authority that encourages their teachers. In the secondary schools, some may be driving ahead, and others may be beyond help. College, however, carries the message that obtaining a degree means obtaining a ticket. The students who present themselves for instruction may, in some cases, be genuinely motivated by the challenge of learning. They may have aspirations and dreams that are entirely intellectual or aesthetic. But most of them have much more tangible goals. They want to get into professional schools, which means they want to learn enough to pass the examinations they need for admission, and they want the grades that will give them an acceptable transcript. They want letters of reference, and they want leisure time to explore relationships and engage in what was known in an earlier generation as "sowing their wild oats."

Furthermore, the subject matter they are offered cannot be neatly divided into categories like "readin', writin', n' rithmetic." College students learn cognition, affect, and behavior. Cognition refers to the acquisition of information, affect to attitudes about the topic of study, behavior to the performance of associated tasks. Chemistry students learn the "facts" about the rules to be followed in combining chemicals or the characteristics by which they can be identified. They take positions on various theories of the elements and on the relationship between organic and inorganic compounds. They also learn enough laboratory technique to qualify them as "chemists" with credentials sufficient to make them useful in industry.

Each discipline contains its combination of these three elements. In addition, there are subtleties, for college students are urged to conceptualize as much as possible; to find ways they can contribute to the advancement of knowledge. Further, in the performance disciplines they learn to recognize quality and how to emulate. College students are educated to become critical consumers of knowledge in general and to adjudicate the controversies in the disciplines in which they specialize. They learn appreciation of knowledge for its own sake, and they learn to carry over, to apply what they learn to the mundane problems of life and work. Problem solving is a vital goal of learning. In fact, it is what most students are seeking. They want to carry something away with them that they can use. Very few of them are willing to commit to the pursuit of learning for its own sake. Those who are usually become committed to careers in higher education.

Good teaching demands an understanding of the teacher's responsibility.
A teacher must have goals. These goals arise with the knowledge that a
teacher invariably changes the student in some ways. Bad teaching can
prejudice students against future learning. Good teaching can inspire
them. The point is, the teacher must have a good idea of what effect he or
she wishes to have on the students and must be able to justify that effect.

The justification must include:

1. What is taught is mandated by university policy.
2. What is taught is essential to an understanding of the subject
   matter.
3. What is taught is useful to the student either in his or her present academic career or in the future.

These are the bare minimum. To the extent that it is possible, what is
taught should be intrinsically interesting or made interesting by the
instructor. The bottom line is almost like the Hippocratic Oath. The
teacher must be very careful to avoid doing harm.

Harm can be done inadvertently. There is no way of predicting
individual sensitivities and proclivities in the classroom. The teacher, in a
sense, must slant teaching toward the middle, toward the least common
denominator. Sometimes teachers decide they wish to direct their efforts
to the best and the brightest or, on the other hand, work with those at the
bottom and attempt to improve them. That is a personal choice, and it
may have a lot to do with a career decision. However, in most cases, the
college instructor must handle the class to which he or she is assigned
and adapt instruction to the students in it.

This is best accomplished by setting careful goals relevant to the
modification of student behavior. How is the student to be changed?
There is no doubt that change will take place and so the following four
heuristics apply in every case:

1. How is the student to be changed?
2. How can the change be justified?
3. What teaching methods will best bring about the change?
4. How can you be assured that the methods will work?

The following review of teaching methods is abbreviated and far
from comprehensive. It is offered merely to suggest some of your options.
If competent teaching is part of your personal mission as well as a requirement for advancement in your profession, it will be useful to you to have
as much experience as possible with a variety of methods.

Instruction proceeds through many modalities. There are no limits to the techniques college instructors can use to reach their students. They range from formal teaching techniques confined to the classroom, to vicarious learning through activities and simulation, to general learning through field trips and study abroad programs. In fact, college instructors need considerable versatility because effective college teaching demands careful adaptation of teaching techniques to students' needs. Most college teachers, however, are given little or no formal training for their task. In their case, the doctrine of imitation applies. They tend to teach as they were taught.

Lecturing. The default method of instruction is lecturing. There is probably nothing so exhilarating as giving a good lecture and nothing quite so taxing as preparing it. How do you know when you have given a good lecture? The answer appears to be obvious—the students hang on every word. They laugh at the jokes. They ask questions. They hang around when you are done and try to engage you in conversation. They may not applaud, but you feel the same sense of approval as a nightclub comic on a good night.

This is not quite true. A lecture is a performance, but it is not a show. There is a purpose to lecturing that transcends the desire for self-display we all feel. The lecture is not supposed to be a showcase for the personality of the professor. The lecture was originally the only way a professor could get information to students. When there were no books, knowledge was transmitted orally. What is the purpose of a lecture today?

Currently, teachers have a variety of means of disseminating information. The book, for example, is a database that contains the means of instant retrieval. It is portable and inexpensive, and it requires no power source. Libraries are full of books, and most teachers have the facilities to make syllabuses that list required readings. Some professors have the unsavory reputation of repeating in their lectures what the students are required to read in books. However excited the teacher may become, this is unnecessary duplication.

In fact, the lecture is a very inefficient way of disseminating information. Speech is transitory. We tend to remember only about 5% of what we hear. Consequently, the information lectures transmit must be carefully focused. A good lecture uses stylized redundancy, that is, a variety of repetitions of a main point so that the students are continually pressured to consider the topic. The adept lecturer tries to motivate the students to focus on the main conclusions of the readings. The lecture is filled with illustrations, applications, definitions, and explanations of what the student has already covered in the text. Conversely, a lecture can be used to motivate curiosity. It can raise questions that can only be answered by a careful reading of the text.

This means that lectures must be carefully planned. That is why preparation is so arduous. First, the lecturer must discover the main point, the residual message, the single capsule of an idea that epitomizes the information he or she wants to cover. Then, the message must be cut so that it is sufficiently uncomplicated for the student to remember. The remainder of the time is devoted to answering redundant questions. Why should the student remember it? How will it be useful in the student's life? How will it help explain other, more complex, concepts about to be covered? Why is it intrinsically interesting to all human beings?

Each of these questions must be answered to motivate the student to listen to the details. What are some examples of the main point? What is the significance of these examples? How are conclusions drawn or discoveries made? What is the reasoning process underlying the main point? All of these explanations focus attention on the residual message. The text and ancillary readings provide the details.

But the teacher's responsibility in lecturing goes beyond that. It is fair, for example, to use the lecture to call students' attention to the issues that will be covered in examinations. There should be coordination between the lectures and the readings. There are some teachers, particularly in advanced courses, who announce that there will be no relationship between the lectures and the readings. They urge the students to make connections if they can. These teachers use their lectures to provoke and sometimes to advance knowledge by sharing their own experiences and those of contemporaries. The lecture is used as a means of sharing state-of-the-art information.

Whatever the purpose the teacher has in mind, lecturers must follow the principles of preparation of a good speech. A lecture is 50 to 75 minutes of talk. Human attention span may be as short as 5 minutes and it's rarely longer than 20 minutes. It is hard to conceive of any teacher in an institution of higher education who does not lecture frequently. The lecture usually is the main contact your students will have with you; thus, the ability to lecture well will have considerable impact on your career.

Discussion. The discussion or seminar method is frequently used as a teaching modality, mostly in upper level or low enrollment courses. Some subjects are not amenable to discussion, for example, those in the sciences. Laboratory methods are more appropriate for those courses.

Discussion is used for a variety of reasons. You may want to motivate the students into active involvement with the subject matter. This can be done by asking students to deal with questions that require them to apply what they have learned to practical problems in society or in their life. Discussion can also be used on a much simpler level, to enable students to think up and phrase important questions. Discussion is a fluid form of instruction. It can be attenuated into semester-long projects or compressed into brief skull sessions that provide variety during lecture periods.

One of the problems with discussion, however, is that it requires a certain ambiance. On the simplest level, students must be able to sit so they can face each other. The groups must be small enough so that participants talk to each other and are not required to give speeches. Questions must be carefully phrased so that the discussants know what their charge is. And, it helps if the students are trained in some simple discussion techniques.

Training in leadership is especially important. Often, when students are left to their own devices, the most talkative one becomes the leader, and the result may be a case of the partially sighted leading the blind. The teacher who uses discussion is well advised to provide a leadership guide of techniques and questions so that, at the minimum, the discussion leader follows a procedure sufficiently orderly to lead to a satisfactory outcome.

Phrasing the discussion questions is also important. The instructor may initiate discussion with a question, for example, "What else could President Nixon have done when. . . . ?" He or she may begin with a case: "Here is a digest of the community hearings on the environment bill. What testimony would you offer if you were called?" It can also center around a question of policy, fact, or evaluation. A question of policy would be any question the answer to which would result in a formal proposal. A question of evaluation would be an assessment of the merits of a work or program or the comparative rating of various ideas. A question of fact would require students to engage in collective activity designed to gather and organize information on some issue, for example, a survey of the press coverage of an important national or international event. Discussion can become the tail that wags the dog, but generally students are excited by it, and when well done, it can be a very effective way of applying subject matter in practical ways.

Discussion is one of the traditional components of the speech communication discipline. It is an object of study as well as a performance training category. The educational value of discussion cannot be gainsaid, but often discussion is misused as a time filler by unprepared instructors. Careful integration of discussion and lecture can provide an exciting learning experience for the students. One constant danger, of course, is that, in any discussion, there are those who monopolize the talk and those who do not speak at all. If students are given training in advance, these problems can be minimized. On the other hand, whether students should be graded on their actual participation in a discussion is questionable. Discussion should not be competitive or contentious, and when grades are at stake, students often compete with each other for the teacher's attention rather than concentrate on the issue at hand.

At the graduate level, the seminar often follows a discussion format. In the traditional seminar, the instructor parcels out topics and requires each student to give a report and preside over the ensuing discussion-and-question period. But discussion can also provide challenging experiences to graduate students, enabling them to make original applications of what they have learned.

Other Teaching Methods. There are a number of other teaching modalities that are worth investigating. The idea, of course, is not to use a method merely because "it is there." You select a teaching method to fit your teaching objectives. We have reviewed lecturing and discussion, which are the two most frequent methods. In addition, there are a great many laboratory experiences that can be devised for your students.

Laboratory experience means that the students actually perform some tasks. This is obvious in chemistry or physics courses. In humanities, social science, and communication studies, laboratory experience can include practical assignments, the performance of speeches, and various simulations. Even term projects and papers can be construed as a laboratory experience, particularly if they are aimed at some specific point and accompanied by effective criticism. None of these experiences should be assigned merely to occupy student time. Each should have some legitimate educational objective, and the teacher should have considerable understanding of the kind of response that he or she is soliciting.

Criticism is always associated with student performance. It is a very volatile kind of learning experience, for the bottom line of criticism is the notion that the teacher is qualified to tell the students what they have done wrong and, more importantly, is able to suggest ways for the student to do it right. In no case should criticism be offered unless the teacher has some suggestion for improvement. Criticism without constructive suggestions for improvement is nothing more than carping, and it can be very destructive to the students. Criticism is sufficiently important to your own career, as well as the life of your students, that we include a separate chapter on it later in this book.

One final suggestion: The teacher should explore the proliferating classroom technology now available. Visual aids, film, television, computerized instruction, asynchronous computerized communication, hypercard, and hypertext are all available. They are complicated, and there is no documented evidence that they are superior to traditional methods of teaching. On the other hand, you may have teaching goals for which they are ideally suited. Your experience with them will help you decide whether they can be applied in your classroom.

Testing is a necessary evil. This book, fortunately, is not meant to be a compendium of pedagogy. But we cannot deal with the topic of teaching without introducing the issue of evaluation. It is one of the requirements. You will be expected to submit grades, and often you will be expected to criticize performance. This is especially true in the communication disciplines in which courses range from the highly theoretical to the applied.

Test construction is a complicated and demanding process. It depends to a large extent on your goals and the understanding you have with your students about the course requirements. If your syllabus is explicit enough, it will contain advisories for students about what you expect them to accomplish in the course. Your testing should remain within the constraints of your requirements. The tests should, in some way, evaluate whether you accomplished your goals, as well as whether your students did.

There are two simple choices to make about testing: when and what. The answers depend on the nature of your subject matter and how much time you want to invest in these measurements. It is possible to test diagnostically without making the results a major part of the grade. It is also possible to make a test into a learning experience. Choosing between multiple choice and essay exams is choosing between a rock and a hard place. Multiple choice tests are easy to grade, but extraordinarily hard to construct, if done properly. Those of you who have studied tests and measurements in your statistics courses understand that you cannot just dash off a few questions. Furthermore, you know that a test must be piloted and analyzed before its results can be taken seriously. And, once you build a good test, it is only a question of time until it becomes public domain. Some students cheat, and to the extent you make it possible for them, you make the situation unfair for the students who do not.

The essay test is a simple matter to construct. You merely need to ask the questions you think the students should be able to answer. On the other hand, it takes a great deal of time to set the criteria for a good answer. What should the student be able to say? What distinguishes between a good answer and an acceptable minimum? These are not easy questions, and essay exams, with a few notable exceptions, have acquired a deservedly bad rap for being notoriously unreliable. There is very little agreement even among experts on what constitutes a good answer.

There are esoteric forms of testing also available. In communication performance classes, you will need to find ways to focus on aspects of performance that can be legitimately graded. For example, there is the recurrent argument in public speaking (and English composition) about the extent to which choice of subject should affect the grade. Do you grade someone down if his or her opinion disagrees with yours? Is it even possible to give a fair grade on use of argument when the student takes a position with which you disagree? What do you do about the talented student who is a good performer without instruction and the inept performer who improves considerably as a result of instruction but who is still inept? The way you deal with these complexities materially affects the way you are viewed as a teacher.

Some cautions and drawbacks about teaching to which we must call your attention. First and foremost, good teaching is very time-consuming. It does not require much to make a pro forma appearance in front of a class on a regular basis and fumble through for the 50 scheduled minutes. You might even get a round of applause if you dismiss the class early from time to time. On the other hand, perfunctory teaching will not advance your career.

Decisions about teaching will not be easy to make. You will have conflicts. For one thing, those of you who elect to teach in a research university will also be required to maintain a research agenda. You will hear the admonition, "publish or perish," and you will take it seriously. The time you spend on your syllabuses and lesson plans takes time away from research, and the time you spend with students will keep you away from your word processor. You will have to adjudicate carefully how much time to devote to your teaching activities. It will be easy to give teaching short shrift. A great many faculty members believe that by playing for popularity with the students, their teaching credentials will be protected. This is easy to do by learning stand-up comedy and easy grading. But in a day of peer evaluation and increasing exercise of caveat emptor by the students, popularity is not so easy to achieve.

Those of you who choose careers at institutions that are more student-centered will have the problem of maintaining enough rigor in your classes to satisfy the demands of your subject matter, and possibly your own conscience. In a school in which good teaching is emphasized, it is easy to dedicate yourself to one group, perhaps the gifted or the disadvantaged, and to ignore the others. Such commitments are sometimes honorably made. It is as much possible to specialize in teaching as in research. On the other hand, and this is especially true in state-funded institutions, the offspring of the taxpayers are all entitled to a fair shake, and if they do not seem to demand it, their parents will.

Another major issue is balancing time between student needs and wants. Some students are capable of getting through school quite comfortably, doing their work, learning what they can, and leaving their teachers pretty much alone. This characterizes the vast majority. Furthermore, every student, at one time or another, may have an emergency that calls for immediate attention from a teacher. A death in the family, personal illness, financial crises, and even shattered relationships can seriously disrupt a student's career, and at those times, a sympathetic ear from a teacher can be very helpful.

The question is, however: What is to be done with or for the student who craves attention? There are a few who seek the teachers' attention in order to "polish the apple." The are others who try to form attachments for psychological reasons, and still others who seek mentors or sponsors. Some will even seek attention because they are very interested in the subject matter or the field. There will be a few who crave attention for its own sake, and a small number who want a sexual liaison or some other form of pathological association. The question is how to distinguish among these types.

There are two governing principles by which you can be advised. First, by limiting the time you are available, or limiting what you are available for, you can keep matters under control. If you maintain regular office hours and confine them to class-related business, you will take a giant step toward controlling the flow. If a student appears to crave excessive attention, it can always be limited on the grounds that there is another student waiting for your time. Emergencies are always clearly labeled.

The second principle is to make it clear that office hours are confined to academic business. A few students may want to chat about anything from their personal angst to the outcome of the Super Bowl. The conversations can be kept to 15-second exchanges, and when it becomes clear that there is no academic business pending, the teacher can cut off the contact. In this regard, it is sometimes useful to have an officemate. When someone else is present, students cannot take advantage by introducing excessively personal topics. If this is not possible, the simple technique of never closing the door when meeting with a student is a wise procedure.

The preceding two paragraphs sound a bit like busy-bodying. After all, as a professor you are a grown-up adult professional, and college students are not quite that immature—are they? The fact is that all of us are flattered by attention. Students want it, and sometimes they will interpret perfectly ordinary teaching techniques as overtures to friendship. And faculty members are not immune to the "con." Most students know how to do a little harmless buttering up. But there is a great difference between the student who calls out "nice lecture, doc" over his or her shoulder as he or she leaves to the same student showing up at your office every day for weeks on end. To maintain your own personal integrity, you will need to think carefully about where to draw the line.

One thing is certain and that is that all students are entitled to a fair share of academic attention and no more. It is as unfair for them to make excessive demands on the teacher as it was in grade school for the teacher to have "pets." The possibilities of pathological relationships are greater in college than in grade school. Older students can be hungry for attention and in great need of affection, and they can be very appealing. In our chapter on professionalism, we deal with some of these issues extensively.

Evaluation of teaching is an uncertain enterprise. One way or another, your teaching will be evaluated. The most obvious way of identifying an incompetent teacher is when students do not sign up for his or her class. Word gets around. On the other hand, many of your classes will be required; students will have little or no choice. They may not vote with their feet, but they can register complaints. When you are unfair or dull or fail to deal with individual differences and personal concerns, students are free to go to your superiors. These complaints can mount up, and if they do, you may be in trouble.

It is very difficult to evaluate teaching. It is a common practice in many institutions to have students evaluate their teachers. The administration may prepare elaborate questionnaires to which students respond. The questions may be specific: "Does the teacher come on time to class?" or "Does the teacher keep regular office hours?" The questions may be somewhat ambiguous: "Does the teacher answer your questions accurately and completely?" And there may be questions to which students cannot possibly give fair answers: "Does the teacher come prepared to class?" The problem is, however, that the students do not know the benchmarks of quality teaching and what eventually is evaluated is instructor acceptability.

Peer review is also used, but it is difficult to maintain criteria as well as to remove political considerations from the process. Many schools provide for a peer evaluation system. You may invite colleagues to come and observe your class and write critiques for your record. The problem is that personal considerations sometimes overpower observation. Furthermore, it is hard to make a good evaluation on a small sample. Visiting one class, especially one for which you are prepared, hardly gives a fair view of your teaching ability. Having a tough evaluator on a bad day may forever blight your career. Of course, reviewing your syllabus and lesson plans and explaining where the one class fits in the overall scheme may be helpful, but no matter how you slice it, it is risky.

In the final crunch, the best way to evaluate teaching may be to look at the record of your students after they leave your class. How do they stand in the next class? Are they motivated to take more courses in your area? This kind of evaluation must be accumulated over time. More to the point, however, is to ask students what they recall about your course a year or two after they take it. If students can ask for reference letters from teachers, it seems reasonable that teachers could use reference letters drawn from a random sample of students to give some kind of picture of their teaching ability.

What students expect from their teachers is very important in the evaluation process. It is a hallmark of good teaching to attempt to ascertain student expectations and take them into account. This does not mean the teacher has to pander to student demands any more than students have to accept the teacher's prejudices. On the other hand, knowing the audience and learning how to adapt tends to create a mutually considerate atmosphere in which you can do your best job.

TEACHING COMMUNICATION

The communication disciplines have passed through considerable history in the last 50 years. In the final chapter of this book, we discuss the nature of the discipline and the special problems it presents to those who choose to make careers in it. Briefly, however, we would note here that oral communication is a central issue in human experience. It holds a peculiar and tenuous place in the canon. Everyone expects students to be able to do it, but it is not universally taught, and often, it is approached as a cognitive issue rather than as one of performance.

There is no question about the fact that virtually every social science and humanities subject has communication as a component. Sociologists study the way people interact; psychologists speculate on why they interact. The special mission of speech communication is the consideration of *how* people interact and especially *how* interaction can be improved. The disciplines of dramatic arts and communication disorders are spin-offs from the antique discipline of speech. They are preoccupied with the nature and practice of performance. The residual in the speech communication discipline is performance on the public platform and in small groups. But even with the decline of performance courses in colleges and universities, performance is becoming a major issue in schools of business. Even science and engineering disciplines show concern about their students' presentational skills.

Historically speaking, the earliest recorded schools had oratory as their main subject. The trivium consisted of rhetoric, grammar, and logic, all of which have combined in contemporary times to form the discipline of speech communication. Cicero and Quintilian wrote of "the good man (sic) who speaks well." The idea of the good man was drawn from the Aristotelian notion of the democratic quality of public speech, and the idea that truth and justice would win out over their opposites if given an equal hearing. The performance component of speech has as its mission equalizing the voices of human beings. In a sense, acquiring skill at oral communication is an empowerment. One displays his or her qualities as a human and a professional by the way he or she speaks. Others cannot know of our qualities until we display them. The errors we make in spoken discourse haunt both our professional and personal lives.

The argument on behalf of teaching speech performance skills can be summed up under three headings. First, a democratic society cannot be maintained without free speech and without an informed and skilled electorate. The subject is not taught in totalitarian states, nor is public discourse honored by dictators. The study of the performance of the spoken word has been centered in the western democracies, and it remains intrinsic to their survival. By teaching everyone speech skills, everyone has an opportunity to influence a democratic future.

The second argument is that human socialization in its most basic forms is carried on through oral discourse. The intimate dyad, the family, and friendship are all fueled by talk. Marriage counselors speak incessantly of the importance of communication. Their wise words are indicators of the vitality of speech skills in sustaining relationships and warding off the pangs of loneliness.

The third argument on behalf of teaching speech performance is very simply that *most people are inept at it*. We learn to speak as we are spoken to. We have already pointed out that speech is not emphasized in grade school, and furthermore, a great many colleges and universities offer no formal training. Yet, it is not possible to socialize without encountering disorganization, hesitation, monotony, and egocentrism in the discourse of others. There are few, if any of us, who can be classified as effective speakers. Virtually all of us could benefit from formal training.

What should be the most important objectives of the speech communication teacher? Training people to do mandated social tasks well so they can assume their appropriate place in their society and contribute and work to obtain their needs. This means teaching how to live in and share the world with strangers. We all need to know how to make requests and give simple instructions. On a more complicated level, we must understand how to negotiate and bargain with others. This is the fundamental unit of living together. In order to run our institutions, we must be able to participate in face-to-face discussion to solve the problems that affect us all and to consider our mutual and individual interests. Finally, we must be able to advocate for our rights and our causes at law and government. Work survives through oral communication from clear instructions to complex solutions. Workers talk to each other. Friends talk to each other. Fellow citizens must talk to each other. Speech is an art, but it is also a skill that can be taught and learned. The study of how to accomplish this is fundamental to the discipline of speech communication. Training in how to do it is the special contribution the discipline makes to the canon of human knowledge.

In recent years, the communication disciplines have put a rather heavy emphasis on theory. Rhetorical theorists attempt to explain the uses of spoken texts and how they are constructed. Communication theorists examine the nature of the influence exerted by communication in normal activities. They are not far from each other in their concerns, although rhetoricians tend to use narrative and critical methods, whereas communication scholars tend toward behaviorist and quantitative approaches to research. Underlying their quest is the notion that the art can be improved by studying the way it is performed. This is the same premise that drives sociology and social psychology and the spoken rationale for the study of literature. Many an English teacher has declared that students learn to write by reading the great literature of the past.

We cannot resolve this issue here, and we do not intend to try. We wish to make it clear that the issue exists throughout the humanities and liberal arts. There is a dialectical tug of war between those that study about and those who study how; the theoretical versus the applied. You will have to take your own position on these issues, not once, but often during your career. The idea of being a professor is to "profess," to take a stand and defend it. It is important to be in tune with the fundamental issues in your professional discipline and to take the time to consider your own stand and cater to your own interests. When we introduce the subject of research we explain how important your personal commitment is in driving your study; the critical nature of personal curiosity in investigation.

On the other hand, when you serve in an academic department, you are often obligated to teach what must be taught. You may not have the luxury of teaching only in your main area of interest. There are required courses to be served, the requirements of the major to be offered, and professionals often must make major adjustments in their commitments in order to fulfill their institutional obligations.

Training teachers of communication is a challenge to the profession. A haphazard approach, like the one the profession has been taking for the past 50 years, may no longer work in the future. We have explained how the existence of a democratic society depends on the speech abilities of its citizens. Part of the problem that seems to plague the discipline is the lack of sensitivity its practitioners have to the centrality of their discipline. We have backed away from the responsibility of teaching performance skills because it has been challenged and demeaned by colleagues in other disciplines. By the same token, we turn to those other disciplines for our inspiration and for basic knowledge in our theoretical investigations and experiments. It is an interesting paradox. But, by reexamining the origins of the profession in classical times, it is possible to construct a mission statement for communication teachers. It is a bill of particulars for their education. Whether we can meet the obligation we have shouldered is an unanswerable question. But we cannot give up trying. It is a mission somewhat like the ephemeral pursuit of truth. Much of our instruction now is routine and ineffective because we do not teach performance and overemphasize theory detached from practice. It is important to note that the preceding is probably a minority opinion. Be on the alert for counterarguments, for it is important that you take your stand where your beliefs truly lead you!

We offer the following note on the training of communication teachers. First and foremost, teachers of communication, whatever their specialized commitment, obligate themselves to the historical tradition of continuing the connection of discourse and human freedom. However dramatic it may seem, the defense of individual rights is mainly in the hands of those who are able to teach others how to defend them. Both individual freedom in human relations and the rights of citizens are inextricably bound up with ability at discourse. We defend ourselves and our causes with words. Those opposed to human freedom use "inartistic" means to advance their ideas. They use brute force, intimidation, bribery, and ritualistic oaths to gain compliance. Aristotle made the distinction between these kinds of persuasions and those done with words more than 2,000 years ago.

As the old saying goes, "the rest is commentary." Communication scholars must understand how the human mind conceives the ideas for discourse and prepares them for delivery. How are ideas composed into extended thoughts? How are they constructed into sentences and phrases? These questions subsume issues of exigency (the need that must be addressed) and stasis (the essence of the issue). By considering these two ideas, scholars are led to the rudiments of analysis of themselves as speakers, their audiences and what can be accomplished with them, and above all, the interactive process, how people respond to one another and how they understand and adapt to those responses.

We must also learn how to select goals and objectives for discourse and how to direct those goals to oneself rather than project them on others. The targeting of the proper audience and an understanding of what is reasonable to expect for yourself and others are fundamentals of this process. The process of composition is exceedingly complex and requires a synthesis of physics, physiology, psychology, sociology, linguistics, literary criticism, and the gamut of research methodologies.

The techniques of composition are not easy to understand and acquire. It is one thing to think up a goal and another to have some idea about what to say in order to reach it. The actual techniques of phrasing those ideas in words and connecting them into extended discourse are demanding. They require analysis, experience, and guidance under the tutelage of a sensitive and trained teacher. This is the ultimate mission of the communication teacher. Add to this the artistic components of oral communication and the process of performance, and you discover that the teacher in the communication disciplines carries the burden of synthesis of many of the social sciences and humanities. As Cicero once characterized the orator as a man (sic) who "knows all about everything," the contemporary teacher of speech communication is the synthesizer of the liberal arts.

Contemporary technology has facilitated the process of both learning about and learning how. Massive computers help in the study and analysis of the process of communication. Equally, they help students learn to do it better. The admonition is clear: What is learned about communication must be connected, somehow, to learning the techniques of communication.

After all these years it is difficult to explain the noetic process that shapes a philosophy of teaching. Scholars were once preoccupied with it, but it now has retreated into a subtle background for traditional teaching patterns, often entirely free of theory. It is not hard, however, to discover a unifying force into these teaching technologies. There is a theory, and it has been with us for centuries.

First and foremost, learning is imitative and experiential. Experience can be through trial and error or conditioning. It is so in all animals, and humans are animals. Because we are symbolic animals we can add vicarious experience, admonition, and detailed instruction in situations of simulation. This provides the teacher with his or her repertoire of behavior.

A cat learns to groom itself, to stalk its prey, to nourish itself, and to copulate. There are observations of older cats teaching younger cats to mount and thrust. Of course, every cat has to experience it for himself, and variation in partners makes life exciting. Humans can read Henry Miller or elementary school primers, as well as watch XXX-rated films. But no matter how, they must learn the skills of living in the world. If they revert to total animal behavior, then they will wipe each other out. In that sense, those who manage the spoken word are custodians of civilization.

This is not a facetious presentation. Learning to speak well is not a trivial enterprise. In fact, given the state of weakness in which the organism exists, it is imperative in the life of the human. Eating and keeping warm are instinctual. Savoir faire at a cocktail party comes about through learning. So does survival in the workplace and in the family. Even the Weltanschauung must submit itself to discourse. What we think is not real, or meaningful or influential, unless and until it is uttered coherently and with purpose.

We talk of acculturation. Acculturation is nothing more than informal, noninstitutionalized learning. We learn family, neighborhood, ethnicity, and commonplaces of etiquette through acculturation. More importantly, we learn the fundamentals of language: when to speak, how to speak, what words to use, how to address others, and how to evaluate response in a most informal way. The notion that language is an "innate" potential is borne out by the fact that we can all learn to do it in "sort of the same way." We make a big to-do about intercultural differences, but by and large, although the words may differ, the forms remain the same. People in other lands must cope with the same situations we do. They exist in families, there are hierarchies of others who must be considered in social living, and they have forms of etiquette although customs may differ.

We appear to be motivated by more-or-less planned discourse or by discourse-free blandishments such as "here's your paycheck, do your work," or "your money or your life." (Subtext: students, e.g., are often motivated by "it will be on the test.")

Segue, artificial, artifice, manipulation—these words have negative connotations. Unfortunately, they are the fundamental words in formal education. What a person does not learn by imitation and the random instruction of the local culture, or through the acquisition of data about threat and reward, he or she learns from formalized procedures, usually administered by "artificial" institutions, such as schools.

The question that applies most directly to the schools (as a simulation) is how much does one learn about *doing* from learning about the thing to be done? How much does one have to *know about* something in order to do a satisfactory job of doing it? The old Greeks and Romans seemed to worry about this a lot. They became involved in learning about the art of oratory, but they also knew how to do it. Somehow, today, there seems to be little or no articulation between theory and practice. In fact, theory seems to explain practice, but practice does not seem to grow out of theory. Aristotle did not dream up a theory about successful oratory and then generate a teaching methodology from it. Nor for that matter did the cosmologists dream up a theory of the heavens. They saw the heavens and tried to explain what they saw and then concluded that if they explained what they saw satisfactorily, they should be able to generate some kind of technology enabling them either to predict new things or find things they did not see. The chemists discovered how chemicals combined, which led to a theory that enabled them to combine elements. So there is an answer to the chicken-egg riddle.

Observation comes first. It can be gross or it can be refined, but we see something or experience something and then try to explain it. We may not go further in our explanation, or we may generate a technology. In communication, we discover that our theory explains what happens when people communicate, but we must acquire our technology elsewhere. What we want to do is find successful movers (however we describe "success") and then try to explain how to get other people to behave that way. There appears to be no other way to get people to learn *how to perform* as opposed to learning about how people perform.

So, we are behavior modificationists in the final crunch. We modify our professional behavior to meet what is demanded of us by the institution for which we work. We adjust our behavior to the demands of family and friends. We control our behavior in order to live in society. And we teach others to do the same. Teachers are, at their best, masters of behavior; at worst, they control it.

The important thing is that teaching is not ancillary to your profession. Even if you are employed at the most effete research institution, you will be a teacher to your colleagues, your assistants, and to the students who come your way. Not only is there no way to escape the task, it is the *raison d'être* for the institutions you serve, and it must be the central thrust of your professional life.

◆ RESPONSE TO CHAPTER SEVEN
DENNIS S. GOURAN

As there is little, if anything, with which I disagree in Professor Phillips's discussion of teaching, my comments on his chapter will be relatively brief and confined to reinforcing two of his major points: (a) teaching well is demanding both for teachers and students, and (b) the role requires a high degree of professionalism.

To the extent that teaching is an art, it probably functions best when the craft involved goes unnoticed. An effective teacher is one whose students achieve determinable learning objectives as a result of instructor interventions that engage requisite abilities and knowledge. One of the unfortunate models on which both teachers and students rely in an educational environment has the former transferring knowledge and skills to the latter. As convenient as this model appears, there is little evidence that any person can transfer what he or she knows and is able to do to any other person.

What one can do is to arrange the conditions for learning in such a way as to increase the likelihood that students can draw upon such knowledge and abilities as they possess to further their understanding; to cultivate their capacities for the processing, interpretation, integration, and evaluation of new information; and to apply these gains to the situations they encounter in their own lives. Professor Phillips, in my opinion, does an excellent job of capturing this notion as well as dealing with some of the more concrete and practical matters of preparation, performance, and assessment of student progress.

An essential task for any teacher, if his or her interventions are to be successful, is determining the probable skill and knowledge level of his or her students. Some of us overestimate it; others seriously underestimate it. At present, underestimation is probably the greater of the two errors in judgment. I cannot prove this, but the frequently reported declines in standardized test scores, knowledge of science and history, reading levels of college students, and the like do not appear to be of any natural origin, but rather the result of a diminution in expectations and instructional delivery systems that require very little of students. The aphorism "no pain, no gain" appears to be apt in late 20th-century education in the United States.

Please understand that I am not arguing that education should be a painful experience. Neither am I unaware of the variety of sociological and economic factors that undoubtedly have played a role in the decline of student performance. My point is that one cannot develop to a great extent without sufficient opportunity, challenge, and activity that requires effort. If we write textbooks at the sixth-grade level for college students, the most reasonable expectation one can have is that they will function intellectually at that level. If we merely repeat what our students already know or require of them only what they are currently able to do, how can we legitimately expect them to become more knowledgeable or more skillful?

I am always distressed by the number of students who appear content to leave an institution knowing or being able to do little more than they knew or were able to do when they entered. I once heard a student following commencement proudly proclaim in front of the university library, "I made it, and I never stepped in that building once." Even at the graduate level, I find students quite willing to exchange the same ideas and information over and over as if in each recounting of what they already know they have learned something new. Unfortunately, we as teachers are often guilty of contributing to such a state of affairs, and we need more conscientiously to execute our responsibilities for creating learning conditions that promote development, not perpetuation of the status quo or regression.

The second point I wish to emphasize relates to my colleague's views concerning professional distance. I agree with virtually everything he has to say on this matter but would add a further consideration. Assessment is a complicated process, and one succeeds only in complicating it more by becoming personally involved with those one must evaluate. This is not to suggest that one must be aloof or refrain from normal human contact with students, but merely to acknowledge that effective evaluation requires reasonable detachment. When likes and dislikes begin to intrude on the process, the likelihood of providing feedback that accurately conveys to students their standing on the particular attributes one has to judge is diminished. To mislead students as to their demonstrated level of knowledge and skill, it seems to me, is a serious disservice and professionally irresponsible. Providing misleading evaluations is always a risk, but is less probable when one has refrained from intrusion in students' personal lives.

◆ RESPONSE TO CHAPTER SEVEN
JULIA T. WOOD

For this chapter I have little response other than applause, I believe Professor Phillips has offered a most insightful and even-handed discussion of teaching as an art and a serious professional responsibility. By and large I agree with the views he expresses, which is not a surprise because I benefited from his enactment of these beliefs when I was a student of his some years ago. Because my views of teaching are so generally harmonious with those of Professor Phillips, my response focuses on suggesting how his ideas pertain to two important pedagogical issues for women and minority faculty. These issues may have been less salient and visible from Professor Phillips's standpoint than they are from my own.

In my earlier chapter I discussed in some detail the special opportunities and problems inherent in teaching material that lies outside of the traditional curriculum. Here I merely wish to reiterate my point that women and minority faculty often wish to teach about issues pertinent to women and minorities, just as men of culturally dominant races have always taught issues pertinent to their identities and experiences. Whether nontraditional teaching is supported, tolerated, or frowned on varies among departments and institutions. It is prudent to assess the climate of your campus and the attitudes of your colleagues before deciding to teach outside of the standard curriculum. In advising caution I do not mean to suggest anyone should forego teaching courses that lie outside of convention; I simply suggest that anyone who does so should be informed about the probable reception and consequences of that course of action before embarking on it.

I would also note that Professor Phillips's sage counsel on maintaining some distances from students is especially relevant to women and minority faculty. For understandable reasons, there are atypical pressures for nontraditional faculty to build close relationships with their students. Sharing a history of being marginalized induces cohesiveness as does the wish to assist younger people who have been disadvantaged by cultural hierarchies. Yet, overly close relationships with students tend to be no more constructive for nontraditional than for traditional faculty. Too much fondness, identification, and personal investment endanger honest perception, feedback, and judgment, and that is detrimental to students in the long run. It is also detrimental to faculty because heavily identified students are usually unable to provide them with honest feedback and a critical perspective on their teaching and advising. In short, excessive closeness between women and minority faculty and students tends to undermine the professional and personal responsibilities of all involved.

Too close an association between nontraditional faculty and students also invites another problem which, for lack of a better name, I will call "cloning." It is easy for a minority or woman student to identify with and attach to a faculty member like him or her. What may follow is an effort to emulate the faculty member, to be just like him or her. The old adage that "imitation is the sincerest form of flattery" is decidedly inapplicable here. A student dedicated to being just like her or his mentor is crippled from developing unique strengths and style, which ideally would incorporate, but not duplicate, those of a mentor. One way to minimize the danger of cloning is to advise students to take courses and seek conferences with a variety of minority and women faculty. This discourages them from adopting a single model and invites them to recognize and learn from a range of ways that nontraditional academics enact professionalism. Through exposure to and interaction with diverse women and minorities, students are empowered to build their own personal and professional images by incorporating and modifying lessons from multiple models and mentors.

◆ RESPONSE TO CHAPTER SEVEN
SCOTT A. KUEHN

In my view, my colleague's description of teaching is elegant. I can do nothing more than provide a few experiences of a beginning academic that may give added perspective to Professor Phillips's discussion.

One's first job often provides the first real experience of working as a teacher, even beyond the valuable experience of being a teaching assistant. For me, I learned that a teacher can exude very subtle influence in unanticipated ways. I discovered this as I was teaching communication law. I was covering first amendment issues as they pertained to seditious libel and prior restraint. After presenting a lecture-discussion, I was fielding questions. Questions began to pop up about how the first amendment would be left without protection from the emerging Rehnquist court. The point of the lecture was to show how freedom of speech and the press has historically been balanced by concerns for national welfare. However, students seemed to become alarmed from my own views of the positions of conservative members of the court.

Later, I noticed many students who had attended other courses I had taught seemingly adopted much the same value system I used to talk about the power of the media, and they brought these positions into our discussion of the Rehnquist court. I got the strange feeling that I was holding a session glorifying many of my own views. As the students became emotionally charged on these issues I backed away and played devil's advocate. But that did little to promote other points of view.

As I read Professor Phillips's description of teaching I remembered this instance and tried to determine what I had done to produce this effect. I believe that many subtle evaluative comments and nonverbal behaviors from different courses were used by the students to form some sort of value system. Because many students had no value system to evaluate many of these topics, they accepted mine.

Today I try to encourage critical thinking on important issues. I believe now that it is not enough to identify a position as one's own, unless some sort of fair treatment is given to opposing views. A hard lesson for me to learn was that teaching is as much a process of creating openness to other views as it is "learning the facts, and my interpretation of the facts."

8

RESEARCH AND PUBLICATION

Dennis S. Gouran

The subjects of research and publication, in one way or another, have entered into the discussion in several other chapters in this volume, including those focusing on the nature of the profession, issues all professionals face, promotion and tenure, criticism, and professionalism. In those instances in which these two topics have surfaced, however, they have not been the primary foci of concern. Instead, they have been treated as matters related to larger issues my colleagues have introduced.

The purpose of this chapter is to explore considerations in research and publication that bear on how successfully one engages in these activities and that may help the reader to keep them in proper perspective.

AN IMPORTANT DISTINCTION

During the 25 plus years I have been a member of a university faculty, I have become increasingly sensitive to an unfortunate equation that many people draw between research and publication. In the case of the general public, undergraduate students, and even some higher level administrators, who may not have engaged in either activity in any substantial way, if at all, the confusion is understandable. At least, it is excusable. It is less understandable that graduate students and professors are so frequently guilty of perpetuating the semantic interchangeability of these two very important aspects of academic life.

183

Research, although having many different referents in common parlance, in a strict sense involves the systematic acquisition, analysis, and synthesis of information that enables one to provide answers to questions having presumably demonstrable import for understanding the matters to which they are addressed. Developing the materials may entail generating information that presently does not exist or examining extant material for that portion that is most pertinent to the question or questions to which the data gatherer's inquiry is directed. Whatever the source, once one has accumulated a body of data sufficient to provide a meaningful resolution of the issue or issues to which it applies, he or she must process it in ways that are judged acceptable, or at least defensible, within the larger, relevant professional community that has determined the norms of admissibility.[1]

Research may lead to publication, and often does, but there is nothing in the set of activities subsumed by the term requiring that research eventuate in publication. Despite putdowns one frequently hears in academic circles, such as "If it isn't published, then it isn't research," the fact remains that research and publication are independent concepts.

Just as research consists of a set of activities one performs in some reasonably organized sequence, so too does publication. The activities and outcomes of the processes they represent are different, however. Whereas the culmination of research, properly conducted, is the production of defensible answers to previously unresolved questions, the process of publication results in the appearance of documents that some entity (person or organization) authorized to print such documents finds acceptable.[2]

The process usually begins with a decision or request to prepare a manuscript for submission to a source empowered to disseminate some version of the contents as a form of intellectual property, for which the source is willing to serve as an official sponsor and distributor. The acquisition of such imprimaturs is occasionally relatively unfettered. More often, however, one encounters numerous obstacles. Depending on the

---

[1]Some issues, of course, are not resolved in the sense of one's discovering unequivocal or definitive answers to questions. The absence of such answers, however, does not disqualify the activities described as research. No answer can be an answer. Research leading to such an outcome, moreover, frequently serves as a stimulus for subsequent inquiry.

[2]The "documents" to which I have referred are usually printed works of written discourse, but publication can take other forms, for instance, works in electronic media, such as film, videotape, and audiotape. With the expansion of research as an evaluative category of professional performance to include so-called "creative-activity" (see Tucker, 1984), the media appropriate to publication have also expanded. Musical scores, documentaries, instructional tapes, and the like all constitute "publications." Since extended written discourse remains the principal type of publication in academic life, I have restricted my discussion to it. The considerations involved in other forms of publication are essentially the same, however, and differ primarily in respect to preparation.

quality of the work one submits and the prospective sponsor's interests and integrity, as well as the qualifications of those whose assistance the publisher enlists, one can even find the path impassable.

The somewhat, but necessarily abstract quality of the preceding discussion of research and publication notwithstanding, I hope that it makes clear at least two fundamental points. First, the two sets of activities to which the terms *research* and *publication* refer are not the same. Second, not all research is publishable, let alone published, nor is everything that is published to be regarded as a report of research.

Unfortunately, even scholars of long and considerable standing speak of "my research" when, in fact, they mean their publications, only a portion of which may have anything to do with their, or anyone else's, research. Although one may undertake research with a view toward publishing manuscripts based on it, there is nothing about the activities involved as such that demands publication. Neither is there anything inherent in the process of publication requiring that the product be an outgrowth of one's research. Having drawn what I hope is a meaningful distinction between research and publication, I now turn to less esoteric aspects of the related processes involved.

CONSIDERATIONS IN DOING RESEARCH

Because the target audience for this volume is the beginning college or university professor and the graduate student preparing for entry into the profession, for purposes of this chapter, I have assumed that readers are reasonably well versed in methods of inquiry appropriate to their scholarly interests and, hence, refrain from offering advice concerning how to conduct research. Instead, I explore some considerations relating to the set of activities, or process, we call research that, in part, determine the manner in which one executes it and the success one may experience. The specific considerations include: (a) motivations, (b) attitudes, (c) resources, (d) qualifications, (e) focus, and (f) execution.

Motivations

Because research aims at the production of claims that presumably advance knowledge and/or understanding in particular domains of intellectual curiosity and pragmatic need, the motives underlying the activities one performs can have an important bearing on the process. What an individual achieves in research can make or break a professional career. It can bring fame or infamy. It can be a source of considerable personal satisfaction or disappointment. It can be a normal part of one's professional life or an obsession. Most importantly, perhaps, it can sharpen our knowledge or seriously misinform us about matters in which we have interest. For all of these reasons, it is of some value to understand what drives the process.

I should point out here that whatever one's motivation, the quality of one's research depends heavily on other factors. In fact, in principle, the quality of research should be independent of the researcher's motivations. In practice, however, motives affect the ways in which one views the task and, therefore, how one goes about performing it. There is virtue, then, in examining the motive/research relationship.

In the years I have been in higher education, it has been a continuing source of consternation to discover how many graduate students and members of the professorate who aspire to positions in research universities have little or no interest in research—or, at least, in doing it. According to Bowen and Schuster (1986), faculty members in public research universities report spending 22% of their time doing research on the average (p. 15), but because many devote considerably more time than this to research, it follows that substantial numbers do little or no research. For all types of institutions, moreover, nearly 70% of the faculty have never published anything (Bowen & Schuster, 1986, p. 18), which would indicate at best very limited involvement in research in many cases.

To these individuals, research is an unpleasant price one has to pay to have the sorts of professional associations one seeks or somehow feels are necessary. Although such professionals often have the capability to do research, the lingering feeling of being forced that they experience can and does result in the same kind of reactance Brehm (1966) has noted in other social contexts when people believe that their freedom of choice is threatened. If those to whom I have referred engage in research at all, they do so reluctantly and with diminished prospects for producing outcomes that are likely to make a difference.

Threat of punishment, whether leading to resistance or reluctant engagement, is not the only avoidance-related motive. Sometimes, the stimulus is fear of failure. The prospect of having one's work rejected or otherwise castigated is frequently at the base of an inactive researcher's (which may be an oxymoron) professed perfectionism, unreasonable demands for resources and research support, and commitment to completely unrealistic goals. Such masking of fear, whether conscious or unconscious, is apt to have the same consequence—little or no output.

Another type of individual is prompted more by a desire to achieve the perceived rewards that follow from success in research (where success is defined in terms of the number of related publications and recognition) than to avoid the costs associated with a failure to produce. Although those active in research tend to earn more than those not engaged in it, differences created by market conditions, compression, disciplinary status, and other such factors reduce the importance of salary as an incentive. More critical are psychological influences.

One of my professional acquaintances, for instance, has the professed goal of publishing the number of articles in professional research journals minimally necessary to achieve standing among the 100 most frequently published scholars in the discipline. The person in question does research, and perhaps even enjoys it, but not because of its perceived intrinsic value. The central purpose in his case is to achieve recognition (a kind of Roy Hobbes of *The Natural* fame mentality). Such motives can lead to shortcuts in inquiry and an indifference to what research supports as reasonable claims about the phenomena it embraces.

Although probably no researcher is completely free of the influence of either of the preceding motivations, clearly some are prompted in their work much more by a sense of intellectual curiosity. They do research because they feel challenged by the opportunity to reduce uncertainty, to resolve controversies (or even contribute to them), or otherwise to unravel life's often puzzling complexities. In short, they are motivated by a need for discovery. Such individuals may be no better equipped than others of differing motivation, but the odds are that in the long run the results of their inquiries will have greater impact in the advancement of knowledge than those of their comparably equipped, but more personally motivated counterparts.

Attitudes

Closely related to motives in their effect on research are the attitudes of those who do research. In fact, one's motives often determine one's attitudes toward the enterprise. If we think of attitudes in Fishbein and Ajzen's (1975) sense, that is, as the evaluative components in belief-evaluation clusters that relate to particular objects of cognition and vary along continua of favorability and positivity, it seems clear that how favorably or positively one views research will influence how one goes about the activity.

In my experience, those who are favorably disposed toward research as an expectation of their positions tend to enjoy engaging in it and require little encouragement or prodding. Some have such a love of inquiry that it could only be described as "passionate." These individuals find reward in the act of research itself. Even when they encounter difficulty or experience frustration, their positive orientation tends to sustain both interest and effort.

In contrast, those whose attitudes toward research are unfavorable and negative are easily discouraged, and they may use the obstacles they confront to rationalize diminished performance, or perhaps even withdrawal from research. The excuses individuals having unfavorable attitudes toward research offer for avoiding it, in terms of novelty and creativity, frequently surpass anything undergraduate students come up with for not having done their work. As Tucker (1984), with more than a tinge of irony, has noted, such individuals "could write books of excuses and reasons for their failure to finish various projects—if they only had more time!" (p. 32).

It is important to note here the focus of attitudes. The attitudes I have been describing are those one develops in relation to one's own involvement. An individual may be, in general, favorably disposed toward research, but not to doing it him- or herself. You should not underestimate the potential influence of broader attitudes, however. There are professionals who eschew the value of research generally on the grounds that we already know what we need to know.

I cannot recall the number of occasions I have heard someone (usually a university or college professor) claim that Aristotle said everything of importance there is to say about rhetoric. Although such declarations frequently are little more than excuses for the declaimer's not doing research him- or herself, at times they appear to represent genuine—albeit patently anti-intellectual, not to mention anti-Aristotelian—expressions of belief. The "If it's good enough for _____, then it's good enough for me" attitude and the "old-time religion" from which it springs foster not only contempt for those who are active in research, but almost absolutely assures that a professor will never engage in it.

Whether or not one holds a position at an institution requiring involvement in research, negative attitudes of the type described above are injurious. As my colleague Professor Phillips has noted more than once elsewhere in this volume, research is at the base of what we are reliably able to teach. Ben-David (1983) refers to teaching and research as "organically related functions" (p. 81). Winks (1983) puts the matter this way: "To teach well is to exemplify research" (p. 189). A lack of appreciation for it, therefore, encourages indoctrination rather than liberation as the *raison d'être* for education. Those who contribute to such a condition might be better advised to pursue some other type of career more befitting to their peculiar brands of truth and, hence, education.

Resources

No matter how properly motivated or favorably disposed to doing research a scholar is, the availability of resources is a factor that cannot be overlooked. Institutions vary considerably in both their ability and willingness to support research, and one must consider how the constraints imposed by access to resources affect what one realistically can expect to accomplish. Even the most well-endowed research universities derive a relatively small amount of money from tuition, state aid, and gifts for direct support of research.

Increasingly, college and university researchers are becoming dependent on grants and contracts and must compete with others in the private and public sectors for research funding. Currently, to expect that an employer will be able to provide all the resources a researcher may see as necessary for the successful prosecution of his or her agenda is naive at best. The problem is exacerbated by the fact that external support for research has not been keeping pace with the growth in activity (Winks, 1983). If that trend continues, finding adequate means to do research will become even more difficult.

The types of resources researchers typically require reduce to some combination of materials, facilities, personnel, and time. Each has a price tag. An individual who does research requiring only access to extant documents may find the materials in his or her institution's library sufficient, in which case the material cost of doing research could be quite small. Even in this relatively rare situation, however, the time necessary for completion of a project could be problematic. For economic reasons, release from other responsibilities is not usually possible, and most researchers are understandably reluctant to take unpaid leaves of absence in order to expedite their work, regardless of its personal importance to them. In addition, it is often necessary to travel to other locations to acquire materials beyond those locally available or to engage in some other aspect of data collection. When one is engaged in projects that are equipment- or labor-intensive, the cost of doing research can be very high. Some research, finally, may require facilities an institution does not presently have. Even if the necessary physical space is available, adapting it for research purposes could entail substantial expense.

For the beginning professional, the associated costs of doing research can be a startling and even discouraging revelation. The response of far too many individuals to such discoveries is to become either defensive, demanding, or both. Criticizing the administration for not providing what, from the researcher's point of view, would be adequate support, however, is unlikely to have any impact. A more constructive response is either to make appropriate adjustments in one's research agenda or to explore avenues of external support. In fact, it is probably wise to do both. As is true for other types of explorations, it is mining, not pining and whining, that leads to paydirt.

The first course of action necessitates coming to terms with what one can accomplish in research in the face of limited resources. In research, there are typically many ways of approaching the task. In my own area of specialty, for example, I have discovered that extant accounts and records of discussions provide an accessible, relatively inexpensive source of information about aspects of decision making I earlier believed could be explored profitably only through much more costly laboratory investigations.

The adjustment of ambition to resource limitations may in some instances be too great a compromise in terms of desired or necessary yield. Collaborative research offers one means for reducing the problem; however, if that possibility is not sufficiently promising, then one has little recourse other than to look to external sources. Most universities have an office of grants and contracts administration and personnel equipped to assist researchers in locating appropriate agencies and foundations for their work, as well as in preparing proposals for submission to them. You should become acquainted with the operations of your institution's office and its staff.

Seeking external funding is time-consuming. In addition, if one is successful in securing it, one runs the risk of becoming dependent. There are the added inconveniences of interim reporting, penetrating the agency and university bureaucracies, and delays in authorizations (Winks, 1983). Bureaucrats are not paid to be efficient. Finally, there is the temptation to adjust one's interests to the continually shifting interests and priorities of the funding agencies. Chasing money can become one's occupation. The unfortunate result is that one loses sight of the concerns that prompted seeking external support in the first place.

University administrators are increasingly exerting pressure to expand the concept of research to mean the funded variety. If you take or have a position at a research university, you will soon feel this pressure. You need to be careful about how you respond to it and recognize that in many instances the sources of pressure could not care less about your particular research interests. They want you to help pay the bills. External funding can be a considerable asset to a faculty member's research, but not if it diverts the individual from the issues to which the research is directed to the means for supporting it.

The resources on which one can draw in doing research clearly affect the extensiveness and, ultimately, the quality of one's research, but the relationship is far from being linear. Ample resources do not assure high-quality research (as former Senator Proxmire's "Golden Fleece Award" used to remind us fairly regularly), nor do limited resources necessarily diminish possibilities for making important contributions. Einstein's greatest achievements, we should not forget, were based on thought experiments. Much depends on how one uses the resources one has. Not the least of those is the researcher's intellectual capabilities, which, in part, are reflected in the discussion of qualifications that follows.

Qualifications

Success in research (viz., acknowledged and meaningful advancement of knowledge) frequently breeds emulation. Aside from its possibly unfortunate impact on originality, the tendency toward imitative behavior often takes potentially productive new scholars into arenas in which they have limited prospects for performing well. It is one thing to learn, and be conversant in, the dominant traditions and modes of inquiry central to given areas of study and to draw on such knowledge in executing one's own program of research. It is quite another to undertake activities one is either unequipped to perform well or does not adequately understand in the hope of creating increased opportunities for a little intellectual shoulder rubbing. In the latter case, one could easily embarrass oneself.

In my opinion, the sine qua non for any serious scholar is to be in command of the issues and methodologies appropriate to the inquiries he or she initiates. It is important, therefore, that an aspiring researcher either work within his or her present limitations or expand his or her knowledge to the base-level requisite for undertaking the sorts of projects he or she wishes to pursue. As a frequent reviewer of manuscripts submitted to professional journals, I continue to be surprised by the number that reveal ambition in research beyond the evident knowledge, skill, and scholarly sophistication of the author. In most instances, it strikes me that the parties involved have used someone else's work as a model without being fully appreciative of either the substantive matters under consideration or the appropriate means for exploring them.

No researcher I know of can ever feel assured of being completely in command of all that he or she surveys, but there is a minimal level of proficiency beneath which one simply cannot fall if one is to make supportable and acceptable claims. Even if one draws appropriate conclusions from research one is not adequately equipped to have done, the person will not understand the bases on which they are warranted and, hence, will be ill-prepared to explain or defend them if called upon to do so.

Avoiding the problem I have been discussing necessitates honest and potentially disturbing self-examination. In the long run, however, one's successes in research are likely to be much greater if a person recognizes what types of inquiries he or she is most suitably equipped to undertake. There is nothing wrong with our grasp exceeding our reach in many areas of life, and that may even be what heaven is for, but in research, it is better if one thinks of aspiration in the context of preparation rather than execution. The consequences are simply potentially too costly even to contemplate undertaking work one is not ready to perform. The proper matching of qualifications to ambition, then, is absolutely crucial if research is to serve the intended function of advancing knowledge in acceptably meaningful ways.

The qualifications necessary to do research vary with the field of study and the types of inquiries one seeks to pursue. In general, however, these consist of a knowledge of accepted norms of inquiry, analytical skill, and the ability to draw the conclusions that follow from the critical examination of relevant data. If one is unable to satisfy any of these criteria for a particular project, one should not undertake that project. In short, don't get in water over your head if you don't know how to swim.

Focus

In any field of study, there are so many issues whose resolution would constitute advancements in knowledge that those new to research sometimes have difficulty choosing which ones to address. This uncertainty may lead one down either of two paths, both of which can be problematic. One path involves efforts to make contributions in a number of different areas. The other, a much narrower path, represents a kind of shortcut to prominence a person assumes will follow from becoming identified with someone else's work. Although researchers are generally free to pursue whatever issues they consider worthwhile, you should understand the risks associated with the choices mentioned above. The following is a discussion of the more serious of these.

That new faculty members enter the academic profession with a diverse set of interests is understandable in light of experiences typical of graduate education. During the three or more years a candidate spends in a Ph.D. program, he or she will enroll in as many as 15 to 20 courses and be exposed to numerous aspects of specialties within the discipline. Even narrowly conceived programs have some breadth, and one is tempted to develop facility in the content relevant to several specialties, especially if faculty members representing them are good teachers and succeed in making their respective areas of study interesting. In addition to the coursework, a doctoral candidate will have written as many as 30 papers—most specifically for classes, but some possibly for presentation at professional conferences and meetings—by the time his or her degree is conferred.

As a result of such experiences, an individual's inclination might be to adopt a so-called "generalist" perspective on research, take advantage of starts provided by past coursework, and pursue many different types of inquiries. Although there is nothing wrong per se in having a broad set of interests, difficulty arises when, collectively, these interests show no coherence. The expected synergy associated with the pursuit of widely diverse interests is more apparent than real. Under these conditions, the novice becomes something of a dilettante or dabbler in the research arts rather than developing scholar.

In addition to the fact that institutions stressing research expect to see faculty members develop programs of research that have focus, direction, and momentum, there is another good reason for being concerned about too great a breadth of research interests. The prospects for making significant advances in any given area are substantially reduced if one is doing research in several others that have no apparent unifying links.[3] Hence, trying to be a "Jack" or "Jill" of all trades in research can have both professional and scholarly consequences any serious researcher probably would like to avoid.

The second path some beginning researchers take entails focus, but not in a necessarily desirable sense. These individuals identify their research interests with those of more prominent scholars, usually the person's major professor or advisor in graduate school. In and of itself, the

---

[3]A person can successfully draw on seemingly diverse strands of interest in developing a coherent perspective on some issue or set of issues. Bormann (1986) is an excellent case in point. Bormann has been able to combine work in group communication, public address, and rhetoric in formulating his "theory of symbolic convergence." Such individuals are comparatively rare, however, and are more apt to make such contributions later rather than earlier in their careers.

practice is not bad, but a fine line often exists between advancing work initiated by another person and discipleship. The side of the line on which one resides may well prove to be critical to the types of contributions one is apt to make in research.

Individuals who further lines of work begun by others out of a genuine interest in the issues involved are more likely to produce research of high quality and measurable impact than ones who merely aspire to prominence through association. Like the shoulder rubbers mentioned above, hero and heroine worshippers fade quickly from the scene because even though their research may be clearly focused, they lack the ability or commitment (or both) to take the kinds of strides forward that distinguish one's work. They also lack the necessary originality of thought.

Few, if any, accomplished researchers remain unaffected in their thinking by the scholarship of others, but neither is their interest in that work driven by a desire to enhance the reputations of those on whose efforts they draw and presumably, thereby, their own. Their inquiries are much more likely to be a consequence of the potentialities and deficiencies they perceive and the intellectual challenges posed by each.

The two paths I have been discussing are not the only ones taken. Still others are chosen on the basis of advice. How to establish oneself in research, unfortunately, is frequently the subject of poor, if not downright disreputable, advice to those at the beginning stages of their professional careers; for instance, "Find a hot topic," "Pick something in which no one else is interested," "Look into the backgrounds of journal editors, and select topics in which they appear to be interested," "Gear up for ____" [e.g., a forthcoming election], and, of course, "Follow the leaders." Although such advice in some instances may have a certain strategic value in gaining acceptance of one's work for publication, acting on it does not auger well for the beginning professional's becoming a productive, contributing scholar in the long run. Such individuals never seem to move beyond what they perceive to be the fashions of the moment.

Personally, I find it difficult to believe that one can reach the point of entry into a professional career with no research interests. Advice of the kind illustrated above, therefore, serves only to cause a person to question the legitimacy of what he or she has just spent three or more years trying to develop and define. If a person is lacking in self-confidence, he or she is especially susceptible to following such advice rather than sticking with his or her original intentions and inclinations. You should remember that the voice of experience is at times perhaps better ignored than heeded.

At the risk of seeming to contradict my caveat and adding to the frustration that can result from conflicting advice, let me offer what I hope are some useful suggestions:

1. Try to identify questions you believe are in need of resolution in those areas in which you wish to do research.
2. Determine what gives coherence to this set of questions.
3. Think about what advances in knowledge or understanding can be derived from the answers to these questions.
4. Establish priorities for conducting inquiries that are appropriate for addressing these questions.
5. Recognize the limitations under which you may be forced to work.
6. Proceed with specific projects in some determined order, and whenever possible, complete each one before moving on to the next one.
7. Be prepared to make personal sacrifices others are not willing to make and for which you may receive some criticism.

Although adoption of these suggestions will not assure anyone success in research, attending to them can be of help in developing not only a reasonably well-focused program of research, but a focused set of related actions as well.

Execution

The final consideration in research I wish to discuss has to do with its execution. However well motivated, qualified, and focused a researcher may be, the quality and, hence, success of his or her research can suffer from a variety problems occurring in its execution. No one, of course, can possibly anticipate every conceivable contingency and difficulty that may arise in conducting a research project. Unwanted intrusions can be minimized, however, through careful planning.[4]

Despite the discipline that graduate students are encouraged to develop in courses in research methodology and through the preparation of thesis and dissertation proposals, the pressure to do research that is sometimes perceived upon entering the profession can and does lead to shortcuts and other lapses in rigor that increase the likelihood of encountering problems in the execution of a research project. The quality of research that a person does, in most instances, will be no greater than the care he or she has taken in planning it. This relationship may be less than perfect, but inadequacies in planning certainly do little or nothing to increase the probability of a high-quality result.

The other side of the coin in respect to research is excessive attention to planning. If you have not already heard someone say of another,

---

[4]Babbie (1992) has an excellent discussion of how to develop and pursue a research plan. For beginning researchers, in particular, the material (pp. 102-112) is most helpful.

"He/she talks a good research project," you will. Although the observation frequently applies to individuals who are unsuccessfully engaging in impression management, there are people of serious intent who become so concerned about designing the perfect (zero-defect) study that they are unable to ever get one off the ground. Instead, they spend a lot of time worrying and talking with others about how best to manage this and avoid that. If one works at it, anyone can "What if?" a study to death. (Given a median of 0 for the career publication rate among academics, presumably, higher education has an abundance of perfectionists.)

Successful scholars are either free of such obsessive tendencies or are able to overcome them at some point and to move forward with their research. Projects do not complete themselves. They have to be put into motion and conducted by human agents. Devoting inordinate amounts of time to achieving flawlessness, at best, assures limited output and, more often than not, no product at all. In the latter case, the quality of one's research is not an issue. There isn't anything to assess. On the other hand, one's professional future may be very much in doubt.

Regardless of how carefully one plans a research project, Robert Burns's observations concerning mice and men and at least one of Murphy's Laws remind us that things can still go wrong. Subjects fail to report for an experiment, the manuscript one urgently needs and was told is available turns up missing, the recording of an interview proves to be defective, or any of a hundred other mishaps. When some problems like these arise, the researcher must assess the damage and, if possible, make appropriate corrections or adjustments. If the problems are too serious to correct, he or she may be forced either to begin anew or scrap the project altogether.

Mature scholars, however disturbing these latter possibilities may be, are prepared to make the necessary choices. Immature scholars, in contrast, often plunge ahead in the hope that others will take into consideration difficulties beyond their control in evaluating the results. Little such charity exists, or should, for that matter, in a discipline deserving of respect. Even if the hope is realized, all that one will have accomplished is the production of claims of highly questionable merit. In addition, the short-term gain could be merely a prelude for later failure.

Whatever the personal consequences, the fact remains that inappropriate responses to problems that arise in the conduct of research do little to contribute to outcomes of high quality. They can do much, however, to provide consumers with misleading information and understandings that seriously misrepresent phenomena in which a relevant population may have reason to be vitally interested.

CONSIDERATIONS INVOLVED IN PUBLICATION

As I mentioned in the opening portion of this chapter, researchers often undertake inquiries with a view toward sharing the results with a larger professional community via the publication of reports based on the results of these inquiries. Not everything suitable for publication, however, relates directly to, or is result of, research. The broader range of materials may include critiques of others' work, philosophical speculations, reviews, arguments related to new directions in a field of study, and, of course, instruction in the form typical of many textbooks.

Like research, publication entails a set of activities one performs with varying degrees of success. Some of these activities are similar to those mentioned in the preceding discussion of research, as are some of the considerations that bear on the probability of success. I have chosen to deal with four matters that are relatively distinct, however: (a) deciding to publish, (b) selecting appropriate sources of publication, (c) readying manuscripts, and (d) working through the process.

Deciding to Publish

One afternoon a few years ago, my secretary told me that one of our graduate students was in the outer office and had a very serious problem about which he needed to see me right away. I was engaged in other work at the time but instructed the secretary to send in the student. When I inquired about this "serious" problem, the student responded, "Here I am at the end of my second year of doctoral study, and I have no publications." When I asked whether or not he had submitted something for publication, his nonverbal behavior seemed to convey a genuine sense of puzzlement. It was almost as if the notion that to be published requires first that one write something and then submit it to an authorized source had never occurred to this individual.

I suspect that the student, who at the time was in the job market, may have been responding to some sudden attack of anxiety resulting from not having received a job offer, or possibly from just having received a letter of rejection. The incident, however, relates to a more general mystification about publication as an aspect of professional life. In the observations that follow, I hope to demystify the process if I can by speaking frankly about the decision to submit a manuscript for publication.

Ultimately, the decision as to whether one's work will be published is that of someone authorized to act on behalf of a publisher, not the individual who submits the work for consideration. Nevertheless, at some point, the prospective contributor has to determine whether or not to prepare and submit a manuscript for possible publication. (I emphasize "possible" because no one empowered to publish another's work has the obligation to do so, regardless of how important, valuable, or well done the contributor considers it to be.) There are two decision points of interest, and the course of action that follows each may differ.

The first decision point occurs when one begins a project that either could or will culminate in the production of a manuscript. The immediate purpose in writing the manuscript may be unrelated to publication; for example, the manuscript is part of the requirements for a graduate course, one has been asked to present a paper at a convention, or the individual simply wants a written record of a project for subsequent reference. (The latter situation is comparatively rare, although one does occasionally find references in manuscripts submitted for publication to other "unpublished manuscripts.") The question the individual faces under these circumstances is whether or not to develop the manuscript in such a way as to serve a different or additional purpose, namely, reaching a larger audience via publication.[5]

At this stage, younger scholars, in particular, are sometimes susceptible to what should be irrelevant, such as lore about "old-boy" networks, editorial conspiracies to exclude representation of certain areas of study, impossible standards, and the like. Listening to this type of commentary, which often originates with individuals who themselves do not publish, can be discouraging and, in some instances, may lead one to drop the idea. In my judgment, it is best to think in a more positive vein at this point.

Far too few graduate students and beginning professionals write with possible publication in mind. The fact that even in research universities nearly 50% of the faculty have never published (Boyer, 1987, p. 129) lends credence to this assertion. To some, publication is always beyond the next horizon or past the next hurdle. The scholarly goals of such individuals are distant in comparison to their instrumental goals; hence, they lock themselves into a sequence that virtually assures they will not publish. It is no secret that those who are successful in publishing their work have usually developed the habit of writing for publication and experience little conflict at this initial decision point.

Once an individual has completed a manuscript or, at least, conceived what such a manuscript would consist of, there comes a second decision point. This stage is typically more conflicted than the preliminary one, even for highly successful published scholars. At issue are such matters as whether one has or will have said anything of substance, whether treatment of the subject written or to be written about is adequate, whether one's motive is simply to add to his or her list of publications, and whether the work represents enough of an actual or potential

---

[5]When one is making a decision concerning a book-length manuscript, having it completed at the point of decision would be unusual. The document on which one has been working is much more likely to be a proposal. I should also note that occasionally both proposals and manuscripts for journals or chapters in edited collections are solicited. In these instances, one's decision has to do primarily with whether or not to accept the invitation.

contribution to warrant the attention of others. How a person resolves these issues will influence the choice he or she makes.

The decision to submit a manuscript for publication is not one you should take lightly. Over 50,000 books are published annually (Weiner, 1990, p. 44), and the number of articles in journals and other periodicals is substantially greater than that. There is a significant probability, therefore, that what one hopes to see in print will be read by relatively few, if any, of the people at whom the manuscript is aimed unless it has something to offer.[6] Within the scholarly community especially, it is difficult for one to achieve notice unless the work he or she produces stands out. Even when individuals have something of importance to say, their work may still go largely unnoticed. Further complicating the problem is that our society, in general, is not given to reading much of anything that has intellectual depth—a condition that Hirsch (1987) and others have noted.[7] Academics are often as guilty of not reading as the more general public. As a result, if you are not convinced that your manuscript (or in the case of books, the one you have underway or envision) contains information of importance and that you can write interestingly enough to command attention, it is probably a good idea to defer action.

Making an intelligent decision about the future of a manuscript obviously requires some skill in self-assessment. At times, however, it is helpful to seek the opinions of others. If you choose this course, do so with the understanding that you may not like the response. If you are merely seeking affirmation, then you will have wasted your time and that of the person or persons whose aid you have enlisted. Whatever the basis of your decision to proceed with a submission, however, there are several other considerations you must confront. How you respond has significant implications for both the quality of the manuscript and the prospects for succeeding in having it accepted for eventual publication.

---

[6]I am dubious about the number of $20 bills that allegedly reside in dissertations, books, and journals on library shelves as an index of how infrequently scholarship is consulted. I am even more dubious that the type of individuals who allegedly made this test with their own publications and, more importantly, their own money, would, in fact, have done so. Nevertheless, it is fair to say that most of what is published is consulted by relatively few people. There is simply too much to read for most of us to expose ourselves to a very great proportion of it. Even if one read a book a week for 50 years, the total would only be 2,600, a little more than 5% of the number of books published in one year.

[7]In his reaction to the emergence of hack writers and the decline of sophisticationof Europeans during the 18th century, Oliver Goldsmith made the following prophetic observation: "As writers become more numerous, it is natural for readers to become more indolent" (from *Enquiry into the Present State of Polite Learning in Europe*, 1759; see Goldsmith, 1970).

Sources of Publication

Where to submit a manuscript for publication depends, in part, on the length, scope, and nature of the work. In Speech Communication, scholarship is typically published as articles (including book reviews) in refereed journals, or as books. Electronic publishing is also beginning to emerge as an acknowledged form, but to date it has not been especially prominent.

Journals are usually published by professional organizations, whereas the vast majority of books are produced and distributed by commercial presses. Some commercial presses do sponsor journals, and, of course, university presses publish a great many scholarly books reporting original research, the development of theories, and critical assessments of fairly limited and narrow interest. Commercial publishers have strong profit motives and, hence, are driven to a much greater extent than professional organizations and university presses by market considerations. They gravitate toward textbooks appropriate for courses that have large enrollments. It is becoming increasingly difficult to find sources of publication for upper-level, undergraduate courses. Commercial presses find the enrollments too small, and university presses are generally not interested in textbooks of any kind.

Once it becomes clear what form is best suited for the material an individual seeks to publish, the choice of a particular source becomes a matter of considerable concern. If publication in a journal seems most appropriate, one needs to be aware of what different journals emphasize, their foci, and their manuscript submission requirements. One can usually find most of this information in the stated editorial policies of the journals one is considering. These policies are reprinted in every issue of a journal and, therefore, are easily accessible. The policies of publishers of books are not so easily accessible, and one is well advised, therefore, to have some discussion with a sales representative or division editor in assessing the suitability of an actual or potential manuscript for a particular house.

For submission to journals, a manuscript must be complete in most instances. With books, there are preliminaries, and publishers vary in what they expect at the initial stages. Sometimes, they require only a proposal as the basis for deciding whether or not to offer a prospective contributor a contract. At other times, they will want to see sample chapters. Still on other occasions, one is expected to produce a full draft of the work one is hoping to have published. However much material must be prepared in securing a contract, book publishers reserve the right not to produce any work until they are satisfied that it is acceptable.

Because it would be an extremely rare situation in which the contents of a manuscript would be suitable for publication in only one journal or by one press, deciding where and to whom one should submit one's work requires some thought.[8] It is to this matter that I shall devote the remainder of my attention in this section rather than to the mechanics of publishing or the particular merits of different sources.

The initial thought one may have in choosing among prospective sources of publication is the likelihood that the one selected will accept the manuscript. This is not an unreasonable consideration, but its frequent primacy in the decision-making process is disturbing. Although (and contrary to some opinions) there are relatively few journals or publishing houses that "will accept anything," sources of publication do differ in their standards. Ease of publication, therefore, is related to how rigorous such standards are. The problem in opting for submission primarily on the grounds of probability of success is that one's relevant peers are apt to be familiar with a source's reputation for lack of rigor and, therefore, may have a diminished appreciation of one's scholarship. If the person's work cannot satisfy the standards of respected sources of publication, then he or she has reason to be concerned about its quality.

At a time when the amount of publications appears to have increased importance in hiring, tenure, and promotion decisions at some institutions, the temptation to publish first and worry about quality latter can be difficult to overcome. That it is difficult to resist is suggested by such comments as, "I need some publications," "How hard is it to get into _____?", and "This article (viz., manuscript) isn't good enough for _____, so what would you suggest?" Attitudes, such as these illustrations reflect, reduce publication to little more than a strategy for professional survival rather than the sharing of knowledge and thought it is supposed to be.

As problematic as selecting a prospective source of publication chiefly on the basis of probability of acceptance, in my view, are choices based exclusively on prestige. In response to the comment, "I am thinking of submitting this manuscript to _____ [supply your own choice for a prestigious journal or publisher]," I sometimes ask, "Why?" If the answer is along the lines, "It seems to me that it is the most appropriate outlet for this piece of work," then I am likely to express my agreement or disagreement with the person's judgment. If the answer is "Because it is the best journal in the field" or something similar, I begin to sense that the individual has misplaced priorities and am reluctant to offer any further comment.

Aspiration is fine; however, quality is of paramount importance and should be. If the quality of one's work is not commensurate with the level of aspiration, one will be disappointed to learn that others (namely,

---

[8]Acknowledging that manuscripts may be suitable for submission to more than one source does not mean that one should submit a manuscript to more than one source at the same time. With book proposals, this is an accepted practice (one, incidentally, that I do not encourage) because publishers resolve possible conflicts with the offer and acceptance of a contract. With journals, however, the practice is frowned on and generally considered to be unethical.

those responsible for publication decisions) have made this discovery. All sources of publication, of course, make poor decisions from time to time, including acceptance of work beneath their ordinary standards. When an individual whose work is not of high quality nevertheless succeeds in gaining acceptance of a manuscript by a prestigious source of publication, the consequence may be a sense of achievement that is unwarranted and subsequent frustration with later publication decisions by these same sources.

If the quality of one's work is uniformly good, then one will always have a broader range of possibilities than an individual for whom this is not an essential concern. Selecting a source, then, becomes largely a matter of intellectual communality, not gamesmanship or ego indulgence. One should, of course, be wary of selecting disreputable sources, even if the type of work for which those sources are known is highly compatible with the contributor's. Within reason, reputation is a legitimate concern. It simply should not be the only, or overriding, concern.

Other considerations that enter—or at least, should enter—into selecting a source of publication include turn-around time, apparent biases toward particular modes of inquiry, qualifications of the members of the editorial boards and reviewers if they are identified, and the potential audience. Information pertinent to these factors is not always easy to obtain, but to the extent that one can, one is more easily able to narrow the range of available choices.

I would be remiss in concluding the discussion of the selection process without acknowledging the need to consider external influences. Those who judge adequacy of professional performance do have certain expectations regarding publication. Deviation from these expectations carries certain risks and consequences. When the expectations are low, deviation may take the form of excess. Rarely does this result in severe sanction unless it interferes with other responsibilities for which expectations are high and clearly defined.

Much more problematic are deviations from clearly defined and demanding expectations, such as regular publication in "top-ranked" refereed journals. If one understands these expectations as a condition of continued employment, then selecting appropriate sources to which to submit one's work is partially completed. If a person does not subscribe to such expectations, he or she confronts a different set of choices: (a) trying to change the expectations or (b) seeking alternative employment. If you are genuinely committed to scholarship and recognize the importance of publication, however, external expectations may not prove to be quite so restrictive. The odds are that your own expectations and standards will exceed those imposed by others.

Readying the Manuscript

Having identified the source to which one intends to submit one's work, the individual must then proceed to prepare what he or she expects to see published. In some instances, the preparation may consist of little more than revising an extant manuscript to satisfy submission requirements. Such is often the case when one decides to submit a piece of work that was originally developed for presentation at a convention to a professional journal. In other instances, the individual may have as a point of departure only the prospectus for a book under contract with a commercial publisher or a manuscript in progress.

Whatever the state of a manuscript at the time the question of where to submit it has been resolved, some degree of further preparation is inevitably necessary. The preparation, moreover, should proceed in accordance with the source of publication's stated requirements. Many a rejection of an otherwise acceptable manuscript is directly traceable to a contributor's failure to take a publisher's requirements seriously.

Preparing a manuscript of high quality is hard work. There is no other way of putting the matter. Prolific scholars, it would appear, either have a relatively easy time composing pieces for publication or are privy to certain "tricks-of-the-trade." Such perceptions tend to be illusory, however. There are few, if any, tricks to publishing. Productive scholars are simply more willing than equally equipped but unproductive scholars to make the sacrifices good writing requires. These sacrifices, moreover, can be substantial. Experience helps, but by no means is it sufficient for producing manuscripts of publishable quality. Persistence and drive are at least as important.

Unfortunately, some beginning professionals, desirous of breaking into print and, thereby, achieving national visibility, do not pay adequate attention to the mechanics of writing or to publication requirements. They are in a hurry and indicate this in such self-characterizations of their work as "quick and dirty." Another acquaintance of mine once expressed an inability to understand why professors have difficulty writing because, according to this individual, his practice was to write an "article" every Friday afternoon. One wonders about the informational value of a piece written in a single afternoon, not to mention an entire list composed on consecutive Fridays. In most cases, however, the question is irrelevant because the products of such limited effort have a correspondingly small prospect of finding their way into print. (I should add here that my acquaintance never bothered to comment about what percentage of his weekly "articles" was published, and I think I may know why.)

To submit inadequately or inappropriately prepared documents for publication is to invite summary rejection. It is also a practice that can waste a great many people's time, including that of the contributor. Good writing is rewriting. If you have ideas and information worth sharing, then it is surely worth the effort to assure that the manuscripts in which such ideas and information are to be aired are properly prepared. Continued neglect of this consideration sooner or later will catch up with the aspiring scholar and, as a consequence, may seriously dampen his or her enthusiasm for what ought to be a rewarding and fulfilling part of his or her professional life.

Working Through the Process

Seldom, if ever, does a manuscript, regardless of its quality, move directly from submission to print. Such prospects are pleasant to contemplate when one is composing, but reaching print is not quite so simple. In fact, the process is very cumbersome—at times, even torturous. If a contributor's responses to the many occurrences that seem disruptive are maladaptive, he or she may succeed in "snatching defeat from the jaws of victory," as it were. So be prepared for an experience that, however necessary, is not usually very pleasant.

The processing of a manuscript, for all practical purposes, begins at the point an editor or managing editor receives it, logs it, and acknowledges receipt. These facets of the process do not always occur in rapid sequence, which in itself can be a source of frustration or irritation. In general, however, this phase of the process is abbreviated and entails limited difficulty.

Following acknowledgement is a period in which the manuscript is under review by presumably well-qualified individuals from whom the editor, or person responsible for the manuscript, has solicited evaluations and recommendations in light of a set of criteria the source of publication considers important. Reviewers are not equally conscientious or competent in acting on their agreements. This can result in seemingly inordinate delays in receiving feedback and conflicting assessments. Depending on his or her knowledge and skills, the editor may decide to seek further evaluations before sharing any results of the review with the contributor.

It is during this review period that people new to the publishing enterprise often make their first big mistake in interpersonal relations. Their impatience breeds hostility, and instead of making legitimate inquiries about the status of their manuscripts, they communicate with the editor in a tone usually reserved for the manager of customer service in a department store, or a comparable public servant. Most editors do not take kindly to such conceptions of their roles or to the attendant communication concerning both how to perform and what they can do with their jobs. (I personally have found no achievement in scholarship so substantial as to warrant this sort of hubris.)

Contributors need to remember that no publisher is obliged to accept their work, even if the publisher is a professional organization of which the contributor is a dues-paying member. Hostility may be a perceived entitlement or prerogative of membership, but its expression does little to improve the prospects for a favorable decision, and it can even lead to cessation of any further consideration of one's manuscript.

Following the initial review, a contributor receives feedback of some kind. This may take the form of a decision either to reject or to accept a manuscript with recommended and required revisions, an invitation to revise and resubmit the manuscript, or merely a summary of concerns the contributor is offered for consideration as to whether to resubmit or withdraw the manuscript. The "ball is in your court" approach reflected in the latter instance can be more frustrating than either specifically directed or mandated revisions one is not enthusiastic about making or outright rejection. The focus of responsibility has shifted from where most of us would like it to be. We would prefer being told what is necessary for favorable action.

It becomes a much more difficult task to determine what types of revisions may be most critical to success if they are not specified. Under these circumstances, the contributor has reached another crucial decision point. Must he or she now engage in some sort of guessing game? Does continuation in the process auger for some potentially serious compromise of the integrity and intellectual content of the manuscript? Would he or she be wasting time preparing a revised version of the manuscript? Have the reviewers identified unsolvable problems? If the answers to such questions are affirmative, one should probably withdraw the manuscript from further consideration and either prepare it for submission to another source or, in the case of uncorrectable deficiencies, redo the work on which the manuscript is based—only properly this time.

If the contributor continues in the process, he or she will need to address the issues raised by the reviewers in some way or another. Sometimes, one simply incorporates specific suggestions in a revised draft of the manuscript. At other times, clarification of some aspect of the manuscript provides an adequate response to a concern or criticism. In still other instances, the contributor may have to contact the editor and explain why he or she either cannot or should not make some of the alterations called for.

Arguing with reviewers' judgments is perfectly legitimate, but the manner in which a contributor advances his or her position is critical. Arrogance and righteous indignation generally do little to convince an editor that reluctance to accommodate recommended or required changes is justifiable. Good reasons, if anything, are what best provides a basis for an editor to reconsider the appropriateness of any particular alteration in a manuscript.

Unless an editor has committed to publication on the condition of adherence to specified changes in the original draft, resubmission is part of an iterative process in which review, feedback, further revision, and resubmission recur until such time as the editor makes a final decision. The contributor needs to be prepared for this frequently prolonged aspect of bringing the manuscript to print, which may well last for one year or longer.

If the final decision by an editor is to accept a manuscript for publication, the contributor may feel that the process is over—or at least his or her role in it. No such luck. Remaining are copyediting, checking references and the accuracy of factual information, reviewing of page and/or galley proofs, supplying biographical data, and, in the case of books, helping define the market and related marketing strategies. At each stage, the contributor will have to do more work and usually on short notice. Some people see this stage as a nuisance and do not take it very seriously. This can result in the appearance of a flawed publication, with mechanical errors, inaccuracies, and omissions. Blaming the editor or publisher for such problems will have no effect. In academic life, scapegoating rarely does. In publishing, moreover, responsibility for preventing problems clearly resides with the contributor and properly so.

In addition to those who show neglect in the final stages of the publication process are those who have new thoughts or ideas. These individuals want to make substantive changes—sometimes major ones—that would require considerable additional work and cost to the publisher. In some instances, last-minute changes may be justified, as in the case of the emergence of some significant piece of information that requires accommodation, lest the published manuscript contain a serious mistake or other embarrassment. More often than not, the request to make changes at this point reflects a contributor's desire to exert control and to engage in silly power games. I confess to having very little tolerance for such individuals, and they should indulge their manipulative impulses in some other arena, such as the local elementary school playground.

Because of the cumbersomeness of the process, the interval between submission and appearance of a published manuscript can be lengthy. Two-year time lags are common. Knowing that to be the case, although it is not comforting, can be of value in developing the patience necessary to achieve a greater measure of success in establishing the record of publication to which the ideas and information the individual wishes to share lead him or her to aspire. The best response to delay is to move forward with other projects.

PARTING THOUGHTS

Research and publication are essential to academic life. Relative to other aspects of professional activity, their perceived and actual importance varies from institution to institution. Whether a given institution emphasizes these activities or not, the health of any discipline is vitally affected by them. This needs to be stressed because all too often, and increasingly so, research and publication are being viewed almost exclusively in terms of their relationship to personal professional advancement and institutional prestige. To the extent that they are so conceived and valued in such purely instrumental and crassly utilitarian terms, the prognosis for the meaningful advancement of knowledge and, hence, the intellectual well-being of the academic disciplines is not good.

That individuals advance professionally on the basis of achievements in research and publication is not in itself a bad thing. In fact, it is a good thing. My concern is with the narrow view that individual advancement or institutional bragging rights are the only justifications for doing research and publication. If one cannot see a larger purpose, the long-range consequence could well be a proliferation of publications without correspondingly useful increments in knowledge. The much touted "knowledge explosion," in fact, is more a publication explosion. The former would be nice if it were true, but I am afraid that it is probably the latter that better defines present reality.

I hope that the treatment of these subjects developed herein helps the reader to appreciate the fact that advancement of knowledge can be entirely compatible with personal advancement and institutional standing. The likelihood that it will be, however, depends heavily on how seriously scholars take research and publication, as well as the ends toward which they direct their energies in these two domains.

◆ RESPONSE TO CHAPTER EIGHT
GERALD M. PHILLIPS

My agreement with my colleague is unqualified. I second the motion. But as one of these prolific authors, I want to respond to the process of publishing itself. I have, over a 42-year career, averaged five articles and one book a year. I have even made some money from some of my writing. I have retired into a literary career as a paid editor for one publishing house, a development editor on commission for another, and as a volunteer editor of a journal. I have served as editor for two major publishers as well as for several university presses; I have edited one major scholarly journal and served as an associate editor on at least two journals per year for the last 30 years. I am an associate editor now of two speech journals, one psychology journal, and one journal in computer science. I am, in short, a sort of professional writer.

With these credentials, I believe I can offer some insights into the publishing process from a perspective different than Professor Gouran. We may begin with an axiom: There is no point to writing unless you have something worth saying. Professor Gouran aptly addresses this point in his chapter. My following comments are based on the presumption that your motives for doing research are "righteous," and you have an idea or discovery that is worth sharing with others.

We must begin by correcting a misapprehension. Many of my young colleagues think that once they have done research they are entitled to have it published. They submit it with a kind of arrogance or the blind confidence of vapidity, and when they receive a rejection letter, they are crushed. I wish to make the point that writing is a skill. It can be learned. Most of us must learn it. Not even Hemingway published first drafts. Publication is not an entitlement.

Professor Gouran made an important point in his chapter: All publishing, in some sense, is a profit-making enterprise—even if we are talking about a subsidized press sponsored by a university or a professional organization. It must, at least, break even. It does this by selling subscriptions or copies.

Publishers are not especially concerned about what they sell. They lay out boundaries of topics and types of books and then leave the content to the authors. They sell what people are willing to buy. Of course, they pay a corps of qualified referees to guarantee the quality of the content. But beyond this, they will not serve as referees in scholarly arguments or publish arcane esoterica merely because it exists. They must have a rationale for publication and reason to believe they will sell enough copies to break even.

Much scholarly research is done because others are interested and find the articles useful. A great deal, however, is done because the scholar believes he or she needs to do it in order to survive in his or her career. But there are over 90,000 scholarly journals. Those in the hard sciences, especially medicine, have serious consequences. Often human lives depend on the content of the articles. Refereeing is rigorous and highly critical. Furthermore, these journals operate under the "Ingelfinger-Relman Rule," that is, they do not release information to the media until it appears in a properly refereed publication.

There are other kinds of publications defined as trade books that include those for which the public will pay. Sometimes research is necessary, as in the case of James Michener, whose work is prodigious. Because a work is fiction does not exempt the writer from doing research. Sometimes, as in the case of most self-help books, the research is often done by someone else, and literally pirated, distorted, and otherwise misused. Various diet books, tomes on how to repair your marriage, and others of that ilk are not research driven. Citations are often sprinkled in to make the book look authoritative, but frequently the content is as much fiction as any detective novel.

Textbooks are driven by the research of others. Some writers of textbooks do massive searches of literature. The books themselves offer nothing new, although they may be very original and interesting in their presentation. In fact, many popular textbooks are now written inside the publishing house by anonymous specialists. The house then contracts with a prominent scholar who, for a price, puts his or her name on the work. A textbook writer can make a profit, however.

Publishing in professional journals is a nonprofit activity for the writers, although the journal publishers must, at least, break even. You, the writer, waive the rights to your work. You put it in the public domain when it is approved. You do not receive royalties. You publish because you have something to say (although many publish because they think they must in order to survive in their job). Scholarly manuscripts are almost always refereed. Experts read them and testify to their quality. A scholarly manuscript does not see the light of day until it passes muster. The only thing that scholarly publishing can depend on for its profit is authoritativeness.

If a scholarly publication or press acquires a reputation for irresponsibility, then libraries do not buy its publications. If libraries do not buy, then not enough copies are sold to make it worthwhile to print. There are already huge warehouses filled with unsold scholarly books. This translates into the economics of scholarly publishing: Very little of what is submitted ever gets into print, and not much of what is printed is sold or read. When I was editor of a national journal, the average publication rate was 1 out of 17 submitted articles (over a 3-year period). I am told by one major journal editor that her rate is 1 out of 23. An editor of a medical journal tells me the rate is one 1 of 7; biologists are notoriously meticulous in their research, and, apparently, in their preparation of manuscripts based on this research.

Another salient fact is that editors concur that most authors of rejected articles do not resubmit them. They give up. They quit. I have had estimates that as low as 10% of articles given editorial comment and an invitation to resubmit are ever actually returned. I do not know whether these figures are true or apocryphal, but they do represent a consensus of editors. As a book editor, I find that less than 1 in 10 proposals ever leads to a contract, and of those contracted, less than one-third ever becomes a book. Consider the amount of wasted time and frustration that represents.

Professor Gouran has already discussed what is involved in the process of scholarly research. I assume that you have done some research and have come up with findings interesting enough to warrant publication (at least, in your opinion). Now we come to the secret of publishing. As a prolific published writer, I can now reveal my secret. I am a terrible writer. I am a very good editor. And I can take lumps. And therein lies the secret of getting published.

The following is some specific advice.

Write as well as you can. Write regularly. Do not wait for the "muse" to touch you. Most professional writers approach it as their job. They set aside a certain amount of time each day and stay with it. Writing is rarely a pleasant task, and it always is a task. The joy comes only when you hold the completed work in your hand.

Learn to edit your own work critically. Yes, grammar counts. Most editors consider sloppy writing to be a sign of sloppy thinking. Make sure you correct as many of your own errors as you possibly can. And read your work carefully, however boring it may be, to make sure it says what you want it to say.

Solicit the advice of others and listen to it before you submit your work. If you use statistics, for example, get a consultant to make sure you have included the essentials, and they are in the proper form. Use a style book to guide your corrections. Get your colleagues to read your work and feed back to you what they understand, so you can be sure you are getting your ideas across.

When you get editorial comment from a potential publisher, take it seriously and apply it. In the final crunch, it is the editor that you have to please. Readers will never see your work if you do not please the editor first.

Your words are not sacred, and sometimes your ideas are silly or foolish. You need other eyes and minds to help you. The editor is not your enemy. He or she must have quality work in order for the journal or the company to survive. Editors do what they have to do in order to obtain such work. Most people fear editing. They cannot do it, and they cannot take it. To be published, you must be edited. You must write, rewrite, and rewrite again. For the past 42 years I have set a goal of not going to bed at night without doing 10 pages of text. I can do the same 10 pages over again for a week until they are in shape for others to look at and then do them three or four times more after the editorial criticism is in. But it must be done. The one thing writers have in common is that they often hate what they are doing, at least at the time they are doing it. Writing is hard work; it is lonely work; it is self-critical work. You make errors and someone else can always find them.

Given that, we can look at the kind of outlets you have for your work.

Scholarly presses and journals look for articles and books that other ranking scholars regard as useful and productive. They tend to avoid provocative essays, expressions of opinion (unless they are well reasoned and carefully documented), and above all, they are repelled by cuteness. The books must either be subsidized by a scholarly organization or university, or sell at least 1,200 copies to libraries in order to break even; hence, they cannot afford to publish an author's efforts to be clever.

Textbook presses look for compliant and well-read scholars, established in their field, who will take careful direction from a development editor. They refer to their books as "products," and they market them like any other manufacturing enterprise markets their products. They think in terms of selling to courses with sufficient enrollment that they can count on 25,000 copies sold the first year. Anything less would be a financial failure. It is for this reason, as well as competition by electronic publishing and course packaging, that most text publishing for midrange and graduate courses is being done by small presses.

Major scholarly presses (such as Harvard or Free Press) cater to established scholars whose ideas have already gained credibility. They will publish exceptionally good work by beginners. They think in 10,000 runs, and usually one-third of those must be remaindered. Small presses are likely to be the wave of the future. They publish books that will sell between 3,000 and 7,000 copies. They try to avoid remainders. They pick up the slack between the high-volume textbook publishers and the scholarly presses.

Most universities have very clear criteria as to what they regard as important scholarly publications, and it is to your advantage to find out what they are. They need not affect the kind of research you do or the topic, but by reading widely in those kinds of publications, you will find alternatives to which you can submit your work. It is very difficult to get published in a journal you do not read regularly.

There is, on the horizon, a new form of publishing. With the advent of technological developments such as *CD-ROM* and *ftp*, the day of the electronic book is approaching. If you do not know these two terms, you are five years behind. There are now more than 20 journals distributed entirely through electronic media. They never appear in hard copy. They promise to revolutionize the publishing industry. We are approaching a technology suitable to make this kind of publishing financially profitable, although, at the moment, it is eleemosynary.

This is the last bit of advice for aspiring writers. The time you spend not writing should be spent reading. It seems there is very little time for social life and that, sadly, is the case. A sustained life as a writer means a limited social life. Sometimes it is even difficult to shoulder family responsibilities.

I have always wondered why some of the graduate students I have encountered wanted academic careers. They did not read much. They could not spell words more complicated than "potato." They found writing term papers an unbearable chore, and they were invariably late turning them in. When they received comments, they were troubled; they complained. They just wanted a grade. They seemed almost like people who have chronic seasickness trying to enlist in the Coast Guard and then begging for shore duty.

Research is the sine qua non of the academic profession, and writing is the most visible evidence you have accomplished it. If you do not enjoy or derive satisfaction from these two activities, in the words of a high school teacher friend, "Why not go where the real teachers are?" Look for a career that does not expect you to advance the frontiers of human knowledge and give evidence of it in print form.

◆ RESPONSE TO CHAPTER EIGHT
SCOTT A. KUEHN

There is but one topic I would like to raise in the context of Professor Gouran's comprehensive treatment of research and publication issues. I believe that beginning academics should consider the benefits of networking with other scholars who have similar interests. Networking can provide training opportunities, collegial criticism forums, and information on publication opportunities.

Networks can provide opportunities to share expertise. I have relied on the advice of experts to help me with complex statistical designs, to name one of a few areas. I have also had the opportunity to share some of my limited expertise. This activity helps me focus my research and provides perspective. The only thing to watch out for here is when someone calls for help on an article and offers authorship credit for help. My advice is to look carefully at the article and research design before attempting to become a mechanic for someone else's problems. If one is to redesign statistical methods of analysis, it is likely that one will find flaws in the research design. However, it can be exciting to work with a group of colleagues carefully designing and conducting research. Much can be learned along the way.

Moreover, bouncing ideas off one's colleagues can help in research design, implementation, and publication. A network of colleagues is useful for sharing rough drafts of written research. One must be careful when reviewing the work of one's friend, however. It does not benefit a friend to be told that his or her work is great when problems are present, just to protect a friendship. Similarly, making light of errors and joking about another's work is a sure way to lose a friend. If you commit to critique another's work, be careful to devote the type of attention that you would want paid to your own works.

Working well with colleagues can provide publication opportunities. Obviously, working together means less work for each individual (and a share of the credit) than if the job was done by one person. Colleagues may have ideas for volumes of collected authorship, or joint articles may come from idea sharing. However, if one is to participate in a network, one must be prepared to meet deadlines and get along with the others to a reasonable extent. It seems that as the process of doing research becomes more demanding and the avenues to publishing become more rigorous, groups of beginning scholars will reap more benefits by working together.

◆ RESPONSE TO CHAPTER EIGHT

JULIA T. WOOD

I found this chapter instructive, insightful, and chocked full of the kind of wisdom and perspective that even the best of professionals rarely achieve. My response, therefore, is limited to underlining some themes in

Professor Gouran's discussion and to suggesting how they apply particularly to women and minority faculty.

I appreciate Professor Gouran's discussion of the *raison d'être* of research. Although I wish this reminder were less necessary, I fear I share his concern that academic institutions and individual faculty sometimes seem to believe that the purposes of research are to expand vita, bolster departmental annual reports, and make the list of most highly cited scholars. Relatedly, it seems to me that "productivity" increasingly is conflated with scholarship. The two are vastly different, and Professor Gouran helpfully refocuses our attention on the more fundamental mission of gaining and sharing knowledge. Knowledge, of course, is more than mere information: It is information within a perspective that gives it meaning and direction.

Scholarship, as distinct from the production of things in print, involves learning from reading and conversations as well as original thinking and databased studies. Genuine scholars are people who are deeply and enduringly engaged with issues they want to understand more fully. They read, think, confer, and conduct study in order to know more about that which intrigues them and to then share their knowledge with a larger community of students, colleagues, and citizens of state and nation. Less important to scholars than a letter of acceptance from a prestigious journal are the personal satisfactions of understanding something better and knowing—usually some time later—that they contributed integrally to the overall knowledge of a subject.

To Professor Gouran's discussion of the review process for articles submitted to journals I would add one qualification. The judgment of reviewers is sometimes limited by their inability to understand traditions outside of their own and their unwillingness to learn about new areas and methodologies of inquiry. If I may use a simple analogy, when you assess how good an orange is by the criteria of appleness, it's unsurprising that the orange is found deficient. Precisely this happens when innovative feminist and minority scholarship is judged by standards that do not fit its assumptions and objectives. Although I do not believe that every rejection of a manuscript on minority or gender issues results from biased judgment, I am convinced that this happens more often than it should. I have seen (and even received on occasion) reviews that dismissed a topic or methodology out of hand by assessing it in light of criteria alien to its purposes and intellectual heritage. This exclusion of anything outside of rigid, a priori views of good scholarship, along with other institutionalized biases, impoverishes the academy and inequitably affects the careers of nontraditional faculty members.

9

CRITICISM AND THE
ACADEMIC PROFESSION*

Gerald M. Phillips

A professional career is built on criticism. Your passage through the academic ranks, your tenure, and your salary depend on it, not to mention your standing with your peers. You will subject your students to it, for it is the most important element of their learning process. And, you will be called upon to criticize others. You will evaluate colleagues professionally, and you may play a role as a referee for scholarly papers and articles or as a writer of reviews for publication. You may even select criticism as your main emphasis in research.

Therapists use criticism to modify behavior, physicians to motivate compliance by their patients. Football coaches and band directors use criticism to decide on first string and first chair; art critics choose the pictures to hang based on criticism; editors are the ultimate critics as they select what to publish and what to send into oblivion. Bosses also employ criticism to decide who gets hired, who gets fired, who gets promoted, and who gets a raise. In fact, a good deal of friendship depends on the exchange of tacit and explicit criticism. Friends modify each other's behavior through criticism in order to cement the bond.

Criticism is not always negative. Several forms of criticism are described in this chapter. But a critic always focuses on an object, a per-

---

*Some of the paragraphs in this chapter are taken in their entirety from Gerald M. Phillips, *Communication Incompetencies*, Carbondale: Southern Illinois University Press, 1991.

son, or a behavior. You must have an object to criticize and a human critic for the process of criticism to take place. Critics can observe both productive behaviors and errors. Productive behaviors are intended to be models to emulate. Errors are pointed out and corrections administered. Enough productive behavior earns rewards; excessive errors are punished. Criticism is commonly used in academic settings to enforce and control compliance behavior among professionals. It is used by all teachers to enforce and control compliance by students.

Teachers select the standard they wish the students to meet. They observe and evaluate student behavior as they direct it. Based on their observation, they proceed to attempt to modify it so that it better meets the standards that have been imposed.

Criticism is variously defined. The following list of definitions is taken from the *Random House Dictionary* (1987, p. 477). Note that some or all of them apply in every academic context: teaching, research, scholarship, and service. All academics are judged by them and use them in making their own judgments. Mastery of criticism is the sine qua non of academic mastery.

Criticism is the act of passing judgment as to the merits of anything. It is standard among academic professionals for professional work to be judged. We have discussed earlier how your academic performance is judged, presumably against a set of standards. We have also mentioned that authorities of various sorts impose standards of judgment when they select papers to be delivered at conventions or to be published in journals. The authors set their own standards for material to be included and for the structure and pattern of the disquisition. When they are satisfied, they submit it to critics for review.

However, rarely are formal standards published. Editors of journals may regulate the form of submissions by requiring conformance to a particular style sheet, but the quality of the content is a judgment call. The same holds true for the evaluation of academic performance. Although most institutions publish standards in some sort of faculty manual, they are often fuzzy and leave a great deal to the individual judgment of those in a position to judge. Consequently, the basis of judgment must either remain a mystery or be negotiated among professionals. The right of superordinates to judge or to arrange for judgments to be made is not questioned. The basis for the standards employed is traditional and consistent, although the application may vary from institution to institution.

Once you enter a contract of employment, you submit yourself to the rules of judgment. Once you submit an article to a journal or a book to a publisher, you submit yourself to whatever critical standards prevail. *It is senseless to argue with these standards.* One can agree to play or not, but it is pointless to argue with a critic about whether or not he or she ought to use a particular set of criteria. It might be useful to consider whether they have been equitably applied, or whether rules and regulations regarding judgments have been violated. But the standards themselves remain as a kind of constitution for the agreement you make with the critic. In the act of teaching, students are required to abide by your standards of judgment. That is the nature of the institution. But many colleges and universities require their faculty members to publish their standards of judgment, that is, their grading policy, in their syllabus, early enough for students who do not wish to play by those rules to find some other game.

We are all familiar with criticism in this form because we have all gone to school. Our parents, in fact, subjected us to it as we learned the rules of acceptable behavior in the home. The person unable to abide by critical control is considered "sociopathic." Civilized society is based on criticism. Freud takes note of this in *Civilization and Its Discontents* (1962), and he tells us that most of us are upset by it. To control the savage and egocentric part of our nature, we must develop a set of critical standards, referred to as our super ego or conscience.

Academics encounter this form of criticism when they begin their graduate study. It controls their application for jobs and determines what job they eventually take. In the prevailing work climate, fair rules must be applied to all hiring. This means that some duly empowered body will pass judgment on competitors for a position, selecting the individual who, in their judgment most closely approximates the critical standards imposed.

Criticism is the act of passing severe judgment, censure, or fault finding. This form of criticism is the standard method of control used in the industrial model of administration. The user presumes, however, that there are clear, published standards. For example, in publishing, manuscripts are generally deemed unsatisfactory unless they conform to a style sheet published in advance and disseminated to all eligible writers. Theses and dissertations represent the initial major exercise in conformance, although style sheets are a major component of pedagogy in rhetoric and composition.

The job description given to any employee provides the basis for this form of criticism. To a large extent, academics are bound by a job description. Although most lack precision, they restrict the behavior of the professional to certain specific areas of interest. Standards are then imposed by those in a position to judge.

To an extent, a college education, including the quest for an advanced degree, is an exercise that provides training in this form of criticism. As an undergraduate, one learns to make correct answers on tests or to produce work that conforms to standards imposed by instructors. Graduate students, similarly, must meet standards imposed by advisors and committees as well as conform to the stylistic requirements of graduate school editors. Failure to conform to official critical standards leads to failure.

In a sense, this form of criticism is probably the most fair, although the most direct in consequences. To the extent that the criteria of judgment are specific and made public, a person can conform or not as he or she chooses or is able. Failure is clear and the consequences are not ambiguous. Because of the directness of the connection between criticism and consequence, this is the preferred method of criticism in any hierarchical organization. Whoever is in charge has the authority to impose the standards. Those who wish the rewards, the paycheck, the rank, the medals, the honor, or whatever, attempt to conform.

When critical standards are not clear, however, it is possible to proceed through sycophancy and self-proclamation. Each candidate for advancement or honors has the ability to conduct whatever kind of public relations campaign that works in order to establish they have met the standards. Alternatively, they attempt flattery on those who judge in the hope that it will tip the judgment in their favor.

Criticism is the act of analyzing or evaluating and judging the merit of a literary or artistic work, musical performance, art exhibit, dramatic production, and so on. The difference between this form and the preceding is that the consequences are not quite so direct. This is the form of criticism applied to personal choice. It is sometimes referred to as "taste."

This is also the form of criticism applied by editors to works submitted. Regardless of how well a document conforms to the submission criteria of a journal or publishing company, at a particular level, there is a question of the editor's taste to be exercised. Submissions are competitive and refereeing follows rules so that acceptance of an article for publication can be used as prima facie evidence of approval of one's work by one's peers.

However, often the process is not as simple as it looks. Editors can influence the outcome of refereeing decisions because they choose the referees. They have the privilege of interpreting the referee's commentaries. When the final decision is made, it is as much a matter of taste as the selection of a mate. Male and female alike, all of us have felt affection for a person of the opposite sex who did not "quite make it," although we would be hard put to specify why.

Often, the exercise of taste implies argument. If more than one person is involved in a judgment, and the rules of selection are less specific than seniority and passing an examination, there can be differences of opinion. The hiring committees of academic institutions are a case in point. An informant notes that at a recent meeting of such a committee, the final decision to offer a position was based on the argument, "well, they all meet the criteria, but I have a feeling about So-and-so!"

Argument of this kind can be about two issues. First is the standards of judgment themselves. Second is the extent to which the individual case meets the standards. If the stasis of the argument is not clear to the participants, disputes about choice may become very loud and difficult.

This form of criticism is also applied by professionals as a form of research. The exercise of critical judgment represents a legitimate form of scholarship in its own right. (It also is a form of criticism that can be sold to the media for profit for those who become effective at it.) In writing this kind of scholarship, the author is obligated to define and defend the standards of criticism as well as demonstrate that the object meets them. Related to this form of criticism are three others used generally by academics as research forms.

Criticism can be a judgmental comment, article, essay, or evaluative assessment. This form of criticism is confined to the scholars. Critical commentary can be applied to any artistic work, but it can also be applied to scientific essays on theory, or to experiments and technical designs. Hard scientists will testify that the conclusions drawn from the most rigid of experiments are still the results of criticism. Was the experiment based on viable theory? Was it well designed? Were there flaws in execution? Were the proper methods of analysis applied? Were the conclusions properly drawn and documented? Were there conclusions that were missed? All of these questions apply in both the sciences and the arts.

Any of various methods of studying artifacts, texts, or documents for the purpose of dating or reconstructing them. This is used largely by historians or students of culture, but sometimes by scientists. In the work, *Wonderful Life* (1989) by Stephen J. Gould, the author examines a set of conclusions drawn about some prehistoric fossils found in a shale bed. He argues that because the original scholar was locked into contemporary theory, he drew erroneous conclusions about how the fossil parts corresponded. Gould then offered his own set of conjectures about the conclusion that could be drawn from the data. Consider how this kind of revisionist scholarship could be applied to the meaning of old documents, the use of rooms in historical buildings, and so on.

Investigation of a text or literary document. This genre includes literary criticism in its various forms. The process of interpretation is a viable and valuable form of scholarship. Any person is entitled to interpret a work, to extract meaning from it. Traditional modes of scholarship, for example, attempt to figure out what a work's author had in mind when he or she wrote it. Contemporary scholars often investigate what a work *could* mean to the persons who read it. Although when carried to the extreme this form of criticism can result in some "imaginative" (read outlandish) conclusions, it is an interesting and often constructive preoccupation.

USING CRITICISM TO MODIFY BEHAVIOR

Let's examine how criticism functions in two aspects of the academic professional's life. First, we can examine how the professional uses it in teaching. Second, we can consider how it is used by the academic's superiors in his evaluation. What is sauce for the goose is sauce for the gander. Professors evaluate and are evaluated. They change students through criticism; they, themselves, change the same way.

Of the possibilities enumerated above, only one actually refers to what teachers do: censure, or fault finding. Students are not appreciated or understood. Teachers do not conduct abstruse philosophical discussions of the qualities of the ideal scholars. Nor do those who evaluate academic professionals spend much time on understanding subtle qualities of expressiveness or thought. Quite the contrary. The nature of the teaching game is evaluation of performance against criteria. That too is the nature of the professional game.

It is quite competitive; not the competition of one team against another (although on the administrative level this is an issue). It is an Olympic-type competition; a struggle to meet standards, to perform according to the rules, to fulfill obligations.

Scholars find it easy to interpret and understand the qualities of the things or ideas they study. In their professional lives, however, they must continually fulfill their obligations to those who judge them. And this is the model they take into the classroom as well.

There is a governing principle, however, that makes the critical environment of academic institutions productive. It is the dictum that *no criticism should be given for which the critic cannot propose a practical remedy.* There is a temptation for those who have the power to criticize to state what is desirable and expect it to be accomplished. This practice, however, is defeating and demeaning. *Learning to distinguish the doable from the desirable* is the basis for all effective criticism. Although interpretation may enable a professor to get lines in print, it is *censure and fault finding* that is fundamental to the practice of their profession. It is modeled after a parental relationship. The orderly relationship between the student and his or her teacher is *parental.* To an extent, despite protestations of democratic governance, academic officials such as department heads and deans similarly exert parental control over the faculties they supervise. The professors have the power to give grades; the administration has the power to grant raises, promotion, and tenure.

Tenure is the initial payoff. It is the initial "A" for good performance in the first semester of an academic career. After tenure comes progression through the ranks and the various other awards, grants, and honors that come to academic professionals. These awards are based on "critical" decisions, that is, they are the results of criticism either through comparison of an individual against standards or against other individuals playing in the same competition. A good metaphor are the cards Olympic judges hold up after an ice skating exhibition. The numbers are recorded, rankings are established, and when one event is over, medals are awarded. For students in the classroom, their entire academic career is often a quest for medals in the form of marks. When they go out into industry, the competition continues, although the payoffs are different. We have noted earlier that the academy is based on an industrial model. Academics play the same kind of game as their students when they enter it.

The Requirements of Fault Finding

Effective criticism is based on orderly procedure. The critic, presumably, can identify an error and call it to a professional's attention. Underlying this system is the presumption that the person who identifies an error in professional performance is capable of suggesting a desirable modification, and, in some cases, of providing advice about methods by which this modification can be accomplished.

We assume that criticism effectively administered in the proper circumstances is successful in maintaining academic standards for an institution or for a professional discipline. The critic of professional performance focuses on errors in the performance of tasks. Simple errors might include not appearing for class or not teaching the subject matter specified. It might also mean not being published, or not playing an active role in the committee process.

In the classroom, the teacher seeks to modify the students' behavior by changing the amount of information they have or the way they perform specified tasks. There are steps or levels coordinated with letter grades. Whereas some professors are rigorous and others "a piece of cake," all of them have levels of judgment. They have ways to distinguish good students from mediocre and bad ones. They have standards of complete success and total failure.

The director of a play may seek to improve movement, intonation, lighting, costuming, and so on. Each time he or she points out a critical flaw, the actor or tech person is expected to remedy it. It makes life so much easier for the person criticized when the critic can offer some alternatives. Directors working with actors operate from a theory of modification. They may use "the method" and try to get the actor to "feel" or "be motivated" to perform in a desirable fashion. They may model the intonation and expression they desire. They may choreograph the movements. They may proceed through trial and error until the desired level of performance is reached. Criticism and response are the essential components of direction, and everyone involved in the process knows it.

Agreement to participate in the critical process is also essential. Criticism can be given by anyone at any time, but only when the recipient of the criticism agrees to be criticized is there any possibility of effective modification. Thus, a writer, submitting a manuscript to an editor makes a tacit agreement to accept editorial criticism. How the writer then responds is a matter of personal choice, but if the writer does not modify, then the manuscript is not accepted. If the actor does not modify, then the director continues to criticize. If the student does not modify, then the teacher reduces the grade. If the employees do not modify, they may be held back or even dismissed. It is pointless to debate criticism. The critic operates from his or her own standards which, presumably, have been made manifest and are part of the agreement. Thus, we have the following essential elements in the critical process:

1. A critic who is qualified in some ways to criticize.
2. A set of standards that serve as the basis for the criticism.
3. A recipient of criticism, a performer (employee, student, etc.) who has agreed to take criticism from the critic.
4. Suggestions or proposals from the critic that the performer may use as guides to the modification of performance.

The Process of Criticism

Critics compare performance to standards derived from theory and experience. When a supervisor or panel of peers act as critics, they imply that they know what the standards are and have both the data and competency required to make a comparison. This, of course, is not always the case. When an academic is evaluated, what is often considered are personality and his or her work. Personality, however, is not really part of the criteria, and yet it cannot be separated from the nature of the work done. Thus, personal likes and dislikes come into play, and the employee is subjected to decisions that could be, but are not necessarily, based on prejudice or whim.

Political considerations are also influential. As teachers are admonished to be objective in evaluating their students, academics claim objectivity as they evaluate each other. In both cases, however, objectivity is an unattainable ideal. The critic has some notion of what an acceptable or meritorious act looks like, compares observed behavior to that standard, and either decides on an appropriate reward or punishment or offers advice designed to adjust behavior until the results conform, in the critic's eyes, to the standards set.

Very often, the concept of *entitlement* is relevant. That is, if an act meets certain standards, various benefits accrue. The notion of entitlement comes from the federal government—Social Security, for example. A worker pays a specified amount of money each pay period. The money is invested and when the worker retires he or she is entitled to another specified sum to be paid back. If the criteria for the entitlement are met, the individual receives that to which he or she is entitled.

When a manuscript meets the editorial standards for publication, it is presumably entitled to be published. But the situation is not quite as clear as Social Security. Editorial standards that go beyond simple conformance of the manuscript to a style sheet require subjective interpretation. Thus, an entitlement exists if, and only if, the subjective interpretation of the manuscript by the editor reaches the conclusion that it matches the standards set. To the writer of the article, this process can seem capricious, political, or arbitrary.

The decision concerning whether or not a manuscript meets the standards represents a primary contingency. If it does, then publication follows. The same thing holds true for promotion and tenure in the academy. Standards, presumably, are published. The person being evaluated submits his or her record to individuals and/or panels charged with the responsibility of comparing that record to the published standards. The judgment results in either rewards or punishments.

What we may forget, however, is that the process is neither immutable nor rational. It is, in the final analysis, based on the outcome of argument, however rigid the criteria appear. For example, the current debate over political correctness vs. the canon is nothing new. Faculties have argued since the earliest days of the university about what should be taught. It is clear, at least since Bishop Isidore of Seville attempted circa 500 A.D. to make a compendium of all that was known, that such an undertaking is impossible. Today, much is excluded from the curriculum. We do not teach astrology or tarot, nor is Tai Chi a regular offering in physical education. As one important scholar pointed out, we do not give the Ku Klux Klan equal time with black studies. Whatever is taught represents a consensus of scholars qualified to pass judgment (Jay, 1992). The situation in the academy is very much like that described by Hugh Blair who considered taste to be a consensus of those of the best intellect and breeding. There is, in short, much folk wisdom in the world that does not qualify for three credits.

The same process of reasoning holds true for criticism on any level. When objective exams are graded, the answers must conform to those on the answer sheet. What is on the answer sheet may conform to the text, and sometimes the answers are quite empirical. At other times, however, the correct answer is an accurate report of what the professor says he or she believes. The situation is much more confused in grading an essay exam. In fact, essay exams are quite idiosyncratic. There is almost no correlation in the grades various professors give.

The proposition underlying all criticism is very simple. The person who does the evaluating carries the burden of proof for the standards used. Sometimes the standards are explicit and amenable to a clear-cut defense. Sometimes they are subtle and obscure. There is no better example than an academic search committee trying to evaluate credentials and what they know about the reputations of the applicants against the explicit statements in the job description and the hidden agendas they all carry with them. Finding a consensus is very difficult; often, it is agreement on the least common denominator.

Labeling and Criticism

Those who seek to modify human behavior generally must discover some stasis on which correction can hinge. The process of discovering stasis takes place during the construction of the therapeutic contract. Stasis is an intriguing old concept. It refers to the central issue in the case. In a sense, the relationship between supervisors and personnel is an argument. The supervisor declares there is an impairment that must be remedied and offers a plan or procedure which, hypothetically, will bring about the desired change. The reason for changing is the crucial issue. Some employees will respond to the supervisor's influence; others will find a need in their own life. Some will reject the advice out of hand either because they deny the authority of the person who offered it or because they do not think it is justified. The effective supervisor must appeal to the employee's need. If the appeal is based on "do it for me," the change is usually temporary and made out of a sycophantic desire to conform in order to qualify for the entitlement. The reason promotion and tenure decisions are so often partially finessed to committees of peers is to maintain the persuasive effect of collective and consensual evaluation. It is presumed that professionals are more likely to take advice from their peers than from those above them in an administrative hierarchy.

What is so often forgotten in criticism, however, is that it is, itself, an argument for change. If there is, indeed, a therapeutic agreement; that is, if one person agrees the other person is qualified to point out flaws and recommend that changes be made, then the basic forensic principles apply. The burden of proof is on the person who proposes the change. This means that there must be a need for a change identified explicitly and to the satisfaction of the person to be changed. Underlying this argument is the moral and aesthetic qualities of the recommended change. These too must be defended. Once this is accomplished, then the critic must propose a method by which the change can be made and demonstrate that it is feasible and in the best interest of the person to whom the recommendation is directed. Simply to say, "be smarter," is a truncated argument and an irrelevant statement. Saying "you need to study harder in order to pass the next exam; here is a study guide to help you" represents a legitimate pedagogical criticism.

If a similar criticism was to be directed at an academic profession-al who, in the opinion of a promotion and tenure committee, was not publishing "enough," there would be the burden of definition. What is "enough?" Is it one good piece in one good journal? Would five pieces in second-rate journals be equal to the one good piece? For that matter, how does one identify a good journal versus a second-rate journal? All of this business must be clarified before confronting the second issue: How does the person being criticized change his or her behavior in order to accom-plish the goal?

The axiom governing this kind of criticism is: Do not point out an error unless you have a remedy. Errors may include a number of things. A disagreement over what to call a thing can be an error. Is it mol-lusk? Or what? Is it a halogen? What is its correct valence? Was the it the "Civil War" or the "War Between the States?" This kind of argument may include negotiating what name to assign to a state of affairs and identify-ing what behaviors are associated with it. For example, it is desirable to be called a "productive" scholar. The question is, how much of what kind of activity can be called "productive" and whether "unproductive" refers to fewer productive acts or specific acts that can be called "unproductive." Careers are made and broken on such judgments.

The process of correction involves specification and agreement on desirable outcomes together with programming strategies to bring them about. *Goal setting* is a process by which the academic professional can become productively associated with his or her institution or discipline. Within most institutions, there are various "games," such as "strategic plan-ning," used to shape the nature and activity of academic departments and divisions. Presumably, when these academic units search for personnel, they attempt to find people whose specialties and skills fit the master plan. When a clear agreement can be made at the time of employment about the role the professional is to play, evaluation becomes a relatively simple and potentially productive process. When professionals are not compatible with institutional goals, there is inevitable clash. Even if the professional is very productive, if the output does not serve institutional purposes, there is great difficulty when promotion and tenure decisions are made.

Agreement on goals makes the role of all parties specific. The cri-teria for judgment can be precise, and standards can be set. Without this agreement there is the possibility of institutional clash. Whenever a profes-sional seeks to break new ground, or attempts a new specialty, it raises ques-tions about evaluations. These questions are difficult to resolve, for a pro-fessional can demonstrate expertise in an area of research and teaching only to be told this is not an area valued by the institution. Advancement and continued employment can be denied on those grounds.

The problem is that it is hard to know for sure when you have agreed on goals. It is one thing to say the goal is to reach the Hamburger

Shop for lunch. It is more complicated if you say, "a *good* lunch." If the goal is to provide proper nutrition for all employees, the situation becomes very complex because the discussion is about some future state of affairs that will look different to each person involved. Thus, even apparent agreement on wording does not necessarily insure that everyone one will be satisfied when some outcome is achieved, even if a dispassionate outsider could say, "Aha, you reached your goals."

During these days of political correctness and diversity, academic issues can become very divisive. A professional can develop expertise in minority studies or women's issues and be negatively evaluated on the grounds that the research is not mainstream. The argument can be raised that it ought to be and that failure to honor it is not politically correct nor equitable to a deprived and denigrated group. The moral issues advanced by one party conflict with the institutional constraints imposed by the strategic plan. Even worse, the issues may not be acceptable to the group that holds the power, in this case, the power to decide the outcome of careers.

The process of evaluation works best when all parties agree on objectives and standards and especially well when the objectives and standards can be specified. The aspiring academic professional serves his or her own purposes best by obtaining a clear definition of institutional expectations at the outset of employment. When evaluations are made for corrective purposes, they only work if the person evaluated respects the critic or values the consequences. There is, in any event, just a suggestion of intimidation in the application of institutional criteria through the promotion and tenure process. Professionals are pressured to conform, even though the pressure often has a democratic appearance, and every attempt is made to ensure fairness (or at least the appearance of it).

The moral is: Whatever the teacher can do to the students can be done to the teacher. Criticism is an endless process. The board of trustees criticizes the president who criticizes the dean who criticizes the department head who criticizes the professors who criticize the associate and assistant professors who criticize the students who criticize the institution to their parents who pay the fees and who can withdraw support if the outcome is not to their liking. And, to add to the mystery, no one in the institution from the president down to the students really knows what is to the parents' liking.

Modification of Behavior

The process of modification is constrained by ability. Limits on performance are imposed by education, experience, and opportunity, not to speak of interest. To put it in simple terms, if you cannot lift 8 pounds easily, you cannot expect to be a proficient bowler. If you cannot coordinate hand and eye movements, you cannot win at pinball; and if you cannot spell words in some modern language, you cannot hope to be a writer. Beyond that, the situation becomes complex. No one really knows how competent a person is until he or she performs an act. When you interview a potential Ph.D. candidate, the best you can do is to make a contingency prognosis. If the candidate passes his or her courses and exams and writes a satisfactory dissertation, then. . . . You can draw your own inferences from past performance. Writing an M.A. thesis offers some presumption of the ability to write a dissertation. Passing undergraduate courses with high grades offers some presumption of passing graduate courses. And so on.

To any student, the institution can only offer the possibility of a degree contingent on surviving the critical process culminating in a satisfactory transcript. Anything else rests with the student and his or her adaptation to the universe he or she encounters. Thereby hangs a tale. Things change for the student with each passing year. Requirements change, faculties change, friends change, habits change, interests change. Whoever the student was at the beginning, he or she will be different at the end, whatever the end.

The institution cannot guarantee to its faculty that its interests and objectives will remain the same, nor can the professional guarantee continued interest and capability. Rules change, and the game changes (like the 2-point possibility after a touchdown or the width of the goal-posts). Thus, at any point in a career, the process of evaluation can skew the relationship between the professional and the institution. Because we cannot fathom the contents of a another person's mind (or even our own, for that matter), "ability" is a tautology. People are able to do what they have been observed to do. We also assume they are able to do what people like them have been observed to do. When people do something they have never done, they are deemed able to do it again; that is, it would not be unreasonable to expect them to do it again. Accordingly, we cannot presumptuously conclude that because people have not performed an act, they are unable to do so. If we assume that, we deny the salubrious effects of criticism altogether. The administration must assume that professionals cannot only continue to perform effectively but can also learn new behaviors. Professionals must recognize that the repetition of approved acts will continue to earn rewards. The process of career development is a careful dialogue guided by criticism administered by the institution through its agencies and the professional seeking privilege and advancement by serving the specified institutional ends.

But, when the rules change, so does everything else. In fact, when anything changes, so does everything else. When the faculty member's interests change or the university changes expectations, there are problems on both sides. The whole therapeutic contract changes; the outcomes are very much in doubt. Academics can count on this happening several times in their career.

THE OPERATION OF CRITICISM IN THE ACADEMY

Given that there is an agreement between student and teacher or employer and employee, then there is a process that makes it possible to change behavior to the mutual satisfaction of all parties involved. Take note that the agreement is generally implicit in the contract of the relationship. A teacher is responsible for administering criticism, and it is a natural component of the learning process to receive and use criticism. Employers are authorized to criticize the performance of employees. The contract need not be etched in stone.

Modifying human task behavior requires the application of a form of technology. Although it cannot be predicted or controlled in a scientific sense, it proceeds on the basis of hypothesis and test. The critic hypothesizes that a comment about a flaw and a directive about a remedy, accompanied with appropriate instruction, will bring about a behavior change. He or she puts the process in motion and evaluates the results. The person who wishes to change submits to the process, collaborates with it, and stays with it until the desired end state is achieved.

In teaching, experimentation with modification of behavior is a generally accepted procedure. Teachers are permitted to have hypotheses based on their professional experience. Students are often subjected to "innovations." However, the bulk of teaching is done by time-tested methods. The situation is not quite so clear when it comes to modification of professional behavior. Professors are not quite like employees of a corporation. Their job descriptions and lines of authority are not crystal clear. Thus, virtually all merit rating is mainly a judgment call, and there are a great many people involved in making the judgments.

Although it may not be possible to devise universally effective administrative and motivational policies to "improve" professional behavior, there are enough alternatives to allow for a kind of "hacking" in an attempt to find ways and means to modify behavior appropriate in each given case. The procedures employed are selected based on precedent and vicarious learning. There are striking similarities in what is done at most institutions. The faculty manual sets goals, however fuzzy they may be. Younger faculty seek mentors or patrons from whom they can receive criticism and protection. Advice is given by department heads and administrators. And, all judgments are hedged by multiple participation by committees in departments and colleges complemented by evaluations from supervisors.

Criticism is objectivized by pointing out models to emulate and by the sharing of experiences. Faculty members tell each other about methods that work; they edit each other's work, and the exchange of gossip also carries warnings about what behaviors to avoid and what behaviors are preferred.

The professional who seeks to change his or her behavior first practices the alteration and receives criticism from people he or she respects on how closely it approximates the set standards. Each subsequent attempt at change evokes more criticism, sometimes in the form of praise. The combination of rewards and punishments can work to change behavior. More often than not, however, professionals are intractable and resistant against criticism of any kind. Attaining professional goals can be construed as a certification of competency and thus as entitlements for innovation and development in creative directions. These, too, are evaluated by others, and the award of praise and blame continues to exert motivation and constraints.

What complicates the process is that it is often exceedingly difficult for critics to avoid brutalizing the people they criticize. It is sometimes equally hard for the people criticized to withstand the challenge to their work. At the conclusion of this chapter, we point to some of the psychological mechanisms that interfere with the operation even of the most legitimate criticism.

Professional criticism proceeds from generalizations about the "good of the order" or the common good. In classes, there is a body of information approved by duly constituted authorities. Teachers on the elementary and secondary levels are required to work from curricula devised by specialists. Whatever the reasons for the content of the curricula and however good those reasons are, they are legitimate and binding on all participants in the process. College teachers, mostly under the umbrella of protection provided by the concept of academic freedom, are empowered to devise and implement their own curricula. It is presumed that most professors are qualified by virtue of their education (demonstrated by earned degrees) to generate curricula and, despite the fact that they have no formal training in pedagogy, it is assumed they can implement it.

Teachers (academic professionals) serve organizations. Within limits, they have freedom of movement, but essentially they are confined in their behavior by the mission and rules of the organization. The organization provides the criteria by which the professionals are evaluated. The organization gives them both identity and a place to achieve intellectual independence. Thus, it is imperative to tailor criticism to the individual case all the while drawing it from institutional interests. College faculties may serve their disciplines or their institutions or both. In any event, save for a few artists and poets, they are not free to engage in unbridled individual effort. Their responsibilities to students make them institutional representatives; their discipline makes them subject to pressure from peers. Their role in the institution subordinates them to the criticism of superordinates.

A norm in many colleges and universities, indeed in most organizations, is talking behind people's backs. Most evaluative decisions are made in private. The person being evaluated is not present, although he or she is obliged to provide information about activities and accomplishments to whatever panel or person is charged with the responsibility of evaluation. The implications of this process for teaching should be obvious. Teachers evaluate classroom performance, submitted work, examinations, and they assign grades. Students may discuss the outcome, but there is no formal appellate jurisdiction. The teacher's decision is final. Although there are cases on record in which students have worked the system and successfully had grades changed, this is exceptional. The norm is that "the judges' decisions are final."

Even professional sports are providing a somewhat more equitable model in the form of reviews through instant replay. In teaching, the instant replays are reviewed by teacher and student, hardly an unbiased panel. When decisions are made, they are entered into the student's record. The permanent record becomes a basis of data on which subsequent evaluations are performed. Admission to graduate schools and eligibility for jobs are based on the written record.

The process differs slightly when the teachers are evaluated. When the decision is made about advancement, tenure, or raises, it is transmitted privately. There is no public record of the failures. Normally, only promotions in rank are publicly announced. Awards of tenure, although not confidential, are also not considered appropriate for public display. When a professional fails in the evaluative process, reasons must be given. In recent years, the process has taken on a litigious air. Evaluative panels usually seek outside advice from various authorities. Persons being evaluated have the opportunity, in most cases, to request (even demand) the reasons for denial of the desired rewards. Sometimes they have an appeal process. Negative news is invariably given in private. When it does not result in termination, its object is to provide an opportunity for the professional to discover how the standards can be met and to understand what is required for a successful evaluation at some future time.

Although peers participate in the evaluation process, they are not normally involved in the administration of criticism. Any professional can seek help in the form of criticism or advice from anyone he or she chooses. To invite peers to engage in public criticism would be like issuing hunting licenses to blind people. The idea is to spare embarrassment in order to provide maximum opportunity for motivation. As we noted earlier in our section on collegiality, however, there is nothing to prevent professionals from developing their own informal critical networks. One has the privilege of asking for advice or critique as well as the privilege of taking or rejecting the advice. The nonproductive aspect of the process lies in debating the advice. It really is not legitimate criticism when you have had to browbeat someone into modifying it to fit your preconceptions.

Labeling

There are a variety of evaluative labels applied to academics: productive, derivative, creative, meticulous, inspirational, pedantic, and so on. There are few empirical criteria associated with these labels. Some are accepted as compliments, others as denigrative. The problem we face is that they become relevant in considering the record for tenure and promotion. A young academic is supposed to be productive and creative but not derivative and pedantic. (There are also criminal-type labels such as "plagiarist," but these have specific criteria associated with them.)

The label assigned is often pervasive and permanent, however. As the "A" or "D" the professor puts on the student's record is done so indelibly, once a label has been fixed on a professional, it may follow him or her throughout the rest of his or her career. It is in this aspect of "creative" that the process becomes very capricious. The following are two not untypical cases:

> Professor X took his first job at a state college that emphasized teaching. He published five articles in the first three years. On one article in a major national journal he was second author. Three were solos in regional journals, and one a solo in a state journal. He was called "productive" by his evaluation committee, but they also showed concern about his "casual" teaching, which they ascribed to an overemphasis on research.

> Professor Y took her first job at a major research university. In her first year she published two articles in national refereed journals which specialized in women's studies. She published two co-authored pieces in her specialty in regional journals; she was first author on one and second author (of three) on the other. She was classified as "creative" but "unproductive" by her evaluation committee, which regarded her women's studies articles as "political." The committee also expressed concern about whether her teaching was also "politicized."

These two stories illustrate how labeling affects the process of criticism as it is applied to a professional career. There are two main ways in which people respond to labeling. Some accept the label and proceed to behave in line with its predictions. Others use the label as a motivation to change. It is implied in the therapeutic alliance that characterizes criticism; behavior and character attributes must be labeled. Productive behavior is reinforced by praise. Nonproductive behavior is often punished on the presumption that it can be reversed. There must be some common reference for the system to be effective. There is, however, no guarantee that praise alone will be sufficient to sustain desirable activities. The activities must be defined explicitly and instruction given in how to carry them out. Thus, tangible rewards such as pay raises, tenure, and promotion usually accompany it. These function as "carrots." Denial of regular progress or tangible reprimands function as "sticks." Advancement breeds good will. Anything negative may generate anger and rebellion or motivate the professional to seek another job. It also provides a substantive rationale by which the professional can explain, justify, and excuse his or her failure to attain rewards.

The contract between the professional and his or her institution must make clear what form official criticism will take, when and how it will be administered, and how the professional is expected to respond to it. Whether the response to negative criticism is productive depends on whether there are viable alternatives provided. Some professionals may be perfectly willing to put up with their "ineptitude" and seek survival within the crannies of the institution or elsewhere. Some choose to do administrative tasks no one else wants. They may actually make themselves invaluable by these means. Sycophancy is also a useful way to avoid adequate performance. Flattery and obsequiousness are used as effective forms of inartistic proof. Sometimes they work; more often, they do not.

SOCIAL BEHAVIOR AND THE CLASSICAL CONCEPTION OF CRITICISM

The social exchange characteristic of the academy is a process of exchanging criticism; people change their behavior to obtain the approval of those they find important. Friends become friends because of the way they respond to each other. Each negative response to one's behavior suggests a behavior to be modified. New academic professionals encounter "stars" in the profession, deans and department heads, competitors for rewards and attention, potential friends, and potential enemies. Each administers criticism, and each person has the privilege of deciding how to negotiate behavioral change.

Essentially, in social dialogue each party evaluates the behavior of the other, decides whether it represents approval or disapproval, and chooses a response accordingly. To sustain a relationship we continue those behaviors that are rewarded and either discontinue or modify those that appear to evoke censure. The effective administrator takes advantage of his or her power to manipulate praise and blame in order to "socialize" the new academic into collaborating to achieve the goals of the institution. Senior members of the profession use similar techniques to shape the next generation of professionals.

With this behavioristic model, the modification of professional behavior can become very scientific. Scientific management is a process of deciding on goals and applying appropriate motivations. Persons being criticized have a modicum of control. For one thing, they can decide whether it is worthwhile to remain within the institution. Second, they can decide whose criticism is relevant and ignore the criticism they decide is irrelevant. Third, they can limit the amount of change they make to what they think would be most influential in obtaining their personal goals.

When people are spontaneously responsive to criticism, they are easily confused and often make errors. Giving and receiving criticism should be a conscious act on both sides in order to be effective. That means the person who is being criticized must, him- or herself, be critical in deciding what is relevant, useful, and feasible. Gratuitous criticism not germane to professional objectives can be easily ignored. Criticism offered "for your own good" is most often malicious and should serve as a warning. Criticism about matters that cannot be changed should be rejected. The questions that must be asked by the person criticized are simple and apply in every case.

Is the criticism about a behavior that can be modified?
Is that behavior germane to my career?
Is there reason to believe that modification would improve any
   thing?
Is the person offering the criticism prepared to offer sugges-
   tions about implementation?
Is there some standard by which improvement can be measured,
and do both parties understand this standard in the same way?

Imitation is a powerful force in criticism. Professionals learn to be what they are by observing the behavior of others. Deciding whom to imitate is difficult. Intrinsic in imitation is transference. We have trouble figuring out why we decide someone is worth imitating. Often, there are highly personal and emotional issues in operation. For one thing, it is important to imitate someone who can be imitated. A 5-foot, 100-pound white woman will not become a Barbara Jordan, and a bulky man of Mediterranean ancestry will not become a Ronald Reagan. On the other hand, the small woman could copy Jordan's intensity, the bulky man could approximate Reagan's timing. It is here that criticism performs its most useful role by helping the professional select performable acts.

Transference complicates matters. Sometimes we respond to others because they take the place of important persons in our lives. This complex psychoanalytic principle shapes a great many of our relationships. In professional life, however, it is especially relevant because of the blending of ages and genders in the workplace. It is all too easy to make a father figure out of a department head or senior professor, or endow a colleague with the romantic qualities of a lost lover. A certain amount of detachment is necessary in order to maintain a modicum of autonomy in selecting appropriate professional moves.

WHAT WE DO NOT KNOW ABOUT CRITICISM

We do not know precisely how criticism motivates behavioral change, although we are quite sure it does. The process is quasiclinical in the sense that the person who administers the criticism assumes the role of therapist. We form a number of our friendships this way, too. We give our friends suggestions and receive criticism from them, and we accept suggestions for modification (improvement) from those whose opinions we respect.

In the academy, suggestions are often made tacitly. One professional would hardly accept public responsibility for changing the behavior of another. On the other hand, the flattery of admiration can motivate countertransference. Many a teacher has been corrupted by the idolization of his or her students. The flattery of emulation and the obvious glee with which some students accept critique can be a heady brew indeed.

In the same sense, one prominent academic can easily be pushed into the role of dominant critic and take over management of the career of another without even being aware of it. The apprenticeship of the intern and law clerk consists of practicing the profession under the scrutiny of a mentor who criticizes and advises. In essence, we are talking about coaching. In any athletic endeavor, the coach is empowered to criticize, correct, and drill the athlete in the "proper" procedure.

In the final crunch, academics relate to each other in both ways. They choose role models who in some cases are masters to apprentices; in other cases, they coach. We have not yet devised a way to directly measure the effect of criticism on behavior. We can argue, generally, that a critic can modify behavior, but we cannot take individual advisories and assess their impact. Parenthetically, we cannot really measure the influence over time a teacher may have on students. We acquire anecdotal recollections, but no real establishment of causal connection. In this sense, the influence of criticism is presumed but not proven.

Occasionally, some junior professional will come back after a decade and recall some bit of wisdom they heard from their role model's mouth and become very maudlin about how influential it was. These bits of sentiment are not to be trusted. Often we are not aware of who influences us to do what. The word *role model* is important, however. The role model becomes the critic, like it or not. Few role models know that they are being modeled and consequently cannot modulate criticism in a formal sense. On the other hand, often those who are charged with the responsibility of modulating criticism do not become role models and consequently their criticism is not influential. What this means, in blunt terms, is that people often ignore the boss. Bosses (deans, department heads) are often disliked, their criticism mistrusted, and their motives questioned.

We cannot predict how people will respond to their role models. They will ignore what some people say, become defensive with others, and tumble head over heels to follow the advice of still others. Some colleagues make them angry; they regard others as irrelevant; some inspire them to great heights of accomplishment. We also cannot predict which words they will take seriously and which they will ignore. In short, people exert influence on each other in unpredictable ways. If it were all random, it would be no fault, no foul. But operant conditioning seems to work. Young academics will fall under the spell of one person or another, and very often senior academics are literally forced into a position in which they become responsible for the career of a younger person, consciously or unconsciously. In any case, advice is offered, taken, or rejected. The advice is based on one person's experience and taken by another as a vicarious experience. When it works, it becomes part of the repertoire. When it does not, it stirs resentment. Most people base their recommendations on conventional wisdom, personal experience, or the social canons of good taste. Very little of this is profound, and in the final crunch, most academics who make it follow the same path.

What appears to be most effective is to select the person from whom to take advice and solicit it consciously. This enables you to evaluate it and be selective about what to try and what to reject. Criticism is most effective when performer and critic collaborate on the identification of flaws and the choice of remedies. Without agreement on the entitlement of criticism and its process, criticism is correction. It is easy to administer moralistic sermons, and something else again to offer sound advice. The young academic ought to be able to tell the difference. He or she also ought to be able to spot a "Knute Rockne" disquisition and modulate the amount of inspiration he or she derives from clichés profoundly uttered. The effective critic detects a need, devises a plan to meet it, and convinces the recipient of the feasibility and desirability of the recommended modification.

There is very little good that can come of the admonition "you must publish more!" Every academic knows it. Every academic would like to do it. What is useful is identification of the impediments to publication (out-of-date data, ungrammatical writing, and so on).

The rub comes when the advice is wrong, or the recipient cannot follow it. When this happens, confidence is breached, and the therapeutic agreement on which effective criticism is based is likely to be abrogated. That is why most formal criticism is greeted with resistance or apathy.

Once the recipient learns that the critic can make errors, it no longer seems sensible to attempt to follow his or her advice. The therapeutic alliance, so essential to successful psychotherapy, is an important feature in the successful operation of the critical process. When an individual plays the major role in deciding what to modify and has some options in the approach, he or she assumes some responsibility for his or her own career. It is not so easy to foist the blame on others. Thus, conscious consent to be criticized or recognition that one has selected a role model is a constructive step toward autonomy.

Furthermore, when criticism is based on explicit rules (or at least rules that are popularly accepted), idiosyncratic behaviors are ruled out. The professional understands that all behavior has consequences and behaves in line with the probabilities, unless, of course, there is an overpowering moral issue at stake. The road to tenure is pretty much the same for everyone. There are exceptions made at the margins, but most obtain their academic goals by performing by the book.

A Brief Summary

There are components of the academic situation that must be considered in any case. These are the relevant questions:

1. How are the decisions made? Who is entitled to be a critic? Who is qualified to be a critic? Whose criticism can actually be used?
2. What are the published criteria? Are they explicit enough to be useful? Do critics base their criticism on the criteria?
3. What are the precedents? What have others done to get their rewards? Can they be imitated?
4. Who makes the decisions? How are relevant decision makers picked? Do they know what they are doing?
5. What is the proper procedure for drawing the attention of the relevant decision makers to the professional's accomplishments? How does anyone find out what you are doing? Is there an orderly procedure for critique?
6. Are there persuasive levers available? For example, would another job offer be persuasive? What essential services does the candidate contribute and can they be obtained from anyone else?

Criticism is "for keeps." On the surface, it is a gentle and effective way of modifying behavior. Deep down, however, it becomes a matter of economic life and death. There are few people who have not, at some point in their careers, encountered a situation in which they had to adapt or get out. You need to know when you are likely to receive criticism and what is at stake.

Versatility is the crucial issue. What I mean here is the importance of being able to adapt to changes in the workplace. One of the main reasons for criticism is the necessity to prepare employees to cope with changes. There is no way to freeze time, and there is no way to stop learning. This may be the essential secret of professionalism. We cannot predict what the academy will look like 10 years from now, but anyone being hired today will have to continue working tomorrow.

RESISTANCE TO CRITICISM

It is easy to ignore criticism. You will get plenty of it, but you do not have to pay any attention to it. If it comes from a teacher or a boss, you will have to look properly appreciative. But you take criticism at your own risk. Furthermore, even if you decide criticism is in order, and you can profit from it, can usually afford to be selective. You need only take the criticism from people qualified and/or authorized to offer it and then only the criticism you think will be in your best interest.

On the other hand, it is pointless to argue with criticism. Getting a critic to change his or her mind does not change the condition at which it is directed. If someone does not like your teaching or your writing, it is important to ask the question: Does it matter? If the person's opinion is going to be influential in your future, then it is important to listen, learn, and change.

Faculty members often resist correction as a matter of principle, the same way students resist instruction and patients resist therapy, just as patients refuse to comply, and students struggle to bend the system, faculty members have their own systems of evading essential criticism. It is not always clear, however, what they are resisting and why. Some may be frightened by the consequences of changing their behavior. Others may recognize a need to change but feel that it is impossible for them to do so. They may not want to risk failure. Still others may feel a need to reject a therapeutic alliance because they do not have confidence in the person giving the criticism.

The critic must understand that there will be resistance. People will not automatically comply. The critic who expects to make some palpable changes will have to do a job of teaching, including motivating and training. People do not usually change on demand. They do not want to, and they frequently do not know how.

Merely recognizing that someone is resisting criticism is not very helpful either. Demanding that they stop resisting does no good at all.

There is no point to digging into the recipient's psyche to find the reasons for resistance. What is important is to understand that there is resistance and to find a way to overcome it, if possible. People have a natural tendency to resist correctives because it is often inconvenient and uncomfortable to change. Whatever they say in response really translates into "I just don't want to." This is usually the first line of defense. Students continually tell their teachers about their fraternity party or how they just "broke up" or had "the flu" or a "hangover." These reasons may sometimes be eloquently stated, but they are normally ineffective. It is equally ineffective when a faculty member complains about a "heavy teaching load" or "the politics of publishing." No editor would even bother to respond to a letter from an aspiring author claiming that he or she would revise but "it would interfere with plans for the weekend."

Tenure and promotion are not granted merely because the candidate wants them. Of course, he or she wants them, but even in the loosest administrations, there are criteria and procedures by which they are granted. The critics are the administrators and faculty committees duly empowered to act. Collectively, their judgments add up to arguments that support the final decision. Customarily, the burden of proof is on the professional to establish his or her case. That means anticipating criticism or soliciting it in advance. "How am I progressing on the tenure track?" is not an unreasonable question to ask one's department chair from time to time. It helps, of course, if you have mentors to speak for you, but even the most powerful mentor can do little in the face of an inadequate record. One of the advantages of keeping posted on criticism of your work is to help you recognize when it is time to "cut bait."

There is no panacea for overcoming resistance. Sometimes the criticism is picayune and not worth considering. Sometimes the remedy proposed is impossible. Whether you try to overcome resistance depends on how intent you are in modifying the behavior of the other. In the classroom, overcoming resistance is a major component of instruction. In personnel supervision, it is an imperative. Any professional who wants to succeed has to learn to be properly critical of criticism and learn how to take it when necessary.

It is, normally, not productive to accuse the trainee of willful resistance. This places him or her in a defensive position. The professional therapeutic alliance tends to rule out resistance at the outset. The professional who is being criticized may protest the ineptitude of the critic or the injustice of the criticism, but the process itself is intrinsic. The syllabus must be adhered to; performance required; practice supervised; no excuses accepted. The student must either perform or fail the course. The client may be dropped from treatment or committed. The employee can be denied tenure, not promoted, or given a minimal raise.

The cost of failure to accommodate to criticism provides the impetus for the trainee to overcome resistance by him- or herself. Some resistances come with built-in remedies. Others are impregnable. There are 10 obvious patterns of resistance: denial, suspicion, rationalization, transference, refusal to participate, self-fulfilling prophecy, programmatic activity, fighting criticism, narcissism, and begging for mercy.

Any person who is criticized is threatened. The whole process is essentially inartistic in Aristotelian terms. The student in class is threatened by the grade. Although it may be only a temporary state lasting a semester or at most a year, failure to respond properly to criticism demands punishment. The same holds true for employees, potential authors, applicants for grants, candidates for tenure, and so on. If you do not do it right, there are consequences. We offer the following list as a guide for critics. The critic can make the choice of whether to persist or back off, but the recipient of the criticism reaps the potential rewards and takes the punishments depending on his or her response.

Denial

Competency cannot be demonstrated merely by asserting it. It can be confirmed by others when they see it. A student who performs well in the classroom gains attention by good test scores or intelligent recitations. A competent faculty member receives favorable teaching evaluations. A competent researcher successfully publishes his or her work. No one earns points for claiming he or she is going to do something tomorrow. Even obtaining grants must be preceded by a formal proposal.

Competent performance has an affect on others. People can hear it, pay attention to it, be moved or informed by it, learn from it; they respond to it in affirming and rewarding ways. It has discernible components: it is well organized, replete with interesting narratives and examples, phrased in attention-getting language, and delivered in a versatile and expressive voice.

Errors are equally easy to spot. But there is a tendency for some performers to deny even their small gains when they make them. They take criticism and improve but refuse to acknowledge their change. Sometimes they are so preoccupied with feelings about their failures that it blinds them to the fact that they have succeeded at performing successfully. It is more comfortable to retain the old feelings of persecution and rejection. To avoid acknowledging success, they may deny what they feel, report it inaccurately, or even purposely misunderstand it. When they get into this frame of mind, they are quite resistant to criticism.

More often they do not want to assume responsibility for repeating their "virtuous" act. If they can make others believe it was an accident or a lucky shot, they do not have to repeat it. Furthermore, our society does not encourage people to crow about their successes. High grades and salary increases are not legitimate topics of conversation. They are considered bragging.

This is odd because athletes and politicians vie for trophies all the time. Students fear disclosing their high grades lest they embarrass others. Academic professionals learn early not to talk about their salaries; promotions are duly announced by public information offices, and frequently, articles accepted for publication are secrets from all but the necessary authorities.

It is, however, de rigueur to complain about failures and peccadillos. Involuted dialogue about social failure, although boring, is normal. It represents a kind of exchange. "You tell me your misery, and I'll tell you mine." This is the substance of some popular TV talk shows and the basis of the 12-step system in overcoming addiction. Unfortunately, inept academics cannot get by with comfort for their misery. There is no obvious habit for them to kick. The acquisition of skill demands discipline, and discipline is a lonely process.

Academics must deal privately with their feelings about themselves. They may flinch when a dean tells them they are not publishing enough, but they must deal with it. The same holds true for students who are told they are not doing well in a course. To overcome the kind of resistance that comes from the hesitation to talk about success requires considerable ingenuity. One method is to offer hard data about accomplishments, but sometimes the urgency to deny is so strong, that the individual can snatch defeat from the jaws of victory. Sometimes people handicap themselves by refraining from repeating what they have already done successfully. It is tempting for teachers and supervisors to try to respond to expressions of misery, but it is much more effective to force the acknowledgment of accomplishment, note that it is prima facie evidence of success, and refuse to allow recidivism.

Suspicion

People are naturally suspicious of others who are more skillful than they, especially when they wish they had the skill. One problem in the critical process is that when you take criticism you tacitly admit the person who gives it is qualified to give it. It is a much more effective defense to question how others came to achieve their skill. By suspecting those who succeed of doing so because of special influence, an unskillful person can justify him- or herself from taking the criticism.

It is easy to suspect the motives of the person who gives the criticism. "The reason he picks on me is that he is trying to demoralize me." "She criticizes me because she knows I won't be able to compete." It is not necessary to pay attention to critics whose motives are suspect.

Because professional advancement is a shared responsibility, incompetent performers must learn to ascribe credit and blame properly. For one thing, they cannot blame themselves for not being able to do what they have not learned to do. People tend to take credit for their successes and if they can, ascribe their failures to someone else. Critics are always a threat. A critic, by his or her very existence, says that something is amiss. People do not like that message; they would prefer to believe in their own perfection. Thus, suspicion of criticism is natural. It is also difficult to overcome.

The process sometimes becomes almost paranoid. Because criticism usually comes from superordinates, it is easy to ascribe base motives to them. They are threats; but wait! It is the critics who are threatened. The young professional develops the clear insight that the critic is jealous of his or her budding genius and wants to cut the person down. Then the suspicion really sets in; malice is the only logical motive for criticism. It could not be that the youngster's work is immature, rambling, incoherent, irrelevant, or done in the wrong style sheet. Once the paranoid notion is established, the critic can be ignored.

Critics may want to allay suspicion. For some reason, they may believe that what they have to say might be useful. A good critic understands that no one has an obligation to take criticism (only to be polite by acting as if they are listening), and those who wish to criticize have the burden of gaining and holding attention until the other person commits to the process. The critic needs to find ways to engage the attention of the person being criticized, to show that there is some mutual gain from the critical process.

Consider the situation of the student who needs help but does not ask for it because he or she believes that it is impossible to get the instructor's attention. When the teacher seeks out such students, they ignore his or her help because the teacher is "picking on them." Follow this model with the young teacher needing help from a senior colleague, department head, or dean. The senior has "authority" and standing as a critic. By simply acknowledging this fact of vocational life, an individual can obtain much useful criticism. At any event, the person who receives the criticism can ignore it, if he or she chooses.

Criticism does not work unless the need for it is acknowledged. By suspecting the critic's motives, it is possible to distract yourself from even considering the possibility that what you are doing might be correctable. This provides temporary peace of mind but long term insecurity.

Suspicion of the process of criticism stems from various myths about it. We have been told in popular literature that we must be authentic. We are told that it is good to "let it all hang out," to be open and frank. Skillful criticism, however, demands careful modulation. We have already made the point that criticism should not be offered without an accompanying remedy. Suspicions can be overcome by constructive suggestions to facilitate improvement. Suspicions are fed by excessive frankness and uncensored fault finding.

The aphorisms of the medical model also breed suspicion. When people discover that they must change their behavior, they take refuge in the claim that the behavior to be changed is natural. It is defined as a sickness. Sickness then allows them the claim of diminished responsibility and the privilege of attacking their critics on the ground that they are criticizing behavior that cannot be changed. The person who needs help can hide behind his or her "handicap." Unfortunately, in the classroom, the teacher is the last resort. If the student needs help, the teacher is the only person authorized and qualified to give it. In the professional world, inept academics can choose to ascribe their inadequate behavior to any cause they like, but the psychiatrists and clergymen to whom they might turn for help can do little to facilitate publication of their research. They may help inept people to adjust to their ineptitude, but this does not help advance a career. Resignation to your lot in life means compromise with your potential.

Rationalization

Inept performers are often skillful at explaining their personal failures to themselves and others. They are surprisingly fluent with their friends and colleagues as they complain about criticism, but remarkably reticent with their teachers and supervisors when criticism is offered. A standard strategy is to display sycophancy with the person who offers the criticism and then ignore it completely. Superordinates are often easily fooled into believing they are relevant because it something they would like to believe.

An effective defense against rationalization is to convince the recipient of criticism that blame for failure can be shared. The poor student can be appealed to by a teacher willing to admit his or her weakness. A truculent junior colleague will be intrigued by stories of a senior professor's early failures. It is important for both parties to criticism to understand that they each have a responsibility. The real antidote to the many available rationalizations is to make the critical contract explicit. "I can help you; will you accept it?" Once the agreement is made, both parties can agree on an acceptable methodology. Some people prefer direct and explicit criticism. Others prefer to proceed through heuristics.

Critics are sometimes trapped by rationalization into doing the job. It is not unusual for a senior professor to end up writing the paper for the junior colleague without claiming co-authorship. Once the paper is published, the junior colleague can rationalize the claim that he or she does not need any further criticism.

It is important that the recipient of criticism be denied an escape by explaining that the critic had no right to interfere or that the methodology was flawed. The problem is, however, that often critics are snobs, clods, or egomaniacs. They regard criticism as a weapon of destruction and often use it to take advantage of their position. Sometimes the rationalizations are quite accurate; critics are inept or cruel. When the critic is incompetent at criticism, he or she is no help whatsoever to the recipient.

Transference

Transference is the most dangerous of the resistances. Students, for example, often improve rapidly once they commit to training. Unfortunately, virtually all of them go through a period when they believe that their accomplishments are entirely due to their teacher. They endow their teacher with "powers." They admire their instructor so much, they seek ways to spend time with her or him. They want to report their successes and be congratulated; they want their papers displayed on the refrigerator with magnets. When they whimper about their failures, they want the teacher to stroke their heads. Once they discover their instructor is available to listen, they try to unload their autobiographies.

We have already noted how heady this attachment can be for an instructor. When a student offers complete trust, it is hard not to take advantage. The same process takes place when a young faculty member becomes attached to a senior colleague. The opportunity to manipulate is often too attractive to resist. Most often, the recipient of the transference is not even aware of his or her advantage and consequently exploits it without being aware of it.

Furthermore, a countertransference often develops. As the student becomes dependent on the teacher, the teacher becomes dependent on the student's respect and affection. Again, the process is repeated when one faculty member attaches him or herself to another.

Transference is not a conscious resistance, but its presence impairs the critical process. When considerations other than professional ones arise between superior and subordinate, in any context, the main business quickly becomes a secondary consideration as the pair works out the confused relationship. It is important that newcomers be careful not to develop transferences. They are perilous in both directions. In any case, transference can be resisted by concentrating on behavior as opposed to relationship. When one becomes aware of strong feelings, prudence demands that a social separation be made, and if contact is necessary at all, it should be centered on tangible work.

The importance of avoiding countertransference cannot be overstated. It is easy for mentors to inflate their egos by accepting the dependency of young faculty members. Their feelings of potency are enhanced, and they may engage in duplicitous strategies to keep the dependency relationship going. However fulfilling an interpersonal relationship might be, success at professional performance (and in the classroom) is best facilitated by a certain degree of detachment that permits objectivity and prevents pathological dependency.

Refusal to Participate

The simplest way to handle criticism is to refuse to accept it. One can be polite, appear to listen, and ignore everything that is said. Teachers often confront incompetent students who listen passively to criticism and do not modify anything. They convince themselves they are doing well enough and need no improvement. That is a fait accompli that keeps authority figures at bay. Teachers are aware that there are students in their class who are resistant, but they do not have the time to bother with them, and when the course is over, the students go on their way; no fault, no foul. The situation is a bit more complicated when a person in authority attempts to offer constructive criticism that is very necessary to a young professor's advancement. The cases of beginning faculty members who cannot get an article published but refuse competent criticism from their department head or older members of the faculty are legion. But there is little that can be done about it. The beginner declares he or she can do "it" well enough whenever he or she cares to, but. . . . The alternative is to say, "I am working on it!"

Denial of error is a logical justification for refusal to be criticized. Refusal to be criticized excuses lack of improvement. Lack of improvement justifies failure. It is a simple process. Unfortunately, professionals keep score. Failure on the first job can easily spell continued failure if the individual cannot make some kind of peace with the critical process.

There is no antidote to this defense. If a person denies needing criticism and avoids receiving it, he or she is entirely responsible for the consequences. We should note here, however, that refusing proffered help from one person does not preclude accepting it from another. We are not concerned about the person who solicits and takes criticism selectively. Our culprit is the person who denies needing criticism and does not take it from anyone.

Self-fulfilling Prophecy

Students often express a "self-fulfilling prophecy" of ineptitude. The student who believes strongly that he or she will fail probably does. Once again, the teacher does not have the opportunity to hear the excuses or even know what rationale the student is using for his or her failure.

Whatever criticism is offered is ignored because the student "knows" he or she is not good enough. They get away with it and take a lower grade than they could have earned had they worked at the course.

Faculty members can use the same excuse. They can reject criticism on the grounds that they cannot possibly be good enough to do whatever it is they are supposed to do. They excuse themselves from trying by declaring the outcome in advance of the contest. A great many beginning faculty members are quite capable of talking themselves into ineptitude. Often, they seem to be upset when things go well. They will sometimes stop a successful effort in the middle and not pick it up again. Characteristic of this genre are those who present successful papers at scholarly conventions and simply do not make the effort to turn them into publishable manuscripts on the grounds that they cannot possibly be revised and accepted.

One defense against this kind of resistance is to pick things up in the middle and become a co-author, but often this does not work because the power of the prophecy is so great, the young scholar will turn the work over to another rather than make the effort to get the paper in shape. Furthermore, senior faculty members who embark on a career of rescue often end up as ghost writers for the incompetent.

The most effective way to counter self-fulfilling prophecies is to try to persuade young scholars of the likelihood of a successful outcome. Helping to set goals and working out collaborative schedules can preoccupy them so they do not have the opportunity to ruminate about their predictions of failure. When persuading people out of their self-fulfilling prophecies, keep in mind that a person who predicts failure and then fails has a 100% record as a prophet despite no record as a published author.

Programmatic Activity

A clever evasion of criticism comes in the form of ritual and routine. By habituating techniques of research and ritualized writing habits, a young professional can resist any criticism simply by saying that he or she is not ready. Students do it all the time. They must lay out the notebook in a certain way, position the textbook, sharpen the pencils, and so on. By the time they are ready to work, it is too late to work. Many unsuccessful young academics have similar work habits. They adhere to whatever pattern of research and writing they used for their dissertation and refuse to modify it, thus increasing the likelihood that they never write anything but their dissertation over and over again.

Another evasion is to stay with topics long after they are out of date. Included are those scholars who keep writing about the works of rejected authors or who use outmoded statistical techniques despite the fact that every effort in those areas has been rejected.

Antipathy to Criticism

One way to avoid taking criticism is to give it. Often, the least successful young professionals are those who are most adept at offering gratuitous criticism to others. If they do it definitively enough, they can put off anyone who might offer criticism to them. They will often take refuge in the argument that "things were not done this way at their old school," or they attack the "power structure" or the "old boy network." They can claim critics are "anti-feminist" or "too politically correct." Their premise is that a good offense precludes any defense at all. One successful senior professional stated the law: *Those who are least able to solve their own problems are the quickest to offer advice to others about theirs.*

Sometimes they are good enough to succeed on their own. Often they are not. Sometimes they will preempt criticism by criticizing themselves and challenging others to do something about it. "I know I am old-fashioned on this topic, but I really believe in it" will stop offered criticism in its tracks. Each time they are offered a technique or system, they respond with extended recitations of the ineffective remedies they have previously tried and recite a litany of their personal faults, which they regard as intrinsic and not subject to remedy.

Narcissism

It is amazing how narcissistic we all can be. We have learned to concentrate on ourselves because of the possibility of social failure. We seem to believe that other people pay a good deal more attention to us than is actually the case. In fact, we notice only a few details about the people around us. We are only concerned when we are engaged with them.

Incompetent performers (students or teachers) are especially sensitive to what others think of them. They believe others evaluate them in advance and try to intimidate and suppress them. For the most part, they place themselves in an adversarial relationship with others. They believe that the other person could not possibly mean them any good. There is, in this sense, a kind of paranoia that can be both protective and destructive. Because of their sensitivity to social evaluation, they keep out of situations they cannot handle or resort to inartistic methods to take control of them. On the other hand, this protective quality also keeps them from making a legitimate effort to perform effectively.

In some, this generates an approach-avoidance paradox. When criticism starts, they are attracted to it because they believe it could be helpful. On the other hand, once they become involved, their natural suspicion keeps them from seeing what they can gain from it and prevents them from conceding that they could improve. They tend to personalize all criticism, make a personal issue out of it, and divert attention from the task to the relationship.

Critics, however, must also take note of the power of narcissism. People will not accept criticism merely because of the status or reputation of the critic. Criticism must be motivated. If you bother to give criticism at all, make sure the person you are giving it to regards it as useful and collaborates with you in using it. Otherwise, it is just so much wind.

Begging for Mercy

Sometimes beginners solicit reassurance and pity. It is clear that some of their habitual behaviors are designed to gain exemption from social responsibility. By demonstrating that they are manifestly unqualified to succeed, they request that others excuse them from living up to the norms. Their behaviors persuade others to provide entitlements associated with diminished responsibility. They are not good enough; they demand to be told they are good enough. Once they are told they are good enough, there is no point in telling them they are not. These kinds of professionals rapidly wear their critics down and eventually are ignored, until they are terminated.

It is important not to be trapped by these people. Unconditional positive regard is not useful because giving it tends to excuse inept behavior. To be effective, critics must be firmly unforgiving of inept behavior. The simple Skinnerian formula of rewarding competent performance and either ignoring or actually trying to extinguish inept performance seems to be the most useful pattern of criticism.

DOING THE DOABLE

There are two possible ways to look at criticism. One is to discover the cause of the social angst that makes it so difficult for some people to accept it. This orientation presumes that we can know why people have problems. We do not! They may have problems because they choose to have them, because they cannot help it, or because they are told by someone else that what they do is problematic. We presume that incompetent people are somehow misoriented to techniques of competent performance. All of this gobbledygook gives way to simple tautology. People are called incompetent because their performance leads to inferences, by themselves or others, that they are incompetent. Once they have the label incompetent, they act it out, and often that is that. This simple theory explains incompetency but does little about it.

The second way to look at incompetence is through the label. Whatever label is assigned a person is associated with behavior. Any modification of either changes the other. Using this approach makes the study of criticism into the design and implementation of technology. Successful criticism requires conscious effort. It cannot be done casually. As the individual seeks a competent critic, the critic must identify a person who is amenable to criticism and able to take it. Together they must identify what is doable and collaborate on ways and means. Explaining why a person is the way he or she is is not within the legitimate purview of an academic relationship. It is distracting and wastes time. A sensible collaboration—what people can do for each other to bring about mutual improvement—is the essence of collegiality and the basis of success in the academy.

◆ RESPONSE TO CHAPTER NINE
DENNIS S. GOURAN

In this chapter, I believe that my colleague Professor Phillips succeeds admirably in discussing such matters as the pervasiveness, various roles, and values of criticism in the academic profession as well as its limitations and the sources of resistance to it. I confess to a certain distaste for his use of the game metaphor in this and other chapters, but on the whole, I find his treatment of the subject both instructive and useful. A dimension of criticism he fails to explore, however, is that which one directs toward him- or herself.

Being appropriately self-critical (reflective, if you will) can be at least as important to one's intellectual and professional development as any external assessments one may receive. In advocating that professionals become critical of themselves, I do not mean to imply the sort of self-effacement to which some scholars are disingenuously given. Such individuals are typically enamored with their own achievements but feign modesty as a means of eliciting expressions of admiration and praise. Rather, I am concerned with honest self-appraisal.

Criticism from others, as Professor Phillips notes, can be highly beneficial. A person is more likely to appreciate the benefits, however, if he or she is able to appraise his or her own performance in a detached manner. Facing oneself honestly can be more imposing than confrontation with even the harshest of external critics; hence, there is often an understandable reluctance to do so and, instead, a tendency for one to turn outward.

In my experience, individuals who ask for criticism often do not want it. Instead, they are seeking affirmation, positive strokes, or other forms of feedback that enhance their self-esteem. Signs of these types of motivations are injunctions that may accompany requests for criticism, such as "Don't bother with . . . ," "Just give it a quick read," or "What I really would like you to focus on is . . . ." The subtext in these cases is "Please tell me that my work is good." Those who have first bothered to step outside themselves and give thoughtful consideration to the merits of their work (whether it be teaching performance, a conference paper, a book review, a committee report, or a manuscript for publication) typically couch their requests in quite different ways; for example, "I am really having a problem with . . . ," "I am not convinced my argument about _____ is clear," or "There is something bothersome about what I am try-ing to do with _____, but I can't quite put my finger on it. Perhaps you can tell me where I am going wrong."

Self-criticism, as the latter set of examples suggests, can contribute substantially to problem recognition and areas in which improvement may be warranted. Even if one is not able to identify what will lead to improve-ment, the ability to discern what is problematic is a crucial first step.

Occasionally, when I am given material to review and asked for my comments, I find myself wondering if the person making the request has given much thought to the content or its articulation. I am similarly perplexed when students and fellow academics profess no ability to judge whether the work they have produced has merit (as in, "I am too close to this"). After all, there are criteria for determining what constitutes a sound argument, coherent prose, novel thought, a convincing demonstra-tion, and the like.

This is not to suggest that the criteria are applied uniformly or that others will necessarily agree with one's own assessment, but that an individual could have no sense of the quality of his or her output is practi-cally incomprehensible. I can only conclude that those who evince such an apparent incapacity have simply never developed the habit of criticiz-ing their own work. They have become too accustomed to having others tell them what to modify and how to do it.

In addition to deriving greater potential benefit from others' assessments, by developing the habit of self-criticism, one eventually becomes less reliant on outside opinion. Although all of us can profit throughout our lives from others' evaluations of our work (as the acknowledgments or the prefaces of many books clearly attest), indepen-dence ultimately is the mark of the mature professional. The scholar must be able to judge at what point a manuscript is ready for submission to a professional journal or publisher. Similarly, a teacher must be able to determine when a course is appropriately attuned to the abilities and knowledge of students. One also has to be able to assess what revisions in one's work are warranted in light of the results it produces. Being able to make such determinations only on the basis of advice from others is to be committed to a life of conditioned helplessness. The academic world needs no more dependence and helplessness than it already has.

The habit of self-criticism has yet another potentially important value. Through it, one can better determine how strong is one's commitment to professional life. In coming to grips with what is likely required to achieve the results one desires—whether in research, publication, or teaching—a person may discover that he or she would derive greater personal satisfaction from pursuing some other line of work or profession. By "results," I am not referring to tenure, promotion, salary increases, or other forms of personal advancement. My frame of reference rather is the achievements in learning and gains in knowledge to which institutions of higher education are ostensibly committed.

Doing research that advances knowledge is difficult, demanding work. Equally taxing is writing for publication, if one takes the task seriously. So is determining the means by which students can most effectively realize their potential for becoming literate, functioning, and productive contributors to society. It is far better to come to these realizations on one's own and to recognize that one lacks either the inclination or ability to perform at the necessary level than to be so informed by others. To this end, self-criticism can be a significant aid and important determinant of how one may fare in professional life.

◆ RESPONSE TO CHAPTER NINE
SCOTT A. KUEHN

This chapter provides a comprehensive and vital look at a central part of a beginning academic's career. I wish to focus some short comments on one aspect of Professor Phillips's discussion: labeling.

Beginning academics find labels of vital importance. In searching for a job, one has to apply labels to oneself to fit job descriptions. Labels are important in defining one's work to others. We aspire to labels that place a positive focus on our careers.

Professor Phillips's point about adapting to conditions in the academe cannot be underemphasized in this regard. Many who aspire to labels come to believe they deserve entitlements that go along with the label, even though their performance is not judged consistent with the label. I know of professors who believe themselves to be excellent teachers, but who would not attempt to even look at student evaluations of any sort, nor engage in peer review of their teaching. They protect their label by avoiding criticism. I know "researchers" who label themselves researchers not because they conduct research, but because they teach research methods courses. Again, their label is protected because no critique of their own research occurs.

I believe it is vital for beginning academics to avoid labeling ruts like those described above and the ones Professor Phillips carefully describes. This can be done through active scholarship and teaching. If one becomes part of the "mix," one learns to use the advice Professor Phillips presents. Otherwise, one stagnates and owns little more than a label.

◆ RESPONSE TO CHAPTER NINE
JULIA T. WOOD

I commend Professor Phillips's extensive attention to the value of criticism in building individual careers and scholarship. Further, I share his view of criticism as a constructive, positive activity to be sought and valued by any academic who is truly committed to improving how she or he thinks, writes, and studies. With Professor Phillips, I also see criticism as being as important to teaching as it is to scholarship.

I would like to expand Professor Phillips's discussion of criticism in two ways: by enlarging the scope of criticism and indicating its value to the field as a whole. Turning to the first of these points, I believe criticism is not restricted to formal evaluations from reviewers for journals and publishing houses. In addition, it is, at least ideally, a favor exchanged between colleagues. Every serious scholar with whom I am acquainted asks colleagues to read his or her work *prior* to submitting it for formal review. This is a natural, common aspect of collegiality, and it is extremely important in the overall process of developing good ideas, cogent arguments, and clear presentations. My service as a reviewer for several journals, however, suggests to me that seeking colleagues' reviews of early drafts and rewriting before submission are not as widely practiced as would be ideal. Far too many manuscripts are submitted prematurely to journals. More than once my response to authors has been along these lines: "This seems more an early draft of what could be a fine study than a final report." Finding colleagues who will make time to read essays in draft and who will do the enormous favor of giving honest criticism is essential to an individual's growth as a scholar.

Reading working papers of other faculty within your own department also tends to enhance understanding and appreciation of one another's interests and abilities. When faculty members understand each other's areas of research and have a sense of what is important to each other, they are more able to build a cohesive intellectual and pedagogical community than when they do not interact over ideas. Thus, exchanging drafts with colleagues and giving generous criticism benefits both individuals and the larger community of a department and a discipline.

I also wish to supplement Professor Phillips's focus on how individuals gain from and respond to criticism by pointing out the value of criticism to overall fields of knowledge. Criticism is incorporated systematically into academic fields not only because it sharpens individual's work, but also because it improves the fund of knowledge on which everyone draws. It is through reading and responding critically to each others' work that scholars interact collaboratively to point out and rectify flaws in reasoning, analyses, and understandings. This process refines ideas, sharpens interpretations, and enhances the collective body of knowledge.

Without criticism there would be no safeguards against unreflective thinking, inadequate analysis of data, incorrect writing, and other impediments to sound scholarship. Anything could be published, regardless of whether it met any standards of quality. Even though most members of every academic field occasionally complain about the poor quality of what is published (despite little consensus on which articles and books are poor and which are good), research that goes through critical review before making it into print is generally superior to that which does not. This is why most institutions place very heavy emphasis on publications that are "refereed" or evaluated by anonymous peers. Refereed articles have greater stature than invited articles or ones accepted without discriminating review because the former have been judged as significant by experts who know an area of study and the range of work published within it. This perspective allows them to render an informed judgment on work they read. Although there are limitations to the perspective some critics employ, as I have pointed out, the shortcomings are not intrinsic to the process of critical review. Instead, they are flaws in how we implement a useful practice. As flaws they merit attention and correction, but they do not justify abandoning the process itself.

Reviewing submissions to journals is time-consuming and demanding work that is uncompensated. Academics do it out of commitment to their field and to the process of working together to create the best possible knowledge for the whole community. Most reviewers offer extensive and helpful responses to authors, particularly when they recommend a manuscript not be published in its present form. This is not done out of malice or a Machiavellian effort to keep others off one's own territory. Instead, the motive is most often a genuine and generous effort to help others think and write better. In sum, I see criticism as vital to the growth of individual scholars and the intellectual integrity of a field.

10

THE FUTURE

Dennis S. Gouran

When my colleagues agreed that I should write a final chapter to this volume that would focus on the future, I was curious about what commended my particular selection. Perhaps the fact that I am still at mid-career led them to conclude that I could in some Janus-like fashion peer into the shape of things to come from a perspective on the past. Such efforts are better left to those of greater imagination, preferably persons on the order of H. G. Wells. In no sense do I regard myself as prescient, nor do I subscribe to the notion that hindsight necessarily gives rise to foresight. Over the years, moreover, I have developed some sympathy for Albert Einstein's observation that he never thought of the future because "it comes soon enough." I cannot claim never to think of the future, but neither do I reside there. The day-to-day business of professional life is sufficiently absorbing to make future gazing an infrequently affordable luxury.

Scholarly discussions of the future, rather than somehow envisioning or predicting it, often reflect efforts to shape it, and usually in respect to the would-be futurists' own teaching and research agendas. This has led some individuals to question their value (e.g., Miller, 1984). Even when the motivation is not self-serving, there is little evidence that the futures spoken of or written about actually come into existence as a consequence of such discussions. That may be the case because the future is determined by events, actions, and circumstances that are not always easy to anticipate or recognize even when they have been correctly anticipated. This is not to suggest that the future is unimportant, but merely to acknowledge that attempts to predict and structure it can prove futile.

251

More constructive, perhaps, is an examination of the implications of trends now discernible, should they continue and take greater hold. It is from this perspective, therefore, that my consideration of the future proceeds. Throughout, I have attempted to confine my remarks to the issues directly or indirectly addressed in this volume and to refrain from commenting on disciplinary substance. In short, I have made no effort to describe where particular fields of study might or could be moving, but only the possible environment in which teaching and research may occur in the future.

INVIDIOUS TRENDS

Since first entering higher education in 1959 as an undergraduate student, I have been witness to substantial changes in what colleges and universities do and in views concerning what they should be. From this ferment the beginnings of three somewhat disturbing patterns have emerged, which, for the sake of convenience, and with apologies to dictionary compilers for their neologistic elements, I shall characterize as *corporatization, professionalization*, and *politicization*. Although these patterns— trends if you will—may merely represent logical continuities paralleling a larger social evolution, they nevertheless relate to almost every aspect of academic life described in this book. For the moment, the patterns are not especially clear and reside largely in the interstices of academe. To the extent that they become more firmly ingrained, however, higher education as we understand it could be altered in profound—possibly profoundly negative—ways. As a result, the implications and possible ramifications of each trend are worthy of our attention.

Corporatization

The rapid growth in the numbers of people seeking some form of postsecondary education following World War II and the Korean Conflict was a product of many factors. Initially, the G.I. Bill brought many returning veterans to colleges and universities who otherwise would not have been able to attend. In addition, soon thereafter the effects of the "Baby Boom" were felt, as later were those resulting from social programs and forms of financial aid not previously available to citizens of lower socioeconomic backgrounds. In the latter case, expansion was attributable in part to the Civil Rights Movement and President Johnson's subsequent Great Society programs. Accompanying expanded possibilities for U. S. citizens to attend colleges and universities was an infusion of growing numbers of international students desirous of the "American style" of education that added both to growth and diversification. Finally, greater numbers of women and older adults began to matriculate as changing life styles, the requirement of greater education for better paying jobs, and the cultivation of a general belief in the potential value of advanced education became more pronounced. So-called "nontraditional" students, that is, those whose entry into postsecondary education had been postponed for some reason, are presently a significant proportion of the college and university population and soon may become the majority.

As a result of these developments, colleges and universities began to find themselves in need of more specialized nonacademic personnel to deal with the numerous added responsibilities following in the wake of rapid expansion.[1] There was also some recognition of the need for an increase in academic personnel, but a general hope as well that advances in technology would facilitate the accommodation of larger numbers of students. Consequently, the addition of academic positions did not always enjoy the same importance or attention as colleges and universities' other perceived needs.

To some extent, what was happening in higher education for most of the second half of this century resembled what one might expect to see in a successful profit-making business. What institutions had to offer was in high demand. Students were seen as a consumer market and colleges and universities as suppliers. Increasingly, the view of higher education shifted in this direction, that is, toward a concept of institutions as business enterprises that must and should be run as such. This development was probably to the delight of some economists and professors of business administration, as it gave their expertise special significance and advantage in important areas of decision making. Because the rest of the academic community was realizing benefits from this growth, movement toward corporatization, if noticeable at all, was not especially disturbing.

Today, large universities in particular are conforming increasingly to various aspects of the corporate model of structure and performance. Their organizational charts are complex and evermore frequently top-heavy with senior vice presidents, vice presidents, associate vice presidents, assistant vice presidents, directors, deans for administration, and no end of technical specialists and support staffs. In such institutions divisions have proliferated, and although the names of them do not always correspond directly to those in profit-making organizations, in fact, many have essentially the same referents as their less cryptic counterparts and relate to such matters as marketing, public relations, contracts and grants administration, finance, personnel, investment, development, and lobbying.

Upper level administrators are now less apt than in previous years to emerge from academic ranks, or, at least, to have had much direct

---

[1]Although the rate of growth began to level off in the 1980s and has now even begun to decline, the diversity of the college population may be greater than ever.

experience in either teaching or research. For many administrative posts, no academic background beyond a baccalaureate degree of some sort is necessary. In fact, such background may even be considered to be a liability by members of search and screening committees because they fear that candidates having scholarly credentials will devote insufficient attention to administrative duties. As one university president once observed, "Higher education is far too important to be entrusted to academic types." Qualifications impressive to some search and screening committees, not to mention the officials who make the final hiring decisions, include a long history of involvement in administration, self-assessed market value, and evidence of movement up the corporate ladder through frequent changes in position. The reasons for the changes are irrelevant so long as the direction is upward.

These elements of corporatization have brought with them an expanded lexicon, including university relations, human resources, employee services, continuing education, governmental relations, legal services, telecommunications, information technology, strategic planning, Total Quality Management, and my personal favorite, regulatory compliance. The professorate is frequently uncertain, even befuddled, about what such terms mean, but they soon become aware that many if not most of them correspond to the operations of some recently created nonacademic unit occupying substantial physical space and possibly having a staff far exceeding that of their own academic units. They also occasionally discover that such units may function with considerable autonomy, little or no faculty input, and the authority to make decisions having impact on instructional programs and research.

Another by-product of adoption of the corporate model has been a rise in image consciousness. Because of the importance they now attach to image, some colleges and universities seek "professional" advice from an array of private consultants and consulting firms on matters ranging from the design of a logo to the latest techniques in "modern management" to the interior design of administrative offices. Those responsible may even boast how reliance on consultants improves the reputation of the institution for being up to date, progressive, and in line with other social trends.

That positive contributions to image are always the result of such uses of resources is doubtful. One university, for instance, retained an opinion survey firm at considerable expense to determine whether or not faculty members were satisfied with their salaries. Months of data gathering and processing led to the not so remarkable conclusions that (a) many employees were not pleased with their salaries, but (b) those in the professional academic units were more satisfied. One is reminded of Saul Alinsky's rather acerbic characterization of a professional sociologist as an individual who needs a $50,000 grant to locate a house of prostitution when he could obtain the same information free from any taxi driver. To return to the point, however, efforts at image building do not always have their intended effect. At least in this particular instance, many members of the faculty regarded the survey as both a waste of time and money. And it probably was. They might have been less unhappy about their salaries if the money spent on finding out that they were unhappy had been used to increase their compensation.

Whether the corporatization of higher education will continue in some sort of linear progression is difficult to judge. With increasing pressures from the public and legislators for educational institutions to become more cost effective and accountable, such a possibility is not unlikely. There is a certain irony in this prospect. To date, I am aware of no evidence establishing that such elements of corporatization as I have mentioned have done anything to contribute to cost effectiveness. If anything, the proliferation of specialized administrative units and new roles appears to have raised the cost of higher education to the point that it may now be moving further from the reach of those very groups whose inclusion led to the view that adoption of the corporate model might be necessary in the first place. Greater subscription to current practices of management evident in the business community, moreover, is not very promising for improving higher education through increased efficiency and better administrative performance. At least, the record of American business for the past decade or so does not exactly appear to have been one of excellence in these respects.

With the prolonged recession of the late 1980s that continues, as of this writing, to linger into the current decade, colleges and universities have been resorting to some of the same kinds of draconian measures to which businesses have in their efforts to keep profits up and the costs of doing business down. "Down-sizing" and "right-sizing" are two additional terms that have crept into the administrative vocabulary of the 1990s. The euphemistic value of such terminology not withstanding, the implications are clear. The problems of escalating costs and insufficient funding will be addressed through cutbacks and elimination of positions. Thus far, the casualties appear to have resided disproportionately in the academic rather than administrative "sector." That such practices, which in large measure contribute to problems in the general economy, should be emulated and adopted on an even greater scale does not auger well for at least the next few years in higher education.

The grip of corporatization, however slight, is not likely to loosen much in the foreseeable future unless administrators begin to recognize that the most serious problems they face are not managerial in nature. Both within the business and educational communities, there has been, and continues to be, an unfortunate equation of management with leadership. As Zaleznik (1991) has observed, this equation is as erroneous as it is widespread. Management has to do with activities routinely related to the day-to-day performance of organizations. Leadership has much more to do with vision, imagination, and the identification of goals for which appropriate means to their realization must be devised. Both management and leadership are important to organizational success; however, there is little evidence that either business or higher education is under effective leadership at the moment or that the situation is in the process of change.

Leadership also involves insight. A perceptive educational leader, at the minimum, should recognize that what is appropriate to the successful functioning of a profit-making organization may not be appropriate in an academic institution. Differences in goals alone should make this clear, but it is apparent in those institutions in which corporatization has taken some hold that most individuals at the highest levels of administration do not appreciate, or even understand, the distinction. In light of the confusion, it seems likely that those who equate management with leadership will continue to look for "the best in modern management techniques" for dealing with matters that fall essentially within another realm.

Further subscription to the corporate model for the administration of higher education has a number of possible consequences, particularly for those at the beginning of their academic careers. One of these is that programs will be market driven. That is not necessarily bad for people in speech communication because it tends to be a popular field among students, and it is of perceived value in many external communities. Efforts to develop programs based on what "consumers want," therefore, are likely to result in the inclusion of some type of communication component. Who might profit from market-based education, however, is not the issue. The prospect should be disturbing to all teachers and scholars whether they stand to gain or not.

Historically, the determination of what constitutes legitimate domains of study has resided within the scholarly community. Intellectual and educational worth was almost always considered to be a matter of informed scholarly opinion. Many profit-making organizations operated under a similar principle. They decided what they wanted to produce and hoped to convince prospective consumers to buy it. The buying public was not always convinced, however, and production increasingly moved toward market-driven considerations. Successful businesses attempted to determine what consumers wanted and then to deliver it—or at least to create that impression. This, of course, was the point of Packard's (1958) popular book *The Hidden Persuaders*, published when market research and analysis were first coming into their own.

The point I am attempting to make here is that what consumers want is not always something that can be reliably offered. Making educational decisions on the basis of an external demand for particular types of courses and programs, therefore, would put faculty and other scholars in the position of adapting to the market, deceiving people, or finding some other line of work. None of these alternatives is especially inviting. In the first instance, one may be forced to offer content lacking in substance or intellectual merit. In the second instance, faculty would be ethically compromised. And in the final instance, a professor would likely be replaced by someone who does not see the first and second alternatives as problematic. In the long run, under any of these scenarios, it would be students and subsequently society who suffer.

Another implication of the continued corporatization of higher education is the increased impact it could have on tendencies to think of scholarly achievements in terms of products. Already, we speak of students as "raw material" transformed by four years of college attendance into finished "marketable" graduates. Research is something in which institutions and agencies "invest." Faculties are part of the "machinery" essential for the creation of such products, but as with other types of "equipment," they do not always "live up to specifications." Personnel decisions more and more frequently entail consideration of "replacement costs." If such language were merely metaphorical, it would be offensive enough, but substantial numbers of individuals in positions of authority appear to use it in a quite literal sense.

Finally, corporatization has implications for the autonomy and independence of thought that traditionally has been one of the hallmarks of college and university life. The pressure for "better trained" graduates to serve external business, political, and social interests can and does have an impact on the types of programs educational institutions provide and the inquiries faculty members are willing to undertake. That the outcomes of teaching and research provide for and contribute to improvement in the larger social, economic, professional, and political environment is not objectionable. The critical question is, in my judgment, where the locus of responsibility should lie.

Educational institutions cannot exist without contributions and economic support from a variety of sources. The contributors, moreover, have every right to expect these institutions to use the resources they provide responsibly. The problem that arises, however, is that contributors can become "clients" to be served, and their special interests may begin to dictate the choices the "servicing agency" makes about academic priorities, program development, and the permissible boundaries of knowledge. Education and inquiry by constituent demand are not a comforting prospect. Should constituent demand become a driving influence, then many institutions of higher education could become little more than "just another business."

Professionalization

Becoming a member of the profession of higher education in 1968 was an interesting experience to say the least. The drug culture was in full flower.

Both Robert Kennedy and Martin Luther King, Jr. fell victim to assassination. Lyndon Johnson announced that he would not accept renomination for the presidency, and Eugene McCarthy was about to run for president as a third party candidate. Sit-ins, protests, and demonstrations of all kinds were becoming almost a daily part of campus life. Recruiters for the military, CIA, FBI, and Dow Chemical, in particular, were not welcome, as angry students took out their frustrations against the military-industrial complex. At issue were the United States's involvement in Vietnam and a host of other alleged as well as actual social ills threatening to divide the country for the first time since the beginning of the Civil War.

Amidst the considerable social turmoil evident across the nation's campuses through the late 1960s and early 1970s developed a strong conservative reaction, as President Nixon appealed to the "great silent majority," and parents, legislators, and representatives of the corporate world became increasingly concerned about the state of higher education. Tragic events, such as the death of a graduate student in the bombing of a research lab at the University of Wisconsin and the killing of several students at Kent State by overly anxious and poorly prepared National Guardsmen brought outcries for the restoration of order. If college and university presidents could not maintain control, then governors, boards of trustees, and other officials would replace them with more "tough-minded" individuals who were more than willing to do so.

To those party to the backlash, higher education was being subverted by socially conscious, but nevertheless, in their judgment, irresponsible students and faculties. They were committed to restoring what they perceived to be its essential and legitimate end—the preparation of students for entry into the professional world.

With the extrication of armed forces from Vietnam beginning in 1972, the climate on college and university campuses began to change. As social conditions became more settled, there was a corresponding escalation in the number of bureaucrats running institutions and growing anxiety on the part of parents about what their sons and daughters would be able to do with their degrees. As a consequence, more and more students began to become career conscious. During this period, the liberal arts not only languished, but in some quarters were an object of derision. "If it doesn't help you get a job, it isn't worth knowing" was reflective of an emergent attitude that increased the popularity of professional education (e.g., journalism, accounting, engineering, law, and medicine) and further strengthened its position in terms of allocation of resources, expansion of facilities, and fundraising. The trend toward professionalization has continued well into the present.

Because individuals have to spend sometimes in excess of $100,000 pursuing their education, their desire to be attractive to prospective employers is entirely understandable. So too is the interest in preparing for a particular type of profession. My concern is not so much with professional aspirations, but with the frequently accompanying attitude that education is meaningful and relevant only to the extent that it specifically prepares one for entry into a given profession. This reduces the potential experience of higher education to nothing more than job training. If that is its only, or even primary value, society could find far less expensive ways to "educate" its citizenry.

Although I have some serious reservations about the excesses to which it led in the first half of the 20th century, Dewey's (1958) notion of education as "preparation for life" retains a strong influence on my own perspective. How one makes a living, to be sure, is an important part of life, but it is not the only part, and to encourage the view that should education deal only with the former is to ignore what, in the words of Whitehead (1929), one needs to know "to live, to live well, and to live better" (p. 8). Continued and increased emphasis on professionalization could leave future graduates even less well prepared than they presently are to cope with social realities that are in no way unique to one's particular vocation. Functioning well in life requires more than knowledge of how to perform in a given line of work.

Even if one restricts the value of education to its occupational significance, the type of training received in professional programs is rarely sufficient for addressing all work-related matters. Managers frequently complain of deficiencies in employees' communication skills (both formal and interpersonal), engineers are sometimes seemingly insensitive to the possible environmental damage their projects can create, lawyers pursuing political office often manifest little understanding of the historical context of issues for which they seek either to enact or overturn relevant legislation, and some "well-trained" investment counselors have been notoriously unmindful of the ethical implications of financial transactions. This is not to imply that professional education is lacking in substance or rigor, but merely that its focus often removes students from aspects of knowledge to which it is beneficial for them to be exposed.

The revival of general education and core curricula in the 1980s was, in part, a response to the growing realization that colleges and universities were graduating far too many individuals who were narrowly prepared and, thereby, less able to contribute to or profit from social and cultural life or to solve problems related thereto. The impact of these reforms has yet to be determined, let alone felt, but it does not appear that they have been greeted with much enthusiasm by very many students or the professional communities they are entering. The favored status some administrators grant to professional units in their colleges and universities, moreover, convey the feeling that general education is promoted more for the sake of appearances than from a genuine commitment to its functional value.

If the overvaluing of professional education becomes much greater than it already is, those entering higher education in the traditional arts and sciences could find themselves experiencing considerable frustration in both teaching and research, not to mention in respect to such matters as compensation, access to resources, and the potential for influence on the academic and scholarly agendas of their respective institutions.

Professionalization has brought with it some interesting and sometimes disturbing consequences. Among these are the inequitable treatment of faculty and programs. Many institutions of higher education pride themselves on upholding merit as the basis for compensation and the allocation of related resources. All too often, however, the administrative champions of merit, in fact, distribute resources on other bases, which makes them appear to be inconsistent, at best, if not downright hypocritical. This can be embarrassing, for instance, when a faculty member may discover that a new assistant professor of business administration is earning more than an established and prominent professor of English literature.

The embarrassment to the responsible parties is short lived, however, and they are quick to explain the differential in terms of market factors. The assistant professor of business administration, they may maintain, could easily command twice the salary in the private sector. Under the circumstances, merit is beside the point. The assumption is that the professor of English literature has no other options and could not even be employed, let alone command a higher salary, in some other line of work. There is also a curious irony in such a view of market value. In many businesses, employee worth is assessed in terms of value to the individual's organization, not his or her potential value to some other organization. In academe, one's worth is frequently determined by the size of a salary offer from another institution.

Another consequence of professionalization about which we should be concerned is the devaluing of the intellectual content of subject matter. I have already noted the emphasis some people have placed on the immediate relevancy of education to particular occupational choices. Along with this view has arisen in some quarters the companion belief that the only meaningful type of learning is experiential. In the 1980s, "hands-on experience" became something of a religion among many administrators, students, board-of-trustees members, faculty in professional units, and other proponents of professionalization. This belief can be a genuine source of disappointment in teaching to anyone who must confront the behavior that accompanies it when one attempts to go beyond the practical aspects of a subject and explore deeper issues. Such explorations, from the point of view of a good many learners, are a waste of time. And they so indicate this, both verbally and nonverbally.

Please understand that I do not reject the value of experiential learning, nor do I contend that it is inherently anti-intellectual. My concern is with an extreme view that unless learning is experiential, what is to be learned is of no value or interest. That view, in my judgment, is patently anti-intellectual.

More important than the anti-intellectual beliefs about what is important that professionalization may foster are the decisions to which they can lead. Good teachers can find ways of helping students develop an appreciation of the broader aspects of what they are studying (Erickson, 1985; Lowman, 1984). They have less impact on those in positions of authority who decide the directions in which an institution will move. Many administrators are themselves career driven and often to a much greater extent than students. To enhance their prospects for advancement, they must establish some record of achievement. As they are in many instances unable to do this on the basis of scholarship, they must think in terms "administrative" accomplishment.

Developing a reputation as a mover and shaker by serving up what external constituencies would like to have colleges and universities deliver in the way of "trained professionals" is one means of enhancing the prospects for upward mobility. Administrators of such inclination are apt to pander to the educational fashions of the moment and to try to impose them on their institutions. When faculty criticize students for an excessive preoccupation with "careerism," they sometimes forget that some of their most influential role models have precisely the same preoccupations. In any event, given a climate in which administrators are committed to professionalization, decisions affecting program planning and development do not always reflect sufficient attention to scholarly and intellectual substance.

The trend toward professionalization, as manifested in favored treatment of professional units, vocational emphasis, and administrative tampering in program development, could transform educational institutions in ways that sharply conflict with traditional conceptions of them as places for thoughtful contemplation, the pursuit of knowledge, and the meaningful exchange of ideas, as, for example, articulated by Russell (1926, pp. 183-192). Such consequences are not inevitable. A concern with the utility of knowledge, which professionalization to a limited extent reflects, is not undesirable, nor is it in principle incompatible with the values mentioned above. The fundamental problems are the narrowness in perspective professionalization can breed and the disregard for any aspect of learning and advancement of knowledge whose pragmatic value is not immediately apparent.

Politicization

Politicization of higher education has both an external and internal dimension. Because of the expense involved in the operation of colleges and universities, very few have been able to survive without some form of state or federal aid. The ability of such sources to control an institution's economic well-being, therefore, gives them obvious potential for influencing other aspects of academic life. At an internal level, the dynamics of colleges and universities can create a climate in which significant aspects of institutional performance take on a decidedly political character. To some extent, of course, politics are unavoidable. As long as there are opportunities for influence, some degree of political behavior is likely to surface. It is the extent to which politics are influential about which one needs to be concerned.

Early opponents of governmental assistance to education were fond of asserting, "Federal aid leads to federal control." As some of these same individuals were apt to issue this warning with respect to every form of federal assistance, it was very easy to dismiss them as possibly well-meaning, but nonetheless misguided, Cassandras. To be sure, the fear was excessive, but history has since demonstrated that it was not altogether without warrant.

So dependent have some colleges and universities become on governmental aid that even the slightest threat of withholding or elimination of this source of financial support reverberates throughout the entire academic community. For institutions whose operating budgets depend heavily on direct state support, the expression of disapproval concerning some condition or local problem by a state legislator, governor, or other official can be intimidating and is usually taken quite seriously. Whereas government support used to be viewed as an obligation, in some quarters it is clearly conceived and employed as a weapon. The shifting view of what support is intended for gives politics a much greater impact on what colleges and universities do. In my own state, for instance, there is a strong feeling in the executive and legislative branches that institutions receiving aid should be contributing substantially to local and regional economic development. University administrators have responded accordingly.

"Control of resources" is a common definition of power (Kipnis, 1976). It is this control that enables the powerholder to induce compliance in targets of influence. The implication for higher education, of course, is that those in external positions of authority will go beyond the legitimate boundaries of control and impose their own personal agendas on institutions and what it is they are expected to accomplish. The example just cited is a clear instance of this.

At present, buzz words popular among some legislators and other politicos are "assessment," "accountability," and "value added." As a condition of continued support, colleges and universities will be expected increasingly to demonstrate what students have learned or are able to do and how such determinations have been made. On the surface, such expectations appear to be reasonable. On the other hand, they could be the portents of externally mandated reforms in such areas as curriculum, instructional content, credentialing of faculty, and delivery systems. Inasmuch as the system of education, in general, has become a target of increasing criticism, such longer range possibilities are not far-fetched. Although I am not an opponent of educational reform, I do worry about who might be doing the reforming and for what purposes. The situation is well worth watching. As in the case of political freedom, the price of academic freedom may also be "eternal vigilance."

As if intrusions from the external political environment are not enough, as a person at the beginning of your academic career, you also will have to contend with internal politics. Although I have indicated in one of my responses to Professor Phillips that I do not see institutional politics existing on quite as great a scale as he does, or playing as substantial a role as he alleges, neither am I unmindful of the impact on individuals politics can have, especially under conditions of uncertainty and scarcity, the twins of adversity that bring out the worst in people at least as often as they bring out the best.

Colleges and universities are currently coming to the realization that their commitments to various areas of study may have exceeded their base of financial support. Program reduction and elimination, therefore, are becoming unpleasant prospects, if not realities, to be confronted. Determining what is essential and what is expendable invites the intervention of political motivations into the ordinary affairs of institutions as individuals and units seek identification with the "center" and escape from possible identification with the "periphery." To be in a peripheral discipline or area of study is threatening in times of economic hardship.

This set of conditions often activates in usually decent and humane people feelings of insecurity that may take numerous forms of expression, including: backbiting, scapegoating, bad-mouthing, ingratiation, narcissistic indulgence, manipulation, competitiveness, self-aggrandizement, and variety of other less-than-admirable attributes. Under extreme conditions, panic may even set in, with some individuals prematurely, and perhaps unnecessarily, seeking alternative employment. Unfortunately, some of the principal "rats" most responsible for inducing the state of panic do not leave the ship they have actively encouraged anyone who will listen to believe is sinking.

Extreme conditions, although contributing to politicization, are usually transitory, and the behavior that accompanies them a product of the moment. Of greater concern are some general attitudes that disturb the essentially apolitical character of higher education regardless of the general economic climate. The ones most often implicated in politicization relate to competitiveness.

In American culture, competitiveness is highly valued, but it is also highly overrated as a mean of achieving excellence (Kohn, 1986). Increasingly, competitiveness is being promoted by those in positions of authority, who may themselves attribute their own professional standing to competitive skill. Such individuals often speak in terms of athletic and military metaphors: "What's the game plan?"; "This is a horse race"; "I torpedoed that"; "I hope you're not thinking about some kind of end-run"; "I cut him off at the knees"; "Let's go for it"; "She's a triple threat"; "We're still in the running"; "Second is for losers"; and "We intend to win this battle" are but a few of the expressions that administrators and others are using with increasing frequency in discussing matters of academic concern. Such language is at once a reflection and reinforcement of the view that competition is a healthy state.

In my experience, competitiveness seldom has the virtues attributed to it. Instead, it contributes to highly self-serving behavior and to the loss of any conception of the collective good. Additionally, it promotes an elitist outlook and false hegemony among disciplines and areas of study within disciplines. Gould (1989) notes, for instance, that within the natural sciences, physicists are prone to devalue such nonexperimental sciences as paleontology. He reports an acquaintance in physics who likened paleontologists to stamp collectors (p. 281). As another example, a good friend of mine in speech communication had a conversation with a scientist who expressed surprise at my friend's heavy teaching load, but then upon further reflection noted, "Of course, in my field, we do research." To this individual, speech communication and research apparently represented a contradiction in terms.

Even as early as high school, elitist thinking begins to surface as students discuss with one another their choices of colleges and universities. An individual whose selection is not from the list of institutions regarded as most prestigious may be treated in a condescending manner. Those who choose not to attend college, or who may find it unaffordable, are dismissed as "just not college material." Elitism probably has many origins, but one that frequently stands out is a misguided conception of Darwinian thought and its applicability to the social domain. This notion is that the "quality" of the species is continually improved by survival of the fittest and elimination of the unfit. The survival mechanism in evolution theory, however, is natural selection, which as Gould (1989) points out, has to do with how well organisms adapt to changes in local environments. It implies nothing about improvement as such or what is better and worse in nature. Nevertheless, many of those who subscribe to a Social Darwinist perspective honestly believe that academic hegemony is the natural outcome of superior talent. "Cream rises to the top," if you will.[2]

Worse, perhaps, is the accompanying belief that the "academic

---

[2]If this were true, then it appears that a number of highly placed individuals in society should be starving to death instead of enjoying the benefits of station, for it is very difficult to discern what particular talents they possess.

stock" is somehow improved by the deliberate elimination of inferior members and replenishment with those of better "genetic" origin, or academic pedigree.[3] In their own way, those who would "purify the academic race" may be every bit as dangerous as those who have in recent history undertaken a different sort of purification of the human race. I have no opposition to the desire for excellence. In my mind, there is a real question about how best to achieve it. Of one thing I am reasonably certain, however: The course that the Social Darwinists among us would pursue is the wrong one.

By creating a competitive climate in colleges and universities in the ostensible interest of improving their performance, those given to elitist thinking may succeed only in heightening the level of political behavior. Rather than concentrating their energies on teaching, research, and scholarly inquiry, some members of the academic community may feel obliged to look to their survival first, and they may begin to manifest the sorts of tendencies to which I earlier alluded. People new to the profession are especially vulnerable to this possibility.

For those to whom competition is a highly valued ethic, politicization is a welcome companion. They might do well to remember, however, that the story of the survival of homo sapiens is not yet complete. To the extent that we have survived, it may well be, as Leakey (1981) has argued, a result of our ability to cooperate, not to compete. If left to our individual survival skills, we probably would have been extinct long ago. If there must be competition, then let be centered on ideas rather than among those who produce ideas.

DANGERS

The previously mentioned problems stemming from the corporatization, professionalization, and politicization of academia are what warrant the label "invidious" for these three aspects of higher education. Although none of them thus far has become so dominant as to make a career in college or university teaching completely uninviting, neither can the aspiring teacher and scholar afford to be unmindful of them. In combination, their continued influence on the course of events could change the nature of higher education in substantial and, in my judgment, seriously injurious ways.

At stake are several historically significant values. Among these is the Socratic ideal of the examined life, whose opposite, you will recall, this great philosopher and teacher felt was not worth living. Whether or

---

[3]Eugenicists like to refer to human beings as "stock"; see, for example, Pearson (1991).

not one agrees with the extremity of Socrates's belief, reflection and the critical examination of ideas have long held prominence in academe and have been important stimuli to human betterment. Colleges and universities exist in large measure for the generation, examination, and dissemination of knowledge.[4] Such vital functions are imperiled when corporatization supports a view of knowledge and those responsible for it as ordinary commodities to be managed and exchanged, when professionalization leads to its devaluation by students and the larger society in which they must function, and when politicization subordinates it to purveyors' preoccupations with survival and the exercise of influence.

Also at risk, as many of my previous comments suggest, are independence of thought and academic freedom. As colleges and universities incline more toward the corporate model, bow to consumer-driven demands, and struggle with external and internal political pressures, the individual faculty member faces the prospect of losing his or her prerogatives for developing and pursuing a desired scholarly agenda. Should this eventuality occur, the meaning of education may well lose its significance, with scholars and teachers relegated to the position of merely informing others of what they already know or want to hear. What people need to know could well become an irrelevancy in academic life.

Yet another danger in the further corporatization, professionalization, and politicization of higher education is the possible sacrifice of collegiality, which, as Professor Phillips has argued elsewhere, is essential to the effective performance of academic units. In many respects, the trends about which I have been speaking, if not inveighing, are highly incompatible with the notion of collegiality. Corporatization breeds specialization, isolation, and disenchantment. As enlightened and up to date on modern methods of corporate management as some administrators believe themselves to be, the fact is that adoption of the corporate model in many instances has represented little more than a return to Frederick Taylor's school of "scientific management" and the philosophy that individuals are simply replaceable parts in a larger organizational machine (see Jablin, 1990). The model did not work very well in business during the early part of this century when it was in vogue, and its imposition on colleges and universities at the end of the century, despite the enriched vocabulary and facade of participation, promises no greater success in this context.

Professionalization, as manifest in the inequitable treatment of

---

[4]Toffler (1990) has noted that especially in the modern age knowledge has become perhaps the most important source and determinant of power. Those who possess and control knowledge can have significant influence on the well-being of others. This social reality, therefore, would seem to make the traditional missions of higher education all the more compelling, if we are to assure that knowledge will be used in constructive and ethically defensible ways.

academic units and in promotion of the view of education as career training, is divisive and provides little incentive for faculty and students to see
themselves as part of a larger community in pursuit of common intellectual objectives. Where harmony exists, it is more likely to be in camps of
like-minded individuals, not throughout the institution as a whole.

Politicization, it should be obvious, does little to promote collegiality
or a sense of community. It does much more to cause people to watch
their backs. External influences may occasionally lead to a "circling of the
wagons" on some issue, but this is hardly the best basis for developing a
climate in which cooperative endeavor is most usefully advanced. More
often than not, external intrusions lead to individuals' taking sides and to
the building of resentments toward one another. When political influences are internal, the impact on collegiality can be serious—even devastating in some instances. So long as colleges and universities contribute to
faculty and students' seeing themselves, in Deutsch's (1949) words, as
"contriently interdependent" with others, competitiveness will reign and
collegiality will suffer.

CONCLUDING THOUGHTS

No particular future is inevitable. However, some become more likely
than others when given sets of conditions align themselves in particular
ways. The trends about which I have been commenting are not so pronounced as to warrant undue concern about the future of higher education. Certainly, they are not sufficient to justify a fatalistic outlook. My
purpose has been to note some warning signs of what could or might happen. My hope is for a better, not a worse, future. Whether that occurs will
be largely the result of what those entering higher education now and in
the years to come do to counteract the ill effects of corporatization, professionalization, and politicization. In identifying some of the more sinis-
ter of these, my colleagues and I trust that you will be better able not only
to deal with the future as it unfolds, but to affect it in positive ways.

◆ RESPONSE TO CHAPTER TEN
JULIA T. WOOD

This is one of the most depressing views of academic life I have encountered in a long time. What makes it so disturbing to me is that I cannot

disagree with the themes Professor Gouran sees as emerging nor can I dispute his prognosis for where they may lead us. In my response I add my voice to his in underlining the invidious consequences invited by the academy's increasing moves toward corporate models, professionalization, and politicization.

The corporate model applies to a world different from academe. It was developed to guide business toward the goal of making money by producing more of something that is valued, doing it better than competitors, and having fewer expenses than earnings for the activity. Although the efficaciousness of this model even for business is open to question (particularly of late as more and more Chapter 11s are declared), it is incontestably inappropriate for academic institutions. The *raison d'être* of the academy is knowledge: creating, extending, revising, criticizing, and sharing ideas and their consequences. To tie a price tag to this and to mete out rewards and penalties by mechanical measures of productivity is to pervert what the academic enterprise is and should be about. When productivity experts replace academics as administrators, dangerous judgments often follow and harm the long-term quality of higher education. For instance, in the face of tightening budgets over the past few years, a number of institutions have had to cut costs. One economizing measure advocated by some "budget experts" is letting senior faculty go—either by encouraging retirement or by not countering better offers from competing universities—and hiring more junior faculty at lower salaries. On paper this looks fine: The same number of faculty require considerably less salary when they are primarily new and recent Ph.Ds. Yet, what is lost are historical perspectives on fields of knowledge, national and international stature, personal and intellectual seasoning that comes with experience, and appreciation of institutions' lives, traditions, and heritage: These are significant resources that only senior faculty can provide. They cannot be measured properly on a balance sheet, yet they are integral to an institution's quality for they underlie both good scholarship and effective, informed teaching. Another economizing tactic favored by cost-management experts is increasing class sizes so that fewer faculty are needed to teach the same number of students. This works, of course, in cutting the costs of instruction. However, it simultaneously dilutes the quality of education in ways that will never appear on a budget plan or a cost-accounting report. Anyone who has been a student and/or a teacher knows that professors are seldom able to get to know students in large classes, so the opportunity to adapt material to individual students' needs and interests and to offer personal counsel is greatly diminished. From the perspective of those who understand eduction, these costs are more excessive and less tolerable than those of the dollars and cents that are the focus of management and cost experts.

I also agree with Professor Gouran's judgment that professional competencies are no substitute for liberal education. Old-fashioned as it may sound, there is value in the idea of education as preparation for life, which is more than getting a job and earning a living. The increasing emphasis on job-related courses is discouraging because it is shortsighted and violates institutional missions that call for creating an informed, reflective, critical citizenry. More discouraging yet is the complicity of faculty themselves in this move. Although many faculty resist pressures to teach that for which students clamor, increasingly some seem unduly swayed by a value-free market logic. Left unchecked, this trend could lead to moral and intellectual bankruptcy in higher education because it entails exchanging the merits of intellectual content for the more dubious values of "what will sell." Along with this outcome there is the tendency to create internal conflict among faculty at an institution over resources, including students. If students become "resources," higher education will have lost its soul. Perhaps the best corrective to trends that threaten the basic integrity of academic institutions lies within them, more specifically, within faculty. Reflective and incisive analyses such as Professor Gouran's should be widely read and discussed among faculty concerned about the future of their departments and higher education. Further, faculty should lead their institutions, not follow them, in defining the value and essence of the academic enterprise. This means that academics who care about higher education and their fields, and who heed the portentous sounding of Professor Gouran's chapter should commit to active efforts to redirect their departments and campuses toward knowledge and learning as the crux of academic life. Resignation, grumblings about legislators' lack of understanding, squabbling with colleagues over who benefits from decreasing resources, and embitteredness will do little to prevent the likely consequences of the trends identified by my colleague. Concerted concern and action just might. Once again, this reminds us of the importance of collegiality and community, both of which are essential if faculty are to come together effectively to work for common and important interests that are being compromised by trends that erode the meaning, vision, and processes of education and scholarship.

◆ RESPONSE TO CHAPTER TEN
GERALD M. PHILLIPS

I got a note the other day from Tom Loughlin, a young colleague at another institution. He has called me his mentor, a title I resist, but we have shared a lot of feelings and ideas. His comments are worth sharing here.

Dear Dr. Phillips,

I've been reading a lot of material lately on the state of higher education, and what I've been reading distresses me more and more. I hope you will indulge a "young turk" assistant professor one more time. I will try to be concise.

"I have of late, but wherefore I know not, lost all my mirth." At our school we went through a torturous year of budget cutting, harangues, and turf wars. The system as a whole is slowly crumbling as a result of poor planning and financing, as documented by a year-long investigation by [a major newspaper]. I am currently reading a series of articles appearing this week in the [another major paper] which document the decline in undergraduate education and overall quality of education at the major state universities.

Yes, it is my problem, but in all honesty I don't know where to turn to begin to fight the wars. Each little skirmish leaves me weaker and weaker, and like you I have had my share of scars fighting for what I believe in. For the past two years I have served as chair of a faculty council subcommittee charged with the improvement of undergraduate instruction. I have been able to accomplish little partly due to lack of funds, partly due to lack of interest on the part of the faculty as a whole. It is even very difficult to get the several members of the committee to agree to take any sort of action whatsoever. Three years of existence has produced no plan of action beyond forming little discussion groups and producing a questionable newsletter (as if any campus needed more paper floating around).

I see myself slowly losing my idealism and my energy for teaching. All about me I can see the changes which electronic technology will bring about, and I can see the obstacles as well, and they loom large. So much time is spent fighting the various little wars to have this or that tool, this or that dollar, access to this or that source of information, that I hardly have time to think out a lesson plan, re-think pedagogical approaches, and all of the necessary things that go into excellent teaching. All my life I have been in academia either as student or teacher. I have trained as a scholar, someone versed in the history, theory and criticism of (my discipline). I set my sights on a university position, and I recall the day when I first sat in my office at [my institution], having achieved my first tenure-track appointment. I was thrilled and proud. I thought of my father, who did not achieve a similar goal until he was past 50, and there I was, at 36, sitting in that chair. Only the tenure hoop remains to be jumped through, and then— FREEDOM! But now I find we are not so free. University administrators shut down whole computer systems due to the ravings of a few. Colleagues laugh when you propose inventive ideas to solve pressing problems. Everyone seems concerned with their own little world, as if each professor were an entrepreneur unto himself/herself; fighting for grants, fighting for publications, fighting for prestige. The prevailing attitude is always "us vs.

them" whenever confrontation arises on any level. It's so depressing. I fear growing old and cynical. I do not want to have to fight the battle anymore. My life is too short, and society changes too fast, for me to have to waste precious time battling short-sightedness. I become angry because I do not see the problem as so terribly threatening, but rather as something we will eventually outgrow. Ten years until E-publishing matures is a good guess, I think, but I do not want to have wasted that time fighting petty battles with people over whether discussions of sex belong on an academic computer. It's too petty an issue to waste time on. We will outgrow it someday, just like young boys outgrow bathroom humor at some point. It's all so medieval; so much of university life at times feels medieval (maybe because it still is structured after medieval patterns).

And I've never been patient. Another character flaw (I was thrown out of my first graduate program for vehemently disagreeing with the master teacher). In my field in the arts, when a problem presents itself, you have no choice but to solve it because the show goes up on Day X. In academia, problem solving usually gives way to problem discussion "ad infinitum," and there are so many levels of people to please.

I am afraid I ramble, and I promised to be short, so to the point. I will do my best to fight the good fight and defend free access to new technology, but I must defend it in all its potential dimensions. The Supreme Court of this country just yesterday struck down the so-called "hate laws" in Minneapolis as unconstitutional, thus defending the right to burn crosses and make speeches against other races and nationalities. The Wisconsin Supreme Court followed the U.S. lead in a similar decision today, and the Supreme Court of Canada also has a flag-burning and "hate law" case pending, as I hear. The trend of universities to institute "gag rules" banning such speech on campus (Univ. of Wisconsin) and to ban certain user groups from computer access flies in the face of such decisions. The question of "who pays" is a completely separate matter, but it should be seen and framed in the same context as "who pays" for books and periodicals in the library (many of which, as I'm sure you'll agree, are just as worthless as many of the news groups). But I cannot say I relish the thought of the fight. And I fear becoming cynical out of anger and bitterness. My dream of a life as a "scholar among scholars" fades, as have my many other dreams (Broadway success, e.g.).

Why?

Peace.

Tom Loughlin

I answered him.

Dear Tom:

When I entered academe 43 years ago, it was a privilege. When I retired last year, it was a relief. I have seen the changes come and never go. I am using your letter and my answer as a response to a chapter by my colleague on the future of the academy. He comments on many things, but mostly he talks about institutionalization taking place apart from the real purpose of the university, a move of power away from the professors and students into the hands of professional administrators. He talks of economics and politics, the same issues you raise here. You ask, "Why?" I answer, because as institutions grow, it becomes more important to preserve the institution than it is to preserve the purpose for which the institution was initiated. Higher education has grown old and tired, and there is only one answer to it. It is a return to the entrepreneurship of medievalism.

We professors are now entrepreneurs, selling our wares, our ideas. As the institution becomes more anonymous and considers us less, we become more powerful. They don't notice us, those people in the big office buildings. I once went to a union meeting, a group of professors were trying to organize our campus and someone suggested a strike. Another replied, "They wouldn't even know we were out until the grades are due."

So it ends with each of us following our muse, reading our books, assuming our professional responsibility as if we were the only people with integrity left in the world. (We know there are countless others, but we are not organized—yet.) When we become impoverished and unimportant and no longer noticed by public and press, then it will be one of us on one end of the log and the student on the other, and there will be books (and microfilm, and CD-ROM, and all the other technology), and we will start the whole process all over again.

My day is over, but I am still an entrepreneur, and I can feel it in you, Tom. Teach, read, write, think, and gather with your trusted fellows. You can form your own collegium in the midst of the anonymous university and the process can go on.

In 43 years, Tom, I never applied for an administrative job, never dreamed I was competent enough to run one of these monstrous institutions, not even a tiny part of one, like a department. I administered a couple of grants and I was a failure at it. I always had money left over to give back. But I have taught several generations of students who will survive me, and they will teach generations who survive them, and the process will go on regardless of the nature of the institutions. We survived the church and the state, and we will survive the business establishment and the bureaucracy, for we hold the future and there is no one who can take that away.

Peace!

Jerry Phillips

◆ RESPONSES TO CHAPTER TEN
SCOTT A. KUEHN

Professor Gouran's analysis of trends in the academe is penetrating and powerful. I am particularly heartened by his treatment of "futurists," and I wish to comment on concerns related to developing technologies and their effect on the academe.

Computer technology is a hot item of discussion in education. I am concerned, however, that there is more attention paid to the seductive "potentials" of the technology and not enough to learning objectives and outcomes. Computers have been used in instruction since the 1970s. The PLATO system was in place in the late 1970s, elementary and secondary education made use of Apple computers in the early 1980s. Two of the authors of this volume have used computer technology in instruction since 1985. Speaking for myself, I have found that the computer can be an effective learning tool, but only when specific learning outcomes are matched to specific computer functions. Many of my colleagues ask me how they can "put their students online." When I ask them why, more often than not they say "because they want to get in on the trend." I would like to see the trend focused more on what the technology can do for learning.

Technology is not a panacea for the limits of our teaching. It does not replace or necessarily enhance teacher/student contact; it only provides specific functions. Any teacher of a computer-mediated course will tell you that they spend more time dealing with students than ever before. Similarly, it would do little good for physics students to create virtual molecules in cyberspace if they have little understanding of the forces of nature that contribute to the creation of the model. As with any form of media in education, computer technology has the potential to augment conceptual understanding. However, the basics must first be provided to students. An interactive video presentation of the biology of a rainforest may be just as perplexing as a real lecture-discussion of the subject, if students have no understanding of basic plant biology.

The new technologies do create challenges, however. If we sincerely wish to provide the best up-to-date instruction using the machines and technology that are used in business and industry, we must keep pace. We can provide students with industry-like experiences using e-mail and group conferencing software, along with wordprocessing and data analysis programs. The challenge is to learn the technology well enough to teach it. The technical jargon can be overwhelming and easy to dismiss when one has deadlines and courses to teach. There are solutions, however. Computer literate friends who enjoy helping others are true resources to cultivate.

The biggest challenge the new technologies present is providing equitable distribution of their services. Two years ago I attended a convention panel made up of deans of colleges of communication from esteemed universities. One prevalent theme of their discussion was that there was danger of a class system emerging: an "upper class" of academics with access to online conferencing and information services and a "lower class" of academics with no access. The idea was that those who had instant access to almost any information they needed had definite advantages over those who had to travel to libraries and use the U.S. postal service. It may well go beyond that. As a graduate student at a large multiversity, I had a computer account that could access a worldwide network of computers. Now, working at a small state university, that advantage is gone. Until my university is connected to the internet, I must use my own Compuserve account.

This book provides a good example of the potential for the new technologies to aid the professorate. Professor Phillips received word-processor files for each of the chapters. I submitted my work to him through electronic mail. We consulted through e-mail. The time saved is measured in days and weeks. Beginning academics will need to cultivate computer literacy to maintain connections with others working through electronic networks. Electronic journals have become a reality. The computer networks also provide discussion forums in which scholars can share ideas. Beyond all the hype about fancy technology is a clear fact: Computer communication in the academe is growing, and those that take advantage of it will gain more opportunities in research and publication and teaching, than those who do not.

REFERENCES

Babbie, E. (1992). *The practice of social research* (6th ed.). Belmont, CA: Wadsworth.

Ben-David, J. (1983). Research and teaching in the universities. In J.W. Chapman (Ed.), *The western university on trial* (pp. 81-91). Berkeley: University of California Press.

Benson, T.W. (Ed.). (1985). *Speech communication in the 20th century.* Carbondale: Southern Illinois University Press.

Bleier, R. (Ed.). (1986). *Feminist approaches to science.* New York: Pergamon Press.

Blum, D.E. (1991, October 9). Environment still hostile to women in academe, new evidence indicates. *Chronicle of Higher Education,* p. 20.

Bormann, E.G. (1986). Symbolic convergence theory and communication in group decision-making. In R.Y. Hirokawa & M.S. Poole (Eds.), *Communication and group decision-making* (pp. 219-236). Beverly Hills, CA: Sage.

Bowen, H.R., & Schuster, J.H. (1986). *American professors: A national resource imperiled.* New York: Oxford University Press.

Boyer, E.L. (1987). *College: The undergraduate experience in America.* New York: Harper & Row.

Brehm, J.W. (1966). *A theory of psychological reactance.* New York: Academic Press.

Daly, J., Friedrich, G.W., & Vangelisti, A.L. (Eds.). (1990). *Teaching communication.* Hillsdale, NJ: Lawrence Erlbaum.

Dershowitz, A.M. (1991). *Chutzpah.* Boston: Little, Brown.

Deutsch, M. (1949). An experimental study of the effects of co-operation and competition upon group process. *Human Relations, 2,* 199-232.

Deutsch, M. (1973). *The resolution of conflict: Constructive and destructive processes.* New Haven, CT: Yale University Press.

Dewey, J. (1958). *Philosophy of education.* Paterson, NJ: Littlefield, Adams.

Erickson, S.C. (1985). *The essence of good teaching.* San Francisco: Jossey-Bass.

Fishbein, M.A., & Ajzen, I. (1975). *Belief, attitude, intention, and behavior.* Reading, MA: Addison-Wesley.

Freud, S. (1962). *Civilization and its discontents* (1st American ed.). New York: W.W. Norton.

Goldsmith, O. (1970). *An enquiry into the present state of polite learning in Europe.* New York: Garland. (Original work published in 1759.)

Gould, S.J. (1989). *Wonderful life: The burgess shale and the nature of history.* New York: W. W. Norton.

Haney, W.V. (1992). *Communication & interpersonal relations: Text and cases* (6th ed.). Boston, MA: Irwin.

Haraway, D. (1988). Situated knowledges: The science question in feminism and the privilege of partial perspective. *Feminist Studies, 14,* 575-599.

Harding, S. (1991). *Whose science? Whose knowledge? Thinking from women's lives.* Ithaca, NY: Cornell University Press.

Hemmer, J.J., Jr. (1986). *The Supreme Court and the first amendment.* New York: Praeger Publishers.

Hirsch, E.D. (1987). *Cultural literacy: What every American needs to know.* Boston: Houghton, Mifflin.

Hochschild, A. & Manchung, A. (1989). *The second shift: Working women and the revolution at home.* New York: Viking.

Irigary, L. (1985). *Speculum of the other woman.* Ithaca, NY: Cornell University Press.

Jablin, F.C. (1990). Organizational communication. In G.L. Dahnke & G.W. Clatterbuck (Eds.), *Human communication: Theory and research* (pp. 156-182). Belmont, CA: Wadsworth.

Jacobson, R.L. (1985, December). New Carnegie data show faculty members uneasy about the state of academe and their own careers. *The Chronicle of Higher Education,* p. 18.

Jaschik, M.L., & Frentz, B.R. (1990). Women's perceptions and labeling of sexual harassment. *Sex Roles, 25,* 19-23.

Jay, G.S. (1992, February 1). The first round of the culture wars. *The Chronicle of Higher Education,* p. 1.

Keller, E.F. (1985). *Reflections on gender and science.* New Haven, CT: Yale University Press.

Kipnis, D. (1976). *The powerholders.* Chicago: University of Chicago Press.

Kohn, A. (1986). *No contest: The case against competition.* Boston: Houghton Mifflin.

Leakey, R.E. (1981). *The making of mankind.* New York: E.P. Dutton.

Lowman, J. (1984). *Mastering the techniques of teaching.* San Francisco: Jossey-Bass.

McMillen, L. (1991, October 23). A mixed message for campuses seen in Thomas hearings. *The Chronicle of Higher Education*, pp. 1, 14.

Mercer, J. (1992, May 6). States turn to community colleges as route to bachelor's degree as 4-year campuses face tight budgets and over-crowding. *The Chronicle of Higher Education*, p. 1.

Miller, G.R. (1984). Where to next? Some thoughts on future research in small group communication. In R.S. Cathcart & L.A. Samovar (Eds.), *Small group communication: A reader* (4th ed., pp. 494-503). Dubuque, IA: William C. Brown.

Nisbett, R., & Ross, L. (1980). *Human inference: Strategies and shortcomings of social judgment.* Englewood Cliffs, NJ: Prentice-Hall.

Okin, S.M. (1989), *Justice, gender, and the family.* New York: Basic Books.

Packard, V. (1958). *The hidden persuaders.* New York: Pocket Books.

Pearson, R. (1991). *Race, intelligence and bias in academe.* Washington, DC: Scott-Townsend.

Phillips, G.M. (1979). The peculiar intimacy of graduate study. *Communication Education, 28*(3), 339-345.

Phillips, G.M. (1991). *Communication incompetencies.* Carbondale: Southern Illinois University Press.

Phillips, G.M., & Wood, J.T. (1990). *Essays to commemorate the 75th anniversary of the speech communication association.* Carbondale: Southern Illinois Press.

Phillips, K. (1991). *The politics of rich and poor.* New York: Harper Perennial.

Russell, B. (1926). *Education and the good life.* New York: Avon.

Smith, D. (1987) *The everyday world as problematic: A feminist sociology.* Boston: Northeastern University Press.

Snow, C.P. (1959). *Cultures and the scientific revolution.* Cambridge: Cambridge University Press.

Snyder, M.L. (1972). *Individual differences and the self-control of expressive behavior.* Unpublished doctoral dissertation, Stanford University, Palo Alto, CA.

Spelman, E. (1988). *Inessential woman: Problems of exclusion in feminist thought.* Boston: Beacon.

Spitzack, C., & Carter, F. (1987). Women in communication studies: A typology for revision. *Quarterly Journal of Speech, 73*, 401-423.

Steiner, I.D. (1972). *Group process and productivity.* New York: Academic Press.

Thonnsen, L., & Baird, A.C. (1948). *Speech criticism.* New York: The Ronald Press Co.

Toffler, A. (1990). *Powershift.* New York: Bantam Books.

Tucker, A. (1984). *Chairing the academic department* (2nd ed.). New York: American Council on Education/Macmillan.

Tversky, A., & Kahneman, D. (1973). Availability: A heuristic for judging frequency and probability. *Cognitive Psychology, 5,* 207-232.

Weiner, J. (1990). *The next one hundred years.* New York: Bantam Books.

Whitehead, A. N. (1929). *The function of reason.* Boston: Beacon Press.

Winks, R.W. (1983). Government and the university in the United States. In J.W. Chapman (Ed.), *The western university on trial* (pp. 184-197). Berkeley: University of California Press.

Wood, J.T. (1992). Telling our stories: Narratives as a basis for theorizing sexual harassment. *Journal of Applied Communication Research, 20,* 349-362.

Wood, J.T. (1993a). Naming and interpreting sexual harassment: A conceptual framework for scholarship. In G. Kreps (Ed.), *Sexual harassment: Communication implications.* Cresskill, NJ: Hampton Press.

Wood, J.T. (1993b). Diversity and commonality: Sustaining their tension in communication courses. *Western Journal of Speech Communication, 57.*

Wood, J.T. (1993c). Gender and moral voice: From women's nature to standpoint theory. *Women's Studies in Commnication, 15,* 1-24.

Wood, J.T. (1993d). *Who cares? Women, care & culture.* Carbondale: Southern Illinois University Press.

Wood, J.T., & Conrad, C.R. (1983). Paradox in the experience of women professionals. *Western Journal of Speech Communication, 47,* 304-318.